Women Who Love Psychopaths

Inside the Relationships of Inevitable Harm with Psychopaths, Sociopaths, and Narcissists

Sandra L. Brown, M.A.

2nd Edition

D1340354

Important Notice

The purpose of this book is to provide accurate and authoritative information about the subject matter covered. The author (and any contributors) has made every effort to ensure the information is correct and complete. However, neither the publisher nor the author(s) is engaged in rendering professional advice or services to the individual reader. This book is not a substitute for mental health treatment. If you require such advice or treatment, you should seek the services of a competent mental health professional.

The material in this book is intended to help women to identify dangerous and potentially dangerous relationships with disordered men. Every effort has been made to provide accurate and dependable information regarding his potential disorder and the relationship dynamics. The contents of the book have been compiled through professional research and by mental health professionals. However, the reader should be aware that professionals in the field have differing opinions.

Therefore, the publisher, author, and editors, as well as the professionals quoted in the book, cannot be held responsible for any error, omission, professional disagreement, or dated material. The authors and publisher assume no responsibility for any outcome of applying the information in this book in a program of self-care or under the care of a licensed practitioner. If you have questions about the application of the information described in this book, consult a licensed therapist. If you are in a violent or potentially violent relationship, please call a domestic violence hotline or law enforcement.

Published by Mask Publishing, Penrose, NC
www.saferelationshipsmagazine.com

Cover Design by: Barry Briggs

Sandra L. Brown, M.A.
www.saferelationshipsmagazine.com

Library of Congress Catalog Number 2008924208

ISBN 0-9841728-0-7

Printed in the United States of America by
Book Printing Revolution
212 3rd Ave. North
Suite 290
Minneapolis, MN 55401
1-866-797-4314

Dedication

This book is dedicated to all the victims whose lives have been devastated by the psychopath's pathology and to a great supporter of this work my mother, Joyce Brown, who died during the writing of this book. I love you Mom. Thank you for being such a pioneer in this work and for so bravely exposing your own pathological relationships. The huge part of my life that we shared will be forever empty...

Many thanks to my family—Ken, Lindsay, Lauren and grandbabies, Aliyah, Bryce and 'new baby' who keep my life balanced in the midst of this work, and to my foster son, Cody who died shortly after the first printing of this book who so clearly has shown me what good and loving mental health looks like in a young man.

Thank you Cody for having been previously and continuing to be today my teacher in this life.

Many thanks to Dixie Lang for not only her support in the concepts of pathology, but her enormous effort in the help with this manuscript. I am very thankful for her help.

Ordering:

This book can be ordered from our websites at:

www.SafeRelationshipsMagazine.com

www.WomenWhoLovePsychopaths.com

www.amazon.com

Coming soon to bookstores near you!

Sandra L. Brown, M.A

Sandra L. Brown, M.A., CEO of *The Institute for Relational Harm Reduction & Public Pathology Education* is a clinician, program development specialist, psychopathologist, lecturer, and an award-winning author. Her books include *Counseling Victims of Violence* (1991, 2006), *How to Spot a Dangerous Man Book and Workbook* (2005) and *The Moody Pews* (2005).

She is recognized for her pioneering work on women's issues related to relational harm with Cluster B/Axis II disordered partners and specializes in the development and implementation of Pathological Love Relationship clinical training and services. Sandra's work, numerous books, CD's, DVD's, other training materials and literature have been used as curriculum in drug rehabs, women's organizations and shelters, women's jail programs, women's prisons, school-based programs, inner city projects, college campuses, various psychology and sociology programs worldwide, and utilized in almost every country of the world.

Her collaborative research on *Women Who Love Psychopaths* was recently presented at the Society for the Scientific Study of Psychopathy. Her work has been presented in lectures across the country including the Ruth Ginsberg Lecture Series *Women and the Law on Domestic Violence* as well as programs related to Domestic Violence Provider and Batterer Intervention Training in which her unique focus on Pathological Love Relationships has been featured.

In addition, her work at *The Institute* has included the development of a comprehensive online psychopathology magazine interviewing some of the country's leading researchers on personality disorders and pathology, the establishment of a Therapist Certification Program in Pathological Love Relationships, a Peer-Support Coaching Program, and the development of a Model of Care Approach for Treatment Centers.

Sandra's previous work included the founding and directing of Bridgework Counseling Center, a Florida-based program from 1987-1997 which encompassed a multi-faceted mental health treatment center for Trauma Disorders, Personality Disorders, and one of the country's first long-term residential programs for women with Dissociative Identity Disorder. She was also a pathologist on the Woman's Trauma Inpatient Hospital Program for The Manors Psychiatric Hospital. She facilitated groups on PTSD and Dialectical Behavioral Therapy as well as individual treatment. Sandra holds a Master's Degree in Counseling.

Table of Contents

Introduction

The Unexamined Victim

"If you're going to care about the fall of a sparrow you can't pick and choose who's going to be the sparrow. It's everybody."

— Madeline L'Engle

We are all aware of one fact—countless hours and millions of dollars have been spent researching and writing about the psychopath. There are plenty of readers ready to devour whatever is written about this subject. That's probably because for many people, the psychopath is a unique blend of the traits 'dangerous + exciting' in a way that sparks both 'curiosity + fear.' This multi-million-dollar research has produced dozens, if not hundreds, of articles each trying to explain the psyche of this mysterious and very disordered person.

Despite all the research dollars spent, academics and researchers continue to debate endlessly over what to call psychopaths, how to assess them, how differing diagnosis compare, and what to do with the psychopaths among us. The intense interest seems to prompt more questions than answers.

o   'How did this person get this way?'
o   'Is psychopathy really a sickness or something else?'
o   'Can they be helped?'
o   'Are they really that rare?'

Although the academics and researchers have produced an enormous body of knowledge about psychopaths, this knowledge does not seem to have helped the victims heal from the aftermath of encountering psychopaths. Current research, programs, and existing books skirt around a profound issue related to psychopathy—their victims.

Very little attention has been paid to the survivors of relationships with psychopaths, despite the fact that the disorder harms almost everyone in the psychopath's way and devastates the women and children who try to love him. Currently, what is being researched, written, and reported about psychopathy often has nothing to do with the victim's healing. The focus, as a sort of cultural fascination, is always on the psychopath related to what is wrong with him and what he's done. Sadly, people are attempting to heal from the psychopath's extraordinary damage, and do so without any real information about what the aftermath is or how to heal from it. The public's appetite for Crime TV-like experiences about psychopaths seems unquenchable. Victim-oriented books still remain largely memoir types—e.g. *My Life With a Psychopath*—fueling more descriptions about the disorder through narrative storytelling, but not much in the way of help or recovery for his untreated victims. In the end, many victims have foregone true acknowledgment, understanding and treatment.

One reason is that not all therapists know how to recognize victims of psychopathic relationships. Professionals in the general field of psychology don't want to wrestle with psychopathy and psychopathology.

Psychopathy remains one of the sub-categories (or sub-terrains!) within psychology that clinicians don't flock to and mainstream mental health professionals are inadequately trained to handle. Without proper training, therapists are likely to miss his disorder and her resulting victimization.

Historically, professionals have often lumped psychopath's victims together with domestic violence survivors, codependency recoverers, sex or relationship addicts, and labeled them with dependent personality problems, none of which have helped the victim's find specific treatment for the unique relationship dynamics for which psychopaths are known. Consequently, victims of psychopaths have yet another victimization scar due to a lack of knowledgeable and specialized treatment for their unique victimization exposure.

My Involvement in the Field of Pathology

I got involved in pathology 20 years ago as a counselor 'treating' personality-disordered men and women. Over decades of working with these relentless disorders, I came to a new appreciation for the depth of permanent devastation they bring. The devastation affects not only the person that has the disorder, but the people around them. Those people include family members, partners, friends, bosses, children, and even therapists. I came to recognize that this type of pathology, in many ways, really is a wasteland. The progress the disordered person makes is measured in millimeters, while the devastation he or she leaves behind is measured in miles. This lack of progress resulted in shifting my practice from working with personality disordered people to working with their family and intimate-others.

Additionally, I initiated psychopathy and pathology education for the community-at-large. Years later, I wrote the book *How to Spot a Dangerous Man Before You Get Involved* to help non-professionals learn to recognize signs and symptoms of pathological disorders, related mostly to personality disorders. After *How to Spot a Dangerous Man* was released, I realized the 'dangerous man' experiences they were trying to heal from were largely due to two types of pathologically disordered men—Narcissists and the whole 'antisocial end of the pathology spectrum' which includes Antisocial Personality Disorders, Sociopaths and Psychopaths. And no wonder! On a scale of 1-10, these two pathological disorders rate #1 and #2 in terms of 'devastation to others.'

As I worked with these women, I noticed that they were remarkably similar in personality traits, the stories of their relationship dynamics were consistent and even the aftermath of their symptoms was identical! I wanted to develop treatment for this particular group of victims. When I searched for books and research, I found nothing written about women who loved psychopaths. Could there be something to the similarities I had found? I decided to test my theory by asking questions such as:

1. Do the women who love psychopaths share a common 'profile'?
2. Did risk factors in women's lives contribute to them having relationships with psychopaths?
3. Are all the relationship dynamics with psychopaths similar?
4. Is there a general and predictable aftermath of symptoms when the relationship ends?
5. If so, can we use this information to develop both a survivor treatment approach and Public Psychopathy Education for all people?

Next, I ran ads asking women to contact me with their stories. The flood I received showed me that the disorders of narcissism, antisocial, sociopathy, and psychopathy are not *that* unusual.

After reading my ads, Liane J. Leedom, M.D. contacted me. Dr. Leedom is a female psychiatrist who had her own personal experience with a psychopath whom she met on the Internet and married. While some issues in her case remain unresolved, the end result was the destruction of

Dr. Leedom's life and medical practice. Her ex-husband was arrested and Dr. Leedom is currently unable to practice medicine until further notice.

Liane offered to assist by searching for research instruments and then gathered data on the women's temperament traits, looking for the cause of their vulnerability to pathological relationships. I was grateful for her offer of help. Utilizing her professional training, Dr. Leedom was very helpful in assisting in developing the *Women Who Love Psychopaths* research survey. Over 75 women worldwide completed the survey. This intensive survey collected data, stories about women's histories, symptoms, temperament traits, along with the dynamics of their interactions with pathological men who I will refer to as psychopaths. I will discuss my reasons for describing them as psychopaths later in the book. This book reflects the study findings as well as my insights from over 20 years of work in the field.

What Victims Can Teach Us about Psychopathy

Given the challenges researchers have faced about how to describe the idiosyncrasies of the disorder, and what psychopaths 'are' and 'do,' why not study his behavior through contact with, and study of, his victims? If researchers wanted a diversified angle or an unexplored view of the psychopath then we have to ask *'Who has gained more knowledge than the intimate partners who have been seriously harmed by psychopaths?'* By studying victims of psychopaths, I believe researchers will find additional information about him, how he thinks in relationships, his motivations, and what he's likely to do in the future. Additionally, understanding the psychopath's aftermath could shed new light on helping his victims. Victim-based research can bring the long-missing impact to the issue surrounding psychopathy. To that end, in this book you will:

o   See psychopaths through the eyes of women who loved them.

o   Meet the women, read their stories and discover the temperaments of many educated and otherwise well-adjusted women who have become 'vortexed' into relationships with men who lack conscience and empathy.

o   Learn how relationships with a psychopath begin, what it's like to be in love with a psychopath, the Jekyll and Hyde dynamics that cause her to emotionally split inside and what the aftermath affects on her are.

o Read about new breakthroughs in neuroscience that help us understand the brain differences in psychopaths.

o Learn about the role of intense attachments, fear, and sex in relationships with psychopaths.

o Answer the age-old question—do psychopaths have attachment and bonding? The answer is not what you think!

o Understand those 'crazy-making' relationship dynamics seen only in pathological love relationships and which contribute to the development of cognitive dissonance in his victims.

o Discover what is behind how a psychopath lures. What about that 'hypnotic stare' he uses that melts and freezes at the same time? How does hypnosis, trance, and suggestibility play into how strongly women are 'held' in these relationships?

o Learn the fascinating truth about how a woman's personality strengths and weaknesses may be a great match for the strengths and weaknesses of a psychopath.

An Update Since the First Book

Since the first printing of this book, I have spent over a year using this specific information and developing new approaches in our treatment programs. I designed the programs exclusively for women emerging from relationships with men with psychopathic behaviors. After treating dozens of clients I have learned a great deal about the unique aspects of the aftermath the women experience. I have added that new data related to my findings and understanding about their aftermath later in the book.

Both my understanding and my clients' intimate first-hand knowledge of psychopathy are different than many conventional and even clinical writings about the psychopath. Considering how the women came to know what they do know, it *should* be different. My understanding about the disorder has grown out of my unique experiences treating the psychopath's victims who have shared their personal life-destroying lessons about their encounters with a psychopath. When you approach the subject of psychopathy through the outcome of her victimization, the view should be distinctive.

My perspective may differ from other professionals such as psychopathy researchers who work primarily with criminal psychopaths in the prison system or those researchers who work in laboratories. My perspective may also differ from instructors in academia who teach about psychopathology.

In most of those cases, the only psychopathic subjects available for study or reported about are those who were caught or incarcerated.

In the cases in this book, the psychopaths are primarily not, and have not been, incarcerated.

This factor highlights one difference in this book's approach. I based the psychopath profiles on information provided by their intimate partners—not through standardized research approaches. The women answered detailed questions about the psychopath's behaviors and their unique relationship dynamics. Experience taught me you can learn a great deal from how victims and witnesses describe the psychopath's emotions and behaviors.

I wrote this book to help the psychopath's victims understand their unique and unprecedented at-risk status—past, present, and future. I hope the book will teach them how to safeguard themselves from other predators and prevent the devastation psychopathy causes. Over 20 years of providing counseling, I have sadly seen hundreds (if not thousands) of lives devastated by varying levels of mixed pathology and psychopathy. This growing global pathology stands as one of the primary public mental health issues facing our world today simply because of the number of victims it will inevitably affect—because that's what psychopathy '*does.*'

More importantly, I believe this book has begun a process in this country towards Public Psychopathy Education. I believe the way to prevent more psychopathic aftermath is through public awareness education.

Education can help women make better parenting choices by explaining:

o   The risk of psychopathic fathers passing their disorders on genetically
o   How psychopathic fathers emotionally damage the children they parent

Pathological parenting always leaves its brutality and twisted-ness upon impressionable souls.

To impact the public's future knowledge, women must know what psychopathic traits look like in men. She can't understand a psychopath until she learns what pathology in the psychopath looks like, acts like, and hides like.

Although technical, the next section will explain the nature of the male psychopath and bring a greater understanding of his pathology. It will also later highlight the unusual relationship features when I discuss psychopathic relationship dynamics.

If you have read this book, please be an 'Ambassador for Change' in your community by teaching youth and adults what you learned in this book. Help by disseminating information through a Public Psychopathy Education Project in your community or by running support groups for those leaving pathological relationships. *The Institute* offers personal training to coaches, counselors, and therapists who want to offer Pathological Love Relationship groups or support in their communities.

Also, why not donate this book to your local women's organization, Domestic Violence Program, Rape Crisis Center, college campus, or any other women's organization that serves at-risk women? Or, bring a Pathological Relationship workshop to your community and change one woman at a time.

'Each One, Teach One'—contact us for more information!

www.saferelationshipsmagazine.com

1 Understanding the Names Related to Psychopathy

Pathology and the Psychopath Himself

"Ye shall know the truth, and the truth will make you mad."

— *Aldous Huxley*

Even within the psychology field, it's been difficult to nail down:

o   what to call these disorders

o   where the cutoff line is on behavior and traits

o   who fits the definition

...and who does not.

If professionals disagree, how can the survivors hope to understand the specifics and why they matter?

This chapter should help clarify some of the discussion around these disorders. I will also define terms to help non-clinical readers, including survivors, understand how I am going to refer to these disorders.

Before I tackle 'phrasing,' I need to explain some of the categories professionals often use to refer to psychopaths, both with and without the term 'psychopath.'

I will begin with the group of disorders called Axis II or Personality Disorders.

Personality Disorders

There are three clusters of personality disorders which form the category of personality disorders:

o   **Cluster A – Odd or Eccentric Disorders:**

    o   Paranoid Personality Disorder

    o   Schizoid Personality Disorder

    o   Schizotypal Personality Disorder

- o   **Cluster B – Dramatic and Erratic Disorders:**
  - o   Antisocial Personality Disorder
  - o   Borderline Personality Disorder
  - o   Histrionic Personality Disorder
  - o   Narcissistic Personality Disorder
- o   **Cluster C – Anxious or Fearful Disorders:**
  - o   Avoidant Personality Disorder
  - o   Dependent Personality Disorder
  - o   Obsessive-Compulsive Personality Disorder

This book focuses on three of the Cluster B Disorders—Antisocial, Borderline, and Narcissistic Personality Disorders.

For many years, psychology professionals thought personality disorders stemmed mostly from lack of nurturing during childhood. They believed the development was caused from abuse, neglect, or something else inflicted by the child's social environment. The debate over the cause of pathology referred to as the 'Nature-VS-Nurture' debate continues to this day. Today, evidence from neuro-science has supplied us with additional data on biological, genetic, and brain malformations. These reasons teach us why the personality does not develop and the brain does not respond correctly leading to pathology and psychopathy.

That doesn't mean the field of psychology is totally up to speed yet about these disorders. In fact, even now many therapists often misunderstand personality disorders and avoid treating or diagnosing them because they don't understand the disorders or know if they are treatable. That's assuming they *recognize* the disorder in the first place. When I teach other therapists about the disorders, I quiz them on how much they remember about the disorders from graduate school. When most of them do 'poorly' on my verbal quiz, I ask how much time their instructors spent teaching them about personality disorders while in undergrad or graduate programs. Sadly, even psychologists have said their instructors crammed all 10 personality disorders into one week of lectures. That's only a couple of hours training in personality disorders—disorders likely to seriously impact other people's lives. Psychiatrists too have said they feel inadequately prepared for understanding these groups of highly impacting disorders.

The therapists' lack of understanding about personality disorders is especially alarming considering a recent study funded by the National Institute of Health (NIH)[1] found 1 in 5 young adults have personality disorders[2] and others in the field quote 1 in 25 have one of the low/no conscience disorders related to sociopathy.[3]

Two 'items' that therapists often forget are:

o   What core issue is identified on Axis II
o   What is 'allowed' to be diagnosed on that line

The axis model is a list of ways that therapists use to identify factors that will influence the person's outcome in therapy. It helps the therapist assess a wide variety of factors in a person's life that may help or hinder their recovery from what they are seeking counseling for.

For instance, Axis I refers to the 'presenting problem' such as "I'm depressed because I am in a destructive relationship." The therapist would list depression and relationship problems as the reason the person sought counseling. The remaining Axis items look at issues such as general medical conditions that might affect the person's mental health, any social or environmental problems that are impacting them, and an overall look at how they are functioning. What therapists often overlook, however, is Axis II. When I ask therapists what Axis II is for, most of them remember it is for Personality Disorders but they don't remember anything else.

Therapists use Axis II to assess what the DSM (Diagnostic Statistical Manual of Mental Disorder IV-TR) calls *'an enduring pattern'* that is *'pervasive.'*

The word *enduring* means 'everlasting, permanent, lifelong.'

The word *pervasive* means 'spreads throughout.'

These definitions imply how permanent personality disorders can be. The disorders affect many aspects of a person's personality and can ultimately negatively affect the person's quality of life. This happens

---

[1] Blanco, C, Okuda, M, Wright, C, Hasin, D, Grant, B Liu-SM, Olfson, M. (December 2008). Mental Health of College Students and Their Non-College Attending Peers, Results from a National Epidemiologic Study on Alcohol and Related Conditions. *Archives of General Psychiatry,* 65(12):1429-1437.

[2] Includes any of the 10 personality disorders, not just Cluster B.

[3] Stout, M. (2006). *The Sociopath Next Door.* New York: Broadway.

because a personality is innate—we are born with it. Our personality relates to how a person thinks, feels, relates and behaves.

A pervasive disorder related to this innate personality would affect all those aspects—thinking, feeling, relating and behavior. Personality disorders are one category of pervasive disorders.

Therapists may forget which *other* pervasive disorders are placed on the Axis II line. Axis II is used for the two major categories of pervasive disorders—any of the 10 personality disorders and mental retardation! The Developmental Disorders (MR, Autism, etc.) are just as pervasive and have a similar global effect on the person as do personality disorders. We have to ask ourselves "Just what does the DSM imply with this? Why does the DSM have personality disorders listed with mental retardation?"

The DSM lists the disorders together because they are both developmental disorders, in a sense. Personality disorders aren't always thought of as 'developmental.' One disorder involves the affected personality, and the other one involves mostly the affected cognition. The pervasiveness is so global that it impacts literally every part of the person's lives including how they think, feel, relate, and behave.

Survivors would never think of asking a mentally retarded person to change the way they are, to function at significantly different levels, or to see and react to things differently because they understand the impact of the disorder on the brain. Yet almost all survivors have unknowingly expected this of the seriously pathologically or antisocially disordered person. When survivors understand the 'pervasiveness' of these disorders, their understanding helps move them towards emotional (and physical) detachment.

Personality disorders encompass personality developmental delays and more often, biological and neurological deficits that contributed to the development of their pervasive disorder. Next I will discuss problems in development associated with the Borderline, Narcissist and Antisocial, all of which are part of the 10 personality disorders. Psychopathy, although similar in features, is not part of the 10 personality disorders. It has been set aside as a disorder unto itself.

What's In a Name?

Experts often disagree about what to call people with the group of personality traits and behaviors we refer to as *psychopathic.* Some clinicians call them:

o   Psychopaths

o   Pathological Narcissists

o   Sociopaths

o   Antisocial Personality Disorder

o   Borderpaths

These disorders have similarities and yet differences from one another.

Antisocial Personality Disorder

While Antisocial Personality Disorder (APD) and psychopathy share what some survivor's would note as similar qualities, APD focuses primarily on verifiable external and/or criminal behaviors. Psychopathy focuses on emotional and temperament traits less measurable than APD, and often less detected. Hopefully the upcoming DSM V will better describe the ever-elusive group of what I refer to as the 'low/no empathy and conscience' diagnoses.

APD Symptoms

The current DSM (IV-TR) states that APD's present symptoms show a 'pervasive' pattern of disregard for, and the violation of, the rights of others:

o   Failure to conform to lawful social norms

o   Deceitfulness

o   Impulsivity or failure to plan ahead

o   Irritability and aggressiveness as indicated by repeated physical fights or assaults

o   Reckless disregard for the safety of self or others

o   Consistent irresponsibility as indicated by repeated failure to sustain consistent work behavior or honor financial obligations o   Lack of remorse as indicated by being indifferent about having hurt, mistreated or stolen from another

APD falls into the category of a Cluster B personality disorder referred to as the 'Dramatic and Erratic' cluster. APD's are known for their criminal behavior that becomes more obvious over time. Their illegal, criminal or impulsive behavior draws quite a bit of attention, making them easier to spot than psychopaths.

Psychopathy

In contrast, psychopathy or psychopaths could be thought of as forming a sort of secondary category. This secondary category includes the worst of the APD traits *plus* additional traits unique to psychopathy.

It's noteworthy to say that this is one of the issues that researchers have disagreements about—whether true psychopathy has any relation to the similarities of APD or whether it is a completely distinct and different disorder. For the ease of survivors, we are considering psychopathy within the whole spectrum of low/no conscience disorders so these points are not critical to us at this time.

Researchers have studied psychopathy for at least a century or more. Obscure references go even further back in history—all the way back to the Bible. Two preeminent researchers in psychopathy are Hervey Cleckley (from the 1940's) and Robert Hare (current day).

Where APD is associated with illegal and/or criminal behavior, psychopathy (as originally described by Cleckley[4]) is not limited to criminal behavior, but includes these personality characteristics:[5]

o   manipulativeness
o   insincerity
o   egocentricity
o   lack of guilt

Cleckley's[6] original emphasis on psychopathy was a personality 'style' not just among criminals but also among successful individuals in

---

[4] Cleckley, H. (1941 First Edition).
[5] *The Mask of Sanity: An Attempt to Reinterpret the So-Called Psychopathic Personality*. St. Louis, MO: C.V. Mosby.
[6] Cleckley, H. (1941 First Edition).

the community. His work has taught clinicians and survivors alike to expand their recognition of psychopaths outside the APD criminals or lawbreakers. Even now, researchers study the differences between law abiding (although not moral-abiding) psychopaths and the law-breaking psychopath. These researchers are concerned that successful, white-collar psychopaths who don't behave violently or criminally (i.e. like APDs) will remain undetected.

Although many psychopaths never get caught and live their lives within our communities, Robert Hare has worked mostly with the psychopaths who have become criminal and ended up in the prison system. He developed The Psychopathy Checklist (Revised) referred to as the PCL-R which helps to differentiate the psychopath from the mere APD. Although by the time most psychopaths are being evaluated with the checklist, they are usually already in prison or somewhere within the legal system. Remember, however, many psychopaths never get to prison.

Psychopathy Characteristics[7]

Hare defines characteristics of psychopathy as:

o   glib and superficial charm

o   grandiose (exaggeratedly high) estimation of self

o   need for stimulation

o   pathological lying

o   cunning and manipulativeness

o   lack of remorse or guilt

o   shallow affect (superficial emotional responsiveness)

o   callousness and lack of empathy

o   parasitic lifestyle

o   poor behavioral controls

o   sexual promiscuity

o   early behavior problems

o   lack of realistic long-term goals

o   impulsivity

o   irresponsibility

---

[7] Hare, R.D. (1991). *The Hare Psychopathy Checklist-Revised.* Toronto: Multi-Health Systems.

o   failure to accept responsibility for own actions

o   many short-term marital relationships

o   juvenile delinquency

o   revocation of conditional release

o   criminal versatility

See Appendix for more information about the similarities and differences between APD, Sociopathy, and Psychopathy.

Some of these characteristics show flavorings of APD. This is why (for those other than researchers) they are often referred together in the same sentence.

Psychopathy further subdivides into psychopath 'types' which help define differences between them:[8]

Paranoid Psychopath:

o   persistent feeling of being constantly discriminated against by everyone

o   tense and continually on alert for adverse reactions towards them

o   spend a lot of time focusing on what is wrong

Schizoid Psychopath:

o   can be totally psychotic (have a break from reality) or simply aloof and introverted

o   avoidant of situations

o   loners

Aggressive Psychopath:

o   explosive anger

o   irritability

o   destructive

o   socially aggressive

Psychopathic Swindler:

o   lie, steal, cheat, break promises since an early age

o   extremely selfish

o   unresponsive to kindness

o   irresponsible

---

[8] Bromberg, W. (1948). *Crime and Mind.* Philadelphia: J.B. Lippincott.

Sexual Psychopath:

o   distortion of sexual impulses

o   needs immediate gratification of sexual impulses

o   often well educated with good jobs

o   can also be sadists and capable of atrocious crimes

Researchers have been studying the psychopath's biology and neurology through brain-imaging and other forms of in-depth testing. Neuro-science is helping find brain differences in much of pathology, including psychopathy. These fascinating findings will be talked about later in the book.

Sociopaths

Sociologists utilize the word sociopath, sociopathic, or sociopathy when referring to the spectrum of low/no conscience disorders that are related to learned behavior as opposed to innate pathological tendencies that psychopaths are born with. The old 'Nature-VS-Nurture' argument says that some no conscience disorders are born that way while others learn to become that way.

Sociologists believe that sociopaths are those who are not born with predispositions to genetic and neuro-abnormalities that give way to innate psychopathy but instead have acquired the disorder through learned conditioning such as exposure to a pathological parent, abuse, neglect, gang exposure or antisocial environments. Sociopathy, like psychopathy, is not considered to be a personality disorder. The sociopath's checklist of symptoms would be similar to the psychopaths listed above. We will discuss later the issues related to the causes of various low/no conscience disorders. Experts often disagree whether to lump sociopaths with APD or Psychopaths.

Borderlines and Borderpaths

Borderline is one of the categories within the 'Dramatic and Erratic' Cluster B of Personality Disorders that also includes the APD diagnosis. The clusters are often looked at as overlaps in some traits. For instance, some APDs could have borderline or narcissistic traits/disorders, some borderlines could have narcissistic or APD traits/disorders, and some narcissists could have borderline or APD traits/disorders. And to complicate matters further, they can also have traits from *more* than one of the personality disorders as well as *other* mental health disorders.

	Borderline Traits/ Disorders	and/ or	Narcissistic traits/ disorders	and/ or	APD traits/ disorders
APD's may also have...	X		X		
Borderlines may also have...			X		X
Narcissists may also have...	X				X

Borderlines also fall into the low empathy spectrum and are now found to have similar neuro-abnormalities also seen in the psychopathic spectrum. New evidence suggests that some women diagnosed borderline (women are diagnosed borderline more often than men) are really under-diagnosed APDs or psychopaths. This new evidence gives us some idea of the similarity in features of the disorders and why they look similar behaviorally in people. This has given rise to a symptom overlap name of 'borderpath' that incorporates symptoms from both borderline and psychopath.

Borderline Symptoms

The current DSM (IV-TR) states borderline symptoms include:[9]

o   frantic efforts to avoid real or imagined abandonment
o   intense and unstable personal relationships that over idealize and devalue
o   identity disturbance with unstable self image or sense of self
o   impulsivity in at least two areas (spending, sex, substance abuse, reckless driving, binge eating.)
o   recurrent suicidal behavior, gestures, threats or self-mutilation
o   emotional instability due to a marked reactivity of mood
o   (intense episodic irritability or anxiety)
o   chronic feelings of emptiness

[9] American Psychiatric Association: *Diagnostic and Statistical Manual of Mental Disorders,* Fourth Edition. Washington, D.C., American Psychiatric Association, 1994.

o   inappropriate intense anger or difficulty controlling anger
o   transient stress related paranoid ideas

Some borderline symptoms are similar to APD, psychopathy, and sociopathy and share some of the coping styles and defense mechanisms seen in the low/no conscience spectrums of APD, psychopathy, sociopathy, and narcissism. Similar coping and defense mechanisms include:

o   noteworthy chameleon-like behavior
o   the ever-present blaming
o   the infuriating narcissistic entitlement
o   the victimizing relationship exploitation
o   tip-toeing due to hyper-sensitivity within the relationship
o   manipulative gaslighting
o   master-level projecting
o   creative splitting
o   chronic high control

Narcissism or Pathological Narcissism

In the last few years, there has been an increase in the number of people and organizations who have created websites, blogs, and other public educational outreaches discussing the 'It's-All-About-You' disorder—Narcissistic Personality Disorder (NPD). NPD is one of the 'Dramatic and Erratic' personality disorders of Cluster B. They share some symptoms and traits with Borderlines and APDs within the personality disorder category, but also with psychopaths, who are not a personality disorder.

Narcissism, when measured against the other Cluster B disorders, is more likely to be seen as a primary, secondary, or additional personality disorder due to its high genetic transmission rate. Estimates indicate a large percentage of people with one personality disorder may also have additional personality disorders. Narcissism is often seen in combinations with other personality disorders in Cluster B.

Narcissism Symptoms

The current DSM (IV-TR) states narcissism symptoms include:[10]

o   A grandiose sense of self importance, exaggerates their achievements and talents, expects to be recognized as superior without commensurate achievements.

o   Is preoccupied with fantasies of unlimited success, power, brilliance, beauty, or ideal love.

o   Believes that he is special and unique and can only be understood by, or should only associate with, other special or other high-status people or institutions.

o   Requires excessive admiration.

o   Has a sense of entitlement, unreasonable expectations of especially favorable treatment or automatic compliance with his expectations.

o   Is interpersonally exploitative within relationships and takes advantage of others to achieve his own ends.

o   Lacks empathy and is unwilling to recognize or identify with the feelings and needs of others.

o   Is often envious of others or believes that others are envious of him.

o   Shows an arrogant, haughty behavior or attitude.

o   The disorders of APD, psychopathy, sociopathy, narcissism and borderline represent a spectrum of disorders most often associated with impulsivity problems, interpersonal exploitation, cognitive distortions, low/no empathy, and varying levels of inappropriate/non-existing conscience and remorse. I refer to these groups as (low empathy/conscience spectrum disorders). For a survivor, this simply means *'inevitable harm.'*

---

[10] American Psychiatric Association: *Diagnostic and Statistical Manual of Mental Disorders,* Fourth Edition. Washington, D.C., American Psychiatric Association, 1994.

Figure 1.1
Low Empathy/Conscience Spectrum

Psychopathy
Sociopathy
Antisocial Personality Disorder
Narcissistic Personality Disorder
Borderline/Borderpath Personality Disorder
Combinations

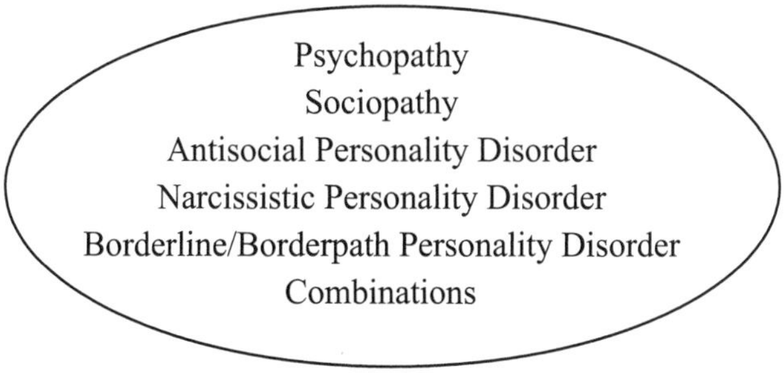

The low empathy/conscience spectrum disorders show how the issue of pathology related to empathy and/or conscience affects a number of disorders. All these disorders render the person capable of harming others by their low/or lack of empathy, conscience, remorse and other emotional deficits. While psychopaths represent those with the least amount of empathy, the other disorders also lack normalized amounts of empathy and related emotional spectrums.

What If They Aren't FULLY Psychopathic?
Why are Traits Important?

Some men are diagnosed with psychopathic or narcissistic '*traits*' as opposed to full diagnoses such as 'APD' 'sociopathy' or 'psychopathy.' Many women don't understand what 'psychopathic traits' are or why they are important.

Many women misunderstand the evaluation checklists. They think fewer symptoms = safety. If the man doesn't have enough 'checkmarks' on the psychopathy checklist or the DSM lists for APD or Narcissism for an official diagnosis, then he is not dangerous. It only takes a few traits for most people to be able to eventually *feel* the negative 'effects' of psychopathy (and other forms of pathology) on their relationship. Women reported that being in a relationship with a psychopath was incredibly different and more damaging than any other relationship. The reason has to do with the 'traits' of their pathology.

Unfortunately, women soon learn even a few traits can do significant damage. The 'traits' apparent (or are later realized) are only the tip of the iceberg. So much of the psychopaths' lives are hidden. Women find out much later what the psychopath has really been doing—after her risky emotional, sexual or financial exposure. Some women never find out all of it. Whether he has full sociopathy/psychopathy according to some experts, or merely a few psychopathic traits according to her, he has the capacity to ruin her life!

The bottom line—all psychopathic traits point to some level or type of psychopathy. Women need to ask themselves "Why am I willing to date a guy with even a few psychopathic traits?"

Combo Packs

What we DO know is that personality disorders and other forms of pathology represent a complex combination of several disorders. Most do not merely have 'just' one disorder—a personality disorder or otherwise. Not only is it common for people with one personality disorder to have more than one (because they are grouped together in clusters and share similar and overlapping features), but they also have *other* disorders peripherally associated with personality disorders. Those with personality disorders also tend to have addictions affiliated with substance (drugs or alcohol) and compulsions (sex, porn, gambling, spending, etc.). They are most likely to also have mood disorders such as depression, anxiety, bipolar or other cycling mood disorders. Many of them have anger and rage problems associated with impulsivity disorders. A low empathy/conscience disordered person's entire mental health list could look something like this:

o   Antisocial Personality Disorder (Primary)
o   Narcissistic Personality Disorder
o   Borderline Traits
o   Substance Abuse Disorder
o   Sexual Compulsivity
o   Intermittent Explosive Rage Disorder
o   Bipolar Disorder or Mood Disorder

Someone within the spectrum of the low conscience disorders most likely has a combo of associated mental health disorders. This adds to not only the complexity of trying to have a normal relationship with someone who has such high pathology, but also adds exponentially to the *lethality risk* for anyone in a relationship with them. The more mental health issues a person has, the higher the relational harm risk.

Creating an Umbrella Term

While these disorders each have their own unique aspects and researchers and academics enjoy discussing the differences, what I have found is that most victims don't find the differences that notable in *their own aftermath experiences.* Why should it be notable? Harm is harm— PTSD is PTSD. Cognitive dissonance, intrusive thoughts, financial ruin, flashbacks, obsessions—it all feels mind-blowing and numbing when she is going through it. To split hairs over "is he this *kind* of low/no-conscience disorder" or "that *kind* of disorder" doesn't matter much to a survivor. Many survivors find it hard enough to concentrate in general to identify any one disorder that completely captures him (thus my point about *Combos*).

Victims experience what I have termed *'Inevitable Harm.'* To approach the teaching about this 'group' of pathology that is a clustered view of the disorder:

~Antisocials-sociopaths-pathologicalnarcissists-psychopaths-borderlines/borderpaths~

I lumped them together in a way most victims can understand for our discussion. I agree with recent research that explained:[11]

"Our results provide empirical evidence that psychopathy constitutes a personality construct made up of different characteristics of the DSM antisocial, narcissistic and borderline personality disorders...One clinical implication of our results is that in cases where a Cluster B personality disorder is diagnosed a high psychopathy value is to be expected, especially where antisocial, borderline or narcissistic personality disorder is involved."

---

[11] Huchzemeier,C., Friedemann G., Brub, E., Godt, N., Kohler, D., Hinrichs, G., and Aldenhoff, J. (2007). The Relationship Between DSM-IV Cluster B Personality Disorders and Psychopathy According to Hare's Criteria: Clarification and Resolution of Previous Contradictions. *Behavioral Sciences and the Law*, 25:901-911 2007.

I chose to use *'psychopath'* in the title of this book because so many people associate that name with severe levels of harm to others. Further, it represents the word that most women were likely to use in an Internet search for assistance. To reach the highest number of searching victims, I selected the keyword 'psychopath' to represent the whole spectrum of men with psychopathic features. I also refer to psychopathic features (related to personality disorders and psychopathy) as 'pathologicals' meaning they have a pathology that is related to low/no conscience and also related to low treatment outcomes.

A Note About Gender

APD, psychopathy, sociopathy, narcissism, borderline/borderpaths, and any combination are mental health issues. They are not gender issues. *The Institute's* primary client is female which is why I have written about male psychopaths and female victims/survivors. However, I certainly recognize that the same disorders exist in women and create devastating aftermath to men as well. *The Institute's* magazine, www.saferelationshipsmagazine.com, carries an e-book for men called *How to Avoid Dating Damaged and Destructive Women.* This book discusses women with these types of personality disorders and other pathologies. Please check there if you are in need of information for men.

So, How Many Among Us?

Based on my work with victims, psychopaths who never get caught— the ones who do not cross the line of breaking the law, or are smart enough to avoid arrest and detection—are a far larger population than many ever dreamed. Psychopaths are such excellent imposters that they can live their entire lives behind what Cleckley called the "Mask of Sanity" and never be detected. A psychopath is likely to dupe nearly everyone. Only those who, over time, have negative experiences with the psychopath end up meeting the true 'man behind the curtain.' The rest of society is likely to believe they have never met a psychopath. In fact, they probably have and didn't know it. This makes psychopaths hard to count and account for.

How many psychopaths and variations of psychopathy are out there? Those who aren't in prison are largely overlooked and go uncounted because they are unrecognized. They are roaming freely in your city, sitting next to you in class, working at your company, and maybe dating your sister. According to some experts, however, three to four percent of the population or possibly eight million individuals (six million men and two million women) in the U.S. are 'sociopathic enough' to get a diagnosis or seriously damage others—if we ever recognize who they are.

Beyond the eight million, even more people show some traits of the low-conscienced. Since clinicians usually restrict the diagnosis to criminal behavior, many clinicians would miss diagnosing a full-blown psychopath hiding behind a well-constructed and non-criminal 'Mask of Sanity.' At most, the clinician who fell under the spell of the mask would only see the psychopath as 'a little selfish.'

Without a traceable criminal history, he'll likely fly under an assessor's radar. What about the numbers of victims he leaves behind whether or not he *is* identified as disordered?

Based on current estimates, if we group together APDs, psychopaths, sociopaths, narcissism, and borderpaths, close to 100 million persons will be negatively affected by these disordered people related to low/no empathy/conscience. These victims could be friends, co-workers, family members, or intimate others whose life path crossed with the group of low/no-conscienced disorders.

This number doesn't include the number of children negatively influenced by pathological parents or exposure to pathological adults. This leaves a huge gap of 'need' for those who require help healing from exposure to someone else's psychopathology.

Conclusion

One of the biggest challenges for both *The Institute* and survivors is finding therapists who can recognize the chameleon-like psychopaths and who understand the Axis II, Cluster B, and psychopathy problem. Our clients tell us how the 'charming psychopath' goes to relationship counseling with her, only to con the therapist who never realizes his diagnosis. Lack of properly-trained clinical professionals is by far the biggest impediment to survivor's recovery.

With millions of 'sociopathic-enough' persons churning out victims by the millions, it's time this country does something in the public awareness venue. Someone needs to teach others how to spot psychopaths, and to teach therapists how to treat the psychopath's devastated survivors.

In this chapter we talked about the diagnostic names of these types of pathological men. In the next chapter, we will discuss how a psychopath becomes a psychopath:

o   What is it that makes the disordered person different from those we consider normal people?

o   What causes a personality disorder and psychopathy?

o   Why are the disorders so destructive to the person who has them?

o   Why can't they be 'cured'?

2 What Causes Pathology?

Let's Talk Nurture

"Since we cannot change reality, let us change the eyes that see reality." — Mikos Kazantizakis

While few experts agree on what to call the groups of low/no-conscience disorders, even fewer agree on what causes these illusive disorders. We will discuss the various theories on what causes forms of pathology (including personality disorders and psychopathy). To consider all sides of the theories, I will discuss my own views about what causes these disorders.

Before I describe theories on what causes the disorders, I need to define the term 'personality' so that we know when a personality is disordered. Personality is a person's own special and unique way of relating to other people and to the world. A 'personality,' as mentioned in the previous chapter, is related to how a person *thinks, feels, relates, and behaves,* and is largely innate (we're born with it.)

Personalities come wired with their own features that make a person, for good or bad, who they are and who they become. Influences along the way tweak who a person becomes. Somewhere in between whom a person is and who they ultimately become is a whole lot of theory!

Here We Go Again—Nature-VS-Nurture

It's hard to get around the Nature-VS-Nurture discussion when talking about personality disorders and/or psychopathy. That's because there are really only three ways to view these unique disorders:

o   You were born that way.

o   You were not born that way, but your environment made you that way.

o   You were born that way AND your environment made it worse.

Nurture or the Lack Thereof

If asked how these disorders form, a sociologist would most likely include a discussion on 'Nurture' and how the psychopath's early childhood environments did or did not support the infant's developing mind and personality. Sociologists believe the low/no conscienced group of disorders is largely produced by negative and emotionally toxic social and environmental exposures. This is why sociologists call this type of disorder 'sociopaths' as opposed to 'psychopaths'—because they believe they have been socially created, not genetically or biologically created.

What can go wrong in early childhood that contributes to forming these disorders? Erik Erickson, who sculpted our view on personality development through the stages of life, taught us about the 'developmental tasks' that must occur for a personality to develop without problems and deficits. Each developmental task builds on the preceding one to 'form' a normal and healthy personality structure.

For instance, the first developmental task a person completes as a baby is to bond. If the baby does not bond successfully, the next developmental step is likely to be adversely effected by the first process. In personality disorder 'theory,' experts have long believed many personality disorders were related to 'over' or 'under' attachment or bonding. For instance, experts assumed Borderline Personality Disorder to be highly predicated on attachment issues to create the 'dramatic and erratic' aspects of the disorder. Psychopathy is often referred to as the 'ultimate attachment disorder.'

The next developmental step a child takes after bonding is individuation and autonomy during which the child begins to wander off and explore their world. If a child is clingy and needy, experts believe the child may have had problems with the first developmental task, bonding, or somewhere in the second task, finding their own autonomy. Personality disorders often predicated their theories on early childhood development or non-development.

Erikson's theory on stages of development takes us from cradle to grave, stacking completed developmental tasks as towers of constructed personality. Even the name 'personality disorder' points back to a causal theory—how the personality did or did not form.

I too have attributed *some* of the personality disorder's various characteristics to malformation in personality development—things which failed to occur but left 'holes in the soul.'[12] These malformations and holes in development become fairly evident when adults have teenage emotional mindsets and matching teenage skill sets. I have often said there is no personality disorder/psychopathy emotionally older than about 14 years old. Imbued into the undeveloped personality are:

o   lack of attachment

o   sometimes-skewed abandonment issues

o   high entertainment/thrill-seeking needs

o   impoverished thinking related to right and wrong and moral decision making

o   high impulsivity, inability to learn from consequences

...just to name a few. These traits all sound like a teenager.

The uncompleted developmental tasks of life take on the armor of irresponsibility, boredom, and excitement-seeking which plague the psychopath's teen and adult life. As parents, they are more like young 'juvies' themselves. Imagine a mere 'emotional 14-year-old' trying to teach a child moral reasoning they don't even understand. Their adult reflections mirror the 'stuck' aspects of their teen mentality. Their chronic infidelity points to their inability to develop normal attachment and bonding. For some of the personality disorders, the intense abandonment and the need to keep constant 'tabs' on their mate all point back to a lack of development in early childhood. Risk-taking in many areas of life reflects their teen-like thrill-seeking and impulsivity as well as their lack of learning from punishment. Their behaviors of stealing, lying, and conning show their defective moral decision making. All of these could be seen from an Erkisonian developmental approach as aspects of the personality that did not form correctly.[13]

These uncompleted developmental tasks create emotional deficits in the child. But the world does not stop because a child is not getting their

---

[12] 'Holes in the Soul' concept by John Bradshaw.

[13] In some of *The Institute's* other materials, I have taken Erkison's Developmental Model and shown how each uncompleted developmental age task then later manifests itself in adult relationship patterns in Pathological Love Relationships.

emotional or psychological needs met. The inner and outer world continues, and so must the child. His emotional growth 'adapts around' his deficits, much like a tree that grows around an obstacle in its path such as a sidewalk or park bench. The tree adapts by creating bulging and knobby protrusions that jut out in odd places. It curls itself around the sidewalk and thrusts itself up and over the concrete that sought to stop its growth. Despite all, the tree continued to grow and develop. Today it is dwarfed here, arthritic there—extended in this section and protruding in that section—it lives and survives to tell a story of its own mangled journey.

Pathology, personality disorders, psychopathy—whatever you call it—is in some ways strangely adaptive, and perhaps a tribute to that strong and *enduring pattern* of misbehavior that is their pathology. As malformed as their personality becomes, the ability to continue on without what they needed does indeed say something about the disorder, if not about them personally.

As you might have guessed, the issue of 'nurture' related to pathology disorders is often related to abuse and neglect. As a child develops, there are times they need an emotional or psychological aspect given to them. The absence of what they needed, when they needed it may form a deficit.

In the long run, deficits create disorders, such as personality disorders or pathology.

As they explored the 'nurture theory,' experts often thought personality disorders and pathology were primarily victims of early and chronic childhood abuse or unrelenting poverty and neglect. While these factors often **are** a contributing factor to pathology and personality disorders (as well as trauma related disorders), they are usually not the **only** contribution to pathological formations. Some psychopaths and other pathologicals have been born to loving and completely normal families. That does not mean 'nurture' does not influence the formation of pathology. It does—maybe more than we realize. 'Nurture' is most likely part of a complex string of social, environmental, and very biological causes. These causes come together causing the poor individual and everyone around them undue harm.

How much does 'nature'—biology or genetics—play in the formation of pathology? I think you'll be surprised.

Let's Talk 'Nature'

According to the 'Nature' theory, people are born with certain innate or permanent personality features. Some of these features have to do with the temperament styles that affect a person's mind. Other features have to do with the brain as an organ as opposed to the mind as a structure. I will talk separately about aspects of temperament and the brain.

People are born with innate or hard-wired aspects in their personality. Some of this is temperament-based. Many mothers can tell within a few weeks or months what 'kind' of temperament their child will have, such as compliant or assertive, good-natured or demanding. Temperament affects many qualities of a person's developing personality. The differences in temperament in both the psychopath and the women will be discussed. But also innate in our personality are motivational drives. Let's take a look...

Motivational Drives

Our motivational drives have to do with part of the innate features of a person's personality. Everyone enters the world wired with motivational drives. These drives help people regulate their needs and interests and push them towards pleasure and away from pain. The women's needs and interests through her motivational drives turn out to be very *differently motivated* than the needs and interests of psychopaths and other pathologicals.

Normal motivational drives are:

1. Food
2. Comfort
3. Possessions
4. Entertainment
5. Sex
6. Affection
7. Social dominance/status/power[14]

---

[14] Contributed by Liane J. Leedom, M.D.

Jacked-Up Super Drives

With psychopaths, the bottom portion of the motivational list becomes much more important to them making their motivational drives super-jacked up on one end while other peoples are more balanced across all the drives.

Psychopaths are highly pleasure motivated and excessively seek out what they enjoy. This includes lots of high-status possessions, the need to be constantly entertained and distracted, hyper-sexual, wanting to be dominant within their social circles, and by all means requiring lots of power. Any of their motivational drives can be seen as excessive compared to non-pathologicals. Their inability to regulate their pleasure seeking behaviors is a major focus of what is discussed in the following chapters.

Suffice it to say that their excessive motivational drives push them towards taking extraordinary risks (financially, emotionally, sexually, physically, etc.) to get what is desired. Most women who have been with psychopaths describe his 'risk taking' behavior and how much pleasure he seemed to take in it. His entertainment drive, also referred to as 'sensation seeking, excitement seeking or novelty seeking,' contributes to his enjoyment of being on the go, exploring new things/people/opportunities and searching for different experiences which often leads to infidelity. Many women wonder why psychopaths are never monogamous. The psychopath's entertainment drive is so high that he is always looking for something or someone new and exciting. This is also why many psychopaths are also very sexually deviant—always looking for the riskier sexual experience. Later in the book I will discuss how this 'excitement-seeking' drive in him serves as a 'hook-up' for women who love psychopaths.

Couple all of that with:

o   a typically very strong sex drive
o   sexual satisfaction stemming from power and control as much as the physical sex act

...and you have a combination for sexual acting out not likely to be quenched.

High Risk Taking Behavior

+ **High sex drive**

+ **High entertainment drive**

_____

= **Infidelity in a psychopath**

Psychopaths are known for their social dominance, status and power drives[15] referred to as the *'antisocial pursuit of power.'* This 'pursuit of power' is a driving force behind making some psychopaths prominent leaders. This is also why we often see psychopaths in prestigious careers such as law, medicine and business. Furthermore, it produces in them the edge of competitiveness, driving the successful ones to the top of their fields.

Rieber and Vetter[16] indicate 'psychopaths are extremely sensitive to power relationships and want maximum power. But they also want to use the power destructively.' Psychopaths enjoy power most when it is equated to, and produces, victimization. The psychopath will not find a victory as 'power inducing' if the victim knowingly gives him what he wants. He prefers to victimize her somewhere in the process. In order for him to feel the most power, someone else must be weak. Many psychopaths, when discussing their feelings about weakness, say the weaker 'demand to be exploited.'[17] Resulting violence is not always a trait of psychopaths and often they seek power (and the consequential emotional victimization) more than exerting violence. This does not mean psychopaths are never violent—they are. The prison system is full of them.

The psychopath's dominance drive is a force behind his pathology. His dominance can be overt aggression and demanding control of his whole environment. Or his dominance can be covert through passive-aggressive use of guilt, pathetic neediness, or pity to dominate her emotions. The end result is the same—the ability to dominate someone's emotions thus dominate their inner world. This issue will be a thread

_____

[15] Rieber, R.W., & Vetter, H. (1994). The Language of the Psychopath. *Journal of Psycholinguistic Research*, Vol 23, No 1.

[16] Rieber, R.W., & Vetter, H. (1994). The Language of the Psychopath. *Journal of Psycholinguistic Research*, Vol 23, No 1.

[17] Rieber, R.W., & Vetter, H. (1994). The Language of the Psychopath. *Journal of Psycholinguistic Research*, Vol 23, No 1.

woven throughout the discussion of his pathological relationship dynamics because his search for dominance, status and power is totally out of control. He will seek to control anything and everything—even the little things in life that shouldn't matter.

While he might be initially outgoing and charming, these irresistible temperament traits are what she will eventually find the most compelling examples of his psychopathy. A public lack of awareness about his pathological use of dominance and power is a reason psychopaths are able to fool everyone—even trained professionals. Since most people don't have a reason to be-come 'acutely' aware of the problems of a super-strong dominant man, the psychopath simply looks like a charismatic leader, revered by many.

Although his dominance may also be camouflaged to the outside world by looking more passive than powerful, yet behind closed doors his dominance is exerted by controlling her through any means he can use. These could include sexual humiliation, suffocating neediness, her every movement is approved or disapproved by him, gaslighting to control her reality—anything overt or covert can be used.

His insatiable need for power and dominance is so non-stop that it feels unquenchable to her. Psychopaths hurt people because power through victimization is much more satisfying to them. They are emotionally rewarded by the harm they cause. Even white-collar psychopaths, driven by their power hunger, squash others as they dash up the corporate ladder.

On top of these power, status, and dominance drives, most (although not 100%) psychopaths are often extraverted as well. An 'extravert' is a person with:[18]

o   a strong personality
o   who is socially outgoing
o   has strong internal motivational drives

All of which most psychopaths have. You can see their extraversion through their:

o   leadership skills
o   ability to work well in groups (or work the group!)

---

[18] Contributions by Liane J. Leedom, M.D.

o   which is why psychopaths often drift (or shark their way) to the top of any career or group they are affiliated with

Extraverts:

o   prefer being with others over being alone (a reason why psychopaths quickly replace romantic relationships and hate being alone)

o   enjoy risk-taking

o   love excitement and change

o   have a strong entertainment drive (the need to be active, distracted or involved)

While these traits are not unique to psychopaths, these traits *in* a psychopath are extremely elevated. These elevated traits cause the psychopath to seek out rewards they want. The rewards can be emotional dominance of someone, as well as physical, sexual or financial manipulation. This reward seeking behavior is a classic trait of psychopathy and significantly influences their behavior.

Extraversion is also linked to impulsivity and often extraverts can't resist an impulse or temptation, even if it's harmful to themselves or others. Impulsivity is also connected to other disorders such as:

o   ADHD

o   substance abuse

o   pathological gambling

o   intermittent explosive dis-order

o   kleptomania

o   pyromania

o   self mutilation

o   sexual impulsivity

...as well as some personality disorders and psychopathy.[19]

Since all of these motivational drives push humans 'towards' pleasure and psychopaths are very pleasure-oriented, **they don't learn from painful experiences.** This separates them from normal people, who do

---

[19] Impulse Disorders, American Psychiatric Association: *Diagnostic and Statistical Manual of Mental Disorders,* Fourth Edition. Washington, D.C., American Psychiatric Association, 1994.

learn from pain. Psychopaths as reward seekers will always go for what they want and won't think enough, or be motivated enough, about the issue of pain or punishment. This is why prison hasn't been a big deterrent for those psychopaths who have made it to the jail cell! Impulsive psychopaths rarely stop to consider the long term consequences of their actions and repeatedly fail to see **their actions = their consequences.** They can't determine when a punishment outweighs a perceived tantalizing reward, and can't resist a harmful temptation. If they could, they wouldn't repeatedly fail in relationships due to their constant infidelity, lying, cheating, and other impulsive behaviors. Whether his consequence was jail or being kicked out of her bed, he isn't likely to learn from either.

These motivational drives are one more issue related to the innate or 'born that way' theories about psychopathy.

More Nature

For many years, the only understanding experts had of personality disorders and various pathologies was the 'Nurture Theory,' even if the experts suspected there probably were some 'nature' issues going on. For instance, what about psychopaths who are born into genuinely loving families and were not abused? What if all their needs were met and their developmental tasks were complete? Why are they disordered if the disorder *only* comes from abuse, neglect, or unmet needs?

Neuro-science provides another possible view. Some important work toward understanding brain differences in pathology has come through not only neuro-science research, but in brain imaging through MRI's and PET scans. How could we have known we could actually *'see'* the differences that explain some of the behavior in pathology? This has given some interesting consideration to the possible neuro, biological, chemical, and even genetic issues that contribute to the malformation of the personality and the brain that drives the personality. This means, the brain as an 'organ' as opposed to just the 'mind' as the structure can be disordered. The flaw in many people's thinking is they always look just at the mind, and try to understand psychopathy as a mind issue, not an organ issue as well.

Why is this important? From *The Institute's* stand point, it is enormously important because survivors usually believe that whatever is wrong with him is only 'willful behavior' or stubbornness. The idea of 'willful behavior' has unfortunately been long supported by areas of psychology and other fields that do not specialize in pathology such as:

o   Relationship counselors attempting to use normal relationship dynamics in the most disordered of relationships by treating his willfulness or non-compromising as an ordinary relationship challenge.

o   The church at-large who label all behavior as 'sin' thus 'willful.' If it's only willful, then it's a spiritual attitude and can be changed.

o   The New Age philosophies that focus on 'Positive Psychology' that 'if you think it, you can change it.'

Women who arrive at *The Institute* are very confused about what he can and can't do about his own biology. Even before the latest neuroscience behind these disorders emerged, experts still had that interesting concept of Axis II and *'pervasive disorders'* associated only with personality disorders and mental retardation. That little tidbit in and of itself suggests an element of *permanent* hardwiring not overcome by mind-over-matter effort. Unfortunately, many women had spent too much time reading psychology books about normal relationships and watching too much daytime TV tele-therapists to believe that what was wrong with him can't be fixed. They clung to the belief that somehow he could be different.

Just an Excuse for Bad Behavior

People don't like the 'brain explanation' for psychopathy or personality disorders because they feel it's a loophole for pathological behavior. If it's a brain-deal, then they are 'not responsible' for a disorder they cannot control. How 'convenient' their behavior isn't associated with simply 'willful behavior'—something they could actually *DO* something about.

A large portion of their behavior is associated with brain function. However, there are still aspects of their behavior that are manipulative, thus willful, in that sense. The overall brain explanation is sometimes offensive to portions of the domestic violence community who have viewed the pathology assertion as an excuse for his behavior. (I won't even get into how defense attorneys would twist and manipulate the disorder to prove he isn't responsible for his behavior. This neuro-biology issue has given rise to an area of study called Neuroethics. What that holds on the legal horizon is unknown but frightening to contemplate.)

Let me clearly state *The Institute's position* on this:

> ***This in no way excuses the behavior of psychopaths. There is no excuse for producing the mangled minds of his victims because of his abuse or the behavioral manipulation that is often willful. This does not mean people should feel sorry for a psychopath and stay in a relationship with him because 'he can't help it.' What he can't help does not make him less lethal. This is simply to understand that 'she didn't break him, and she can't fix him either.' What is and is not inside his brain determines his future. Not her. There is a difference between making an excuse for someone's behavior and understanding what is behind it.***

For *The Institute*, understanding brain function problems in pathology actually *closes* the loophole. This should make it easy to call. For those whose brain function is so permanently and dangerously altered, their cases should be approached differently and strictly. Without the ability to adjust the dangerous and unbridled impulsivity associated with pathology, these psychopaths should be held accountable for every act and punished and contained with the knowledge that **it isn't going to be different next time.** Sending them to batterer intervention, anger management or some other treatment is to waste resources and gives women the false impression that they have been 'treated' when what is wrong with them is actually highly untreatable or treatment-resistant. Therefore, *The Institute* believes that those with serious brain malfunctions should be given the strictest interventions, legally and criminally, since the best predictor of their futures is not only their past behavior, but their permanent behavior as well.

Many people don't know my father was murdered by a psychopath. I share victim-hood with many women who will read this book but who are alive to make different choices about psychopathy than my father had available to him. My 25+ year journey into *trying* to understand psychopathy has finally been quenched in understanding the biology behind this insidious disorder. Understanding the behavior of 'Mr. Manley' who plunged a knife into my father's gut and ripped out his aorta was pretty hard to understand in light of a 'merely bad childhood theory.' For 25+ years and 20 years as a therapist in the very field of pathology, many things did not quite 'add up' in theory for me about 'why' pathology causes people to act in certain, not just violent ways. After hundreds and hundreds of patients, I-knew-that-I-knew-that-I-knew something *'else'* was at play. Mr. Manley's bad childhood, alcoholic condition, and willful behavior were icing on the cake to what brewed beneath the surface in the organ of his brain.

There is a lot of hard science now behind the hard-wiring of pathology for us to look at which will be discussed in more details in a chapter later in the book. Hard science has helped me 'connect-the-dots' of theory that had not previously added up for me. Today, I believe that psychopathy, and for that matter, the Cluster B personality disorders, are a complex weaving of many factors which include biological, neurological, brain malformations, chemical disruptions, brain circuitry issues, uncompleted childhood developmental tasks, and often abuse and neglect that form a seriously disordered framework of innate and created pathology.

Implications

So what are the implications of a disorder that can be both nature-**and**-nurture-oriented? First of all, it should relieve partners, parents and anyone else from the 'guilt' related to "I did something that caused this" or "I made this person worse." *The Institute* receives hundreds of emails a year from guilt-ridden mothers who feel personally responsible for having pathological adult children who bilk the system, who don't take care of their own children, and whom resemble no one in the family regarding conscience, morality or empathy.

Partners believe if they had 'just been a little more tolerant, patient, giving, sexual, etc.' that the relationship would have worked out. There are no approaches, theories, or manuals called *How to Make a Relationship Work with a Psychopath*—sounds ridiculous, right? Yet many women believe that he will be 'happy' with the next person because the failure of the relationship had to do with her or what she did or did not do in the relationship (and of course he told her this). He won't be—he doesn't have the ability to turn on and off his pathology when he wants it to be 'gone,' so he can have a healthier relationship this time around. In his case, this has nothing to do with her anymore than any congenital disorder he might have been born with is about her. His disorder is not about her relationship. It's only *manifested* there.

Mothers often feel guilty that they keep their children away from him even though he is the biological father. What in the world does a psychopath have that is healthy or productive to give in parenting? Understanding the entire package of pathology should help parents, partners, and others make safer decisions for theirs and their children's future.

Hopefully, this information about 'Nature-VS-Nurture' has relieved survivors of the burdens of:

o   She isn't strong enough to 'overcome' his genetic propensity for pathology.
o   She isn't going to 'love' him into genetic-repair.
o   She isn't going to 'understand' his neurology into functioning.
o   She isn't going to 'pray' him into good neurobiology.

Beyond her ability to fix him lies the bigger issue—what these forms of pathology 'imply' to his future functioning. I call these 'The Three Inabilities' that help women to balance future expectations about the psychopath (not to balance the future *with* the psychopath, but to align her expectations with what is realistic given his disorder).

The Three Inabilities

1. The inability to grow to any authentic emotional and spiritual depth.
2. The inability to sustain positive change.
3. The inability to develop insight about how his negative behavior affects others.

These three inabilities represent the future potential of any relationship. Non-pathological people continue to grow emotionally and spiritually, sustain positive emotional and behavioral changes that they make, and have insight about how their behavior affects others while the psychopath doesn't and can't. Counseling is only effective if a person has the ability to grow emotionally, to sustain the positive changes that are encouraged, and to have insight about their own behavioral affects on others. Even spiritual counseling is predicated upon the ability to grow, change, and develop insight. Without these three rudimentary abilities, nothing else can happen in them or their relationships. This is why to a large degree pathology is not curable. For progress to be made, a person has to begin with the fundamental abilities to change, grow, and develop insight. Throughout this and subsequent chapters, we will see more of the many reasons associated with the psychopath's emotional developmental deficits, their neuro-abnormalities, their brain functioning, and why these groups of low/no conscience disorders do not sustain change, grow, or develop true insight.

Conclusion

Understanding the causes of pathology helps us lay the groundwork for examining in the rest of the book the behavior, communication processes, and relationship dynamics attached to pathology.

Now that we have finished discussing the 'Nature-VS-Nurture' argument and the explanations behind it, in the next chapter we will talk about why psychopathy is hard to spot—starting with its own unique birthmarks.

3

He's Flying Under the Radar
Why She Misses the Clues

"People don't change. Only their costumes do." — *Gene Moore*

What makes psychopathy so different, so surreal, so much like a relational b@$*tch-slap that it nearly knocks her head off?

o   The sensation of being emotionally 'jumped' from behind.

o   The inability to wrap her head around the emotional-physical-spiritual-sexual gang-bang that just happened when she thought she was with the most wonderful person.

No one can figure out how a dangerous psychopath curled up to them like a purring cat. Half of recovery is just trying to figure out 'what was THAT?'

The longest portion of therapy is always helping the woman understand 'what' the psychopath *is*. What he does, how he feels, how his brain thinks, what he says, what is at his core—all these traits are far outside the average person's experience. To understand what happened to her, she must learn to understand his peculiar traits. Most people, not just her, fail to recognize these traits and identify his pathology.

Unrecognizable! Didn't See the Chameleon Coming

These women tend to see others as a reflection of themselves—trusting and open. The psychopaths slide right by her because this country does a poor job teaching psychopathy to the general public— what it is, does, and how it affects others. You can't spot what you aren't aware of. Without proper education, our idea of recognizing psychopathy is based on the cardboard cutouts from media, books, television and film. As a result, while the average filmgoer/TV viewer might recognize *Jason* in a hockey mask, they will probably miss a real psychopath until after the damage is done. The real psychopath has unique traits that are contradictory, dichotomous, just plain abnormal, yet well hidden!

Women often feel ridiculous that they let someone *this* disordered into their lives and they didn't even recognize the symptoms until she was way in over her head and emotionally destroyed. Welcome to the world of psychopathy where many—even most—don't recognize them either! The main characteristic of this disorder is social behavior and social hiding. Psychopaths blend in as 'normal' and manipulate others into believing them. These unique chameleon-like traits help them to move about freely and remain largely undetected. This is why Cleckley called these traits 'The Mask of Sanity'—because psychopaths can look and act (at least for periods of time) like a normal person. Even Robert Hare, a psychopathy expert, often tells stories about his own miscalculations of psychopaths and how he's been taken in by them. He shows up to work at a prison *expecting* a psychopath to at least try to con him, and he's *still* been drawn in by them.

As a rule, women don't think psychopaths will show up in their lives as potential dates. They think all the Hannibal Lecters are locked up and that psychopathic bank robbers with masks and guns are easy to identify and avoid during Happy Hour hook-ups. As a result, people tend not to 'be on the lookout' for psychopaths in their lives. If you ask people on the street, most would tell you they've never met one and don't expect to. The erroneous, yet common view about psychopaths is the belief they are:

o   rare
o   primarily killers
o   at the very least criminal
o   unable to succeed in the work force or social settings
o   probably come marked and branded between the eyes like Charlie Manson

It seems clear from the evidence of their victims that the sheer number of psychopaths who are *not* criminal is much larger than many people realize. Wearing an Armani suit and carrying a $500 brief case, sporting a contagious amount of energy or maybe a love for the great outdoors, they slide right under a woman's radar *because they do not meet her expectations of what a psychopath looks and behaves like.* It is estimated that 1 in 25 have a 'no conscience' disorder. The next time you are sitting around at Happy Hour, count off every 25 people and there's likely to be one!

Beyond not recognizing psychopaths, there are other aspects of psychopathy that fool the average normal-ite. These include the psychopath's often successful careers, non-violent approaches, unusual emotions, manipulative behaviors, abnormal brain functioning, and the spiritual manifestation of 'evil'—all of which we look at here and in the following chapters.

Favorably Fortunate

Women are often 'success-struck' by the psychopath's true or surface success. This blinds them to his psychopathy. There are millions of pathological personalities who destroy people's lives—with or without breaking the law. These people unfortunately never go to prison, so their true criminal nature is never unmasked. They are outwardly successful, and can be seen in high-ranking CEO positions, politics, and prestigious positions in law, medicine, and the military. When trusting women expect psychopaths to be criminals, they don't look for them in the pulpit, the penthouse corner office or on Capitol Hill.

Cleckley noted psychopaths seek out positions with power over others:

o   medical doctors

o   psychiatrists or other positions within other fields of psychology

o   religious leaders

o   political leaders

o   lawyers, etc.

Pathological power-mongrels seek any place they can have a client, a constituent, a patient, a congregation, or a following. Some career titles such as medicine, psychology, and theology imply empathy. This assumption allows conscience-less psychopaths to hide among truly empathetic professionals. Other popular careers psychopaths use to 'cloak' their lack of empathy include politics, law, and criminal justice. The psychopaths blend into human service fields so well they are often 'missed'—even by their own colleagues.

However, all psychopaths are not successful. Ironically, the women in our survey met up with a slightly different career-type psychopath. I want the reading public to know, however, many psychopaths are very successful. The more successful they are, the better they blend in, and the harder it is for anyone to recognize or believe they are as pathological as the day is long.

Slick But Not Always Violent

Women don't recognize the psychopath for what he is because they assume people with dangerous disorders are always violent. As many of our clients can attest, there are many ways to harm a loved one without actually beating or killing them. Though he never laid a hand on them, the psychological, spiritual, sexual, financial, or emotional harm he did to them generated long-term Post Traumatic Stress Disorder and other disorders. Very often the victims describe this harm as bad as death.

Without physical violence in the relationship, many women miss other signs of pathology that could have clued them in. Women blame either the relationship dynamics or themselves, completely missing his psychopathy. She never saw him for what he really was until she was extremely damaged.

Swaggering Swindlers

A woman didn't suspect his psychopathy because she never expected a man to wipe her out financially. She believes men are there to be mutually supportive including financially, so she didn't look for a financial rip-off artist. Many psychopaths are con-men or swindlers that confiscate financial resources, help themselves to life savings, steal stock pensions and yet never get caught. One of the signs of pathology is the 'parasitic' lifestyle in which they live off others, even if they don't need the money. This past year, the news has been filled with examples of psychopathic con-men, white collar snakes and swindlers. Almost 90% of the women coming out of relationships with psychopaths have gone from six figure incomes to financial destitution. Many can't understand why he took their money and ran when he had the ability to earn his own or had his own money. Before you judge them, remember Bernie Madoff and his astounding financial salesmanship.

Menacing Mind Games

Women misjudged his pathology because of his prolific brain-games. He used gaslighting techniques to convince her she had a break with reality. Some survivors called it 'The Ultimate Mind Screw'—sending prominent female executives, attorneys, and doctors into mental institutions to recover from him. Coercion, psychological warfare techniques and Stockholm Syndrome symptoms have left the survivors sawed off at the emotional-knees by a smooth-talking and ear-to-ear grinning psychological terrorist. Instead of realizing she never felt more psychologically sick she wonders why she isn't up to par in the relationship. Something must be wrong with her—just like he said. Although normal people accept blame for their behavior, a psychopath won't. Such is the makeup of psychopathy. He keeps her mentally off-balance by playing the 'Hector Projector' game. In this game, he projects blame for his own behavior onto her. She then spends most of her mental energy focused on him, trying to figure out why he is doing that to her. She also misses his ability to lie while staring her in the eye, because it's not a common feature people are use to. In fact, the psychopath lies readily even though he knows he may eventually be found out by others. His menacing mind games are just another reason why his pathology goes unrecognized.

Exploitive Ethics

Women get confused by the psychopath's dichotomous behavior—his actions do not agree with his words. While he may *espouse* an ethical belief system, his behavior diametrically opposes those ethics. Although unbelievably persuasive, psychopaths can only respond to ethical values verbally and superficially. Their careers positions have nothing to do with their ethics—they can be a youth minister, a special education teacher, or a medical missionary and have the ethics of a snake. Women miss who he actually is when they listen to what he says he believes.

Impression Management While Conscienceless

Women are sideswiped by his ability to 'put up a good front' even as he exploits them. She doesn't realize psychopathy lies behind his charming exterior. He social-climbs into everyone's good graces using charisma, a good sense of humor, and an optimistic outlook (at least on the surface). If his mask should slip a bit, he simply 'impression manages' his way right back into positive believability.

He deceives women into believing that impression management = good character. She doesn't recognize that at his core, he does not have the capacity (based on brain function) to develop conscience. Instead, he compensates with the gift of gab, good impression management, and often success and intelligence. Throw in a little gaslighting every time she starts to get close to his real behavior, and you have someone flying so far under her radar that it takes her months, if not years to realize it. Once she realizes it, it takes others, including family members and friends, many years to realize it too—if they ever do.

Flying under the radar and hiding his psychopathy are not the only unusual things about psychopaths. There is one adjective used repeatedly to describe the psychopath. This adjective provides yet another reason he seems to defy detection—when they're dating, who is looking for *'evil?'*

The Spiritual Experience of Evil

Lastly, a unique trait that hides his psychopathy from her is his spiritual 'twistedness.' There isn't a woman alive who thought she was looking for Satan to date. She most likely projected her own spirituality on him, giving him a quality he was not likely to have.[20] In the classic book on evil *People of the Lie,*[21] M. Scott Peck describes how evil hides:

> *"We see the smile that hides the hatred, the smooth and oily manner that masks the fury, the velvet glove that covers the fist. Because they are such experts at disguise, it is seldom possible to pin point the maliciousness of the evil. The disguise is usually impenetrable."*

Whatever the women's spiritual beliefs—heathens, pagans, Christians, Jews, Buddhists—the most popular adjective the women used to describe the psychopath was 'evil.'

Women frequently described the psychopath as nothing short of a Soul Slayer. He slew her existential essence—her spiritual self. Women intuitively labeled their experience of his harm as 'spiritually evil,' not just

---

[20] Remember, one of the Inabilities mentioned is the inability to develop authentic spirituality.
[21] Peck, M. Scott (1983). *People of the Lie: The Hope For Healing Human Evil.* New York: Simon & Schuster.

in the context of another negative personality trait, but something only experienced by the spirit.

Is this Soul Slayer's evil merely psychological, or is it spiritual evil, or both? Those who write about the demonized psychopath have all tried to spiritually explain what he 'is.' They have described him as 'lost to humanity' and 'a catalog of human evil.' Peck devoted an entire chapter of his book *People of the Lie* to the subject. In the chapter *Toward a Psychology of Evil,* he discussed whether it is psychological evil, spiritual evil, both, or totally unrecognized.

> *"Human evil is too important for a one-sided understanding. And it is too large a reality to be grasped within a single frame of reference...We do not yet have a body of scientific knowledge about human evil deserving of being called a psychology. Why not? Yet it is virtually absent from our science of psychology."*

In psychology, our cultural inability to define the psychopath's evil has also hindered female victims the same way—they can't recognize the psychopath's evil either. As a result, she ends up with a personification of evil.

The psychopath is often compared to, or even assumed to be, the Devil, Satan, Lucifer, Spiritual Darkness, the Fallen Angel, and many other references to religious manifestations of serious badness.

Reiber & Vetter referred to the 'devil' as the incarnate of conscience-lessness—everything the psychopath 'is.' For the psychopath, the demonic is a way of life and has evolved through the centuries, acquiring a 'host of representations ranging from the truly bestial to the suave silk-clad sophisticate.'

The *'Mephisto Syndome'* might indeed be the psychopath's syndrome as well. It's described as the personification of the demonic. Psychopathy has been referred to by the same phrase. Mephisto was a character in the classic literature writer Goethe's drama in which the demon who bought the soul of Faustus described himself as 'a part of that force which always wants the bad' (an attitude obviously shared with the psychopath).

In the drama, although Mephisto appears to Faustus as a devil—a worker of Satan—critics claim that he does not search for men to corrupt, but comes to serve and ultimately collect the souls of those who are already damned. Mephisto does not appear to Faustus as a devil on earth tempting and corrupting any man encountered. He appears to Faustus because the devil already senses *he is already corrupt,* that indeed he is already *'in danger to be damned.'*

Perhaps this is where psychological evil and spiritual evil meet—in the middle of the superhighway of both genetic predisposition and spiritual domination. So the mask of the devil is equally worn as a mask by the psychopath—hiding behind it not only as Jekyll and Hyde, but as Satan too. Whether the psychopath has always been evil or became evil as Peck alleges in *People of the Lie,* most who have encountered him are sure of his spiritual status of 'Satan-like.'

We shouldn't be surprised to find scriptures from the Old Testament (The Torah, Jewish) and the New Testament (The Bible, Christian) chocked full of examples of pathology. If we believe that we are triune— representing body, mind, and spirit—then surely spiritual writing will also show us how mind and spirit can go astray and be evil.

The Institute is always asked how this is, or is not, supported in spiritual doctrine, namely Christianity. Although *The Institute* is planning a book in the future about how pathology is referenced to in scripture and shown as early as the Garden of Eden forward, I thought I would take a few paragraphs to address the issue of psychological and spiritual evil as documented in Jewish and Christian doctrine.

To review, *DSM-IV, Women Who Love Psychopaths* and other literature has described the psychopath's behavior as:

o   fails to follow laws or rules/uses unethical

o   unlawful and immoral behavior

o   deceitful

o   lies

o   cons for fun or profit

o   impulsive

o   wants it/takes it

o   sees it/does it

o   aggression

o   disregard for the safety of others

o   puts others at risk

o   irresponsible—bad with supporting others

o   lack of remorse

o   rationalizes stealing, lying

o   pretends to be wonderful, helpful, supportive

This description also matches many spiritual references to the devil masquerading as an *'Angel of Light'* or *'Satan'* in some of his more appealing and beautiful forms—calling others to himself before exposing who he really is.

The following table compares pathology traits side-by-side. The material in the first column is from the DSM-IV which describes Cluster B personality disorder traits/sociopathy/psychopathy, from *Women Who Love Psychopaths,* or other literature about pathology referencing the traits.

The second column is from Old Testament (of the Jewish faith) and New Testament (of the Christian faith) as examples of the definition of 'evil.' You could most likely find similar definitions of evil in other religious texts from other religions as well.

Table 3.1
Examples of Pathology –
DSM-IV, Women Who Love Psychopaths, and Other
Literature vs. Scripture

DSM-IV, Women Who Love Psychopaths, and Other Literature	Scripture
Grandiose, self important and pre-occupied with self	Wants people to worship him
Fantasizes about power, brilliance, success, and money	Says to God "I WILL ascend, I Will Rise..." (Showing power fantasies)
Requires excessive admiration	Says "You WILL bow down to me"
Is entitled	Wants the same power as God, feels he's as powerful as God
Exploits all relationships	Tries to lure others to do his dirty work in the world
Lacks empathy	Envious of others

DSM-IV, Women Who Love Psychopaths, and Other Literature	Scripture
Superior attitude towards others	Is superior to other angels in power and authority
Contempt for others especially authority figures	Fights against God and wants His power
Use power and authority over others	Called the 'Prince of Power'
Prideful	Heart is filled with pride and contempt
Splits people against each other	Turned 1/3 of the angels against God and took them
Destroy and deceive others (and enjoy doing it)	Called 'The Destroyer' and 'Deceiver'
Often charming or attractive	Lucifer called 'the most beautiful,' name means 'the shining one'
Often rejected, expelled, dismissed, broken up with because of behavior	God expelled him from Heaven
Places are created to contain them: jail, prison, mental institutions, probation	Created a place to contain him in the future—'Lake of Fire'
Fights against any rules and others who try to make him conform	Fights against God to ruin and hinder His plans
Masquerades as anything you want him to be	Masquerades as the 'Angel of Light'
Likes to scare others and show power so others fear him	Prowls like a roaring lion
Bold, cunning, self ambitious	Boldness, subtlety in his cunningness
Self willed and strong, prideful self will	Narcissistic wanting to be better than everyone Said "I will be like the Most High"

DSM-IV, Women Who Love Psychopaths, and Other Literature	Scripture
Fakes being wonderful, helpful, virtuous	Many false prophets have gone in the world (like him), performs lying 'signs and wonders'
Accuses others	Called 'The Accuser'
Adversary, enemy to any who turn against him	Called the Serpent or 'Adversary'
Liar, tempter, thief	Satan referred to as a liar, thief and tempter
Motives are destructive to others	Motives are to deceive and afflict

It is clear in some spiritual texts that spiritual evil has almost no separation from psychological evil, or vice versa. In the end, there are some things we don't totally understand such as how the spirit realm can affect the psychological realm, or how one's pathology may taint their spirit. But it has been clear to me, and hundreds of survivors, that 'evil' straddles vocabularies and worlds of both psychological definitions and spiritual ones as well. The spiritual union of souls when united to a psychopath is like none other. Those who have united in the spiritual realm can attest to the evil witnessed in that sharing. There is still much to learn about how psychology and theology meld. One thing is for sure— 'evilness' flew in under the radar because who expects they are dating Mephisto?

Conclusion

In this chapter we looked at some of the issues related to the unique traits of the psychopath and why they manage to fool so many people for so long. Women often need to forgive themselves for being conned by someone so sick. In all honesty, this is a disorder that hides well in the midst of society. Acceptance is probably a more appropriate description than forgiveness.

Flying under society's radar included their unique traits related to:

o   being unrecognizable and hiding well

- o   not always violent
- o   side-swiped her financially
- o   prolific brain games
- o   exploitive ethics
- o   impression management while conscienceless
- o   the spiritual experience of evil

With unusual symptoms that most people don't look for in someone else, the psychopath is free to blow in and blow out of people's lives, leaving wounded women in his wake. Yet his behavior and emotions are not the only unusual things about a psychopath. The biological differences in his brain open up a whole new territory to explore.

4 The Neuroscience of His Pathology

Differences in Brain Function

"If you want to truly understand something, try to change it."

— *Kurt Lewin*

The brain as an organ has the same proclivity to be born damaged as does the heart, the lungs, or the immune system. We don't question that a child can be born with a heart defect, but we don't believe that a child can be born with a brain defect that mostly affects behavior primarily within their relationships. It's hard to fathom that the best way to *'see'* this disorder is to *'see'* the dysfunction of it within relationships. This clearly is part of why people don't suspect psychopathy—because they don't suspect brain problems in someone who looks normal from the outside and is often so bright. Understanding brain differences has had a huge impact on *The Institute's* pathology education with others. This may be the single most important aspect we teach in changing her view of him and the intensity of their connection.

Let's take a look at brain functioning and its impact on pathology. The research findings below are related to the brain of:

o   unsuccessful psychopaths (those caught)
o   antisocials
o   other psychopathic types
o   Cluster B personality disorders
o   and/or violent perpetrators

In our umbrella term for psychopathic persons in Chapter One, I lumped these disorders together for the women's understanding. Following the same approach with the umbrella term, I am lumping brain problems together for an overview of the extensive foray of problems associated with the low/no conscienced group. *Take note of how the similar problems of impulsivity and the inability to learn from negative consequences are repeated in various brain regions and brain functions strengthening the dysfunction.*

Limbic

The limbic region of the brain:

o   is related to emotional language
o   communication
o   emotional processing

The limbic region includes the hippocampus and amygdala which are covered below.

The limbic region is weak in psychopaths causing them to struggle in understanding (yet ironically still manipulating) the emotional language. While they may not totally understand some aspects of emotional language (because they don't appear to have the full emotional spectrum of feelings) these deficits become very apparent later in relationships when she finally notices he can't authentically understand, relate to, and/or express real emotions. Although the psychopath learns to 'mimic and parrot' emotional words back to her, this is not the same thing as having true emotional intelligence, understanding, and the corresponding emotional language.

Normally, the limbic system allows people to consciously and willfully self-regulate their emotional responses. Yet in weak limbic systems, such as the psychopath's, the inability to self-regulate impulse and emotional responses are fraught with disastrous possibilities.

Hippocampus

The hippocampus is part of the brain that:

o   regulates aggression and impulsivity
o   transfers information into memory
o   helps people learn which situations to be afraid of

The issue of non-regulated aggression and impulsivity is related to various brain regions and brain functions including, but not limited to, the hippocampus. It fuels the psychopath's dangerousness, and in some aspects connects to his 'inability to sustain positive change.' This particular brain malfunction stands as one of the hallmark characteristics related to psychopathy as well as other personality disorders.

Psychopaths have problems transferring information into emotion and into the making of new memories. Those with hippocampus deficits have problems living in the present and are stuck in the past of old memories.[22]

Many psychopaths talk a lot about the past and only vaguely 'carrot dangle' about their future and the women's part in it. One wonders if the inability to be concerned about the future is why they are not highly invested in what happens in the relationship in the future.

This inability to transfer relational information into emotion may also be related to why their attachments seem to be surface and shallow. I refer to this in The Inabilities related to the inability to grow to any emotional or spiritual depth. The inability of the emotional system to live in the present moment, experiencing the emotion of the moment has much to do with their inability to grow to any emotional depth. Portions of their emotional spectrum are deficient of emotions they do not experience or have a reduced capacity to feel (such as empathy, conscience, remorse, fear, sadness and disgust).

Also negatively affected is the process of learning which situations to fear which is called 'contextual fear conditioning.' Raine has been comparing successful psychopaths (those not caught) with the unsuccessful psychopaths (those who were caught). In unsuccessful psychopaths, the fear conditioning plays a role in learning the concepts of what to do and not to do—how to learn from the consequences of their wrong choices. Those with more damage to the hippocampus seem to miss the cues that helped them predict punishment and respond to it by changing their behavior. Raine also noted that the unsuccessful psychopath showed differing sizes and shapes of the hippocampus. The differing sizes may reflect an abnormality in the neuro-development process which resulted in emotional regulation problems and not enough fear or concern about getting caught.[23]

---

[22] Raine, A., Ishikawa SS, Arce E., Lencz T., Knuth KH, Bihrle S., LaCasse, L., Colletti, P., (2004). Department of Psychology, University of Southern California, Hippocampal Structural Asymmetry in Unsuccessful Psychopaths. *Bio Psychiatry.* Jan 15;55(2):185-91.

[23] Raine, A., Ishikawa SS, Arce E., Lencz T., Knuth KH, Bihrle S., LaCasse, L., Colletti, P., (2004). Department of Psychology, University of Southern

The women have difficulty understanding *why he doesn't sustain positive change.* One aspect of it is the inability to profit from their negative experiences.

Lastly, structurally there is a disruption of the circuit linking the hippocampus with the neighboring brain region contributing not only to the impulsiveness and lack of control previously mentioned but also to their overall emotional abnormalities.[24]

Hippocampus problems and resulting impulsivity are not just in psychopaths. These were also noted in some personality disorders which increased the behaviors of lying, stealing, and infidelity. All of issues ultimately damage their relationships.[25]

This is why these clusters of behavior are so often seen in the low conscienced group of disorders.

Corpus Callosum

The corpus callosum region of the brain is a bundle of nerve fibers that connect the two hemispheres of the brain helping them to work together in:

o   processing information

o   producing emotions and social connectedness

o   regulating acting out behaviors

Normally, the left hemisphere processes information analytically, sequentially, aids understanding and the use of language while the right

California, Hippocampal Structural Asymmetry in Unsuccessful Psychopaths. *Bio Psychiatry.* Jan 15;55(2):185-91.

[24] Raine, A., Ishikawa SS, Arce E., Lencz T., Knuth KH, Bihrle S., LaCasse, L., Colletti, P., (2004). Department of Psychology, University of Southern California, Hippocampal Structural Asymmetry in Unsuccessful Psychopaths. *Bio Psychiatry.* Jan 15;55(2):185-91.

[25] Oakley, Barbara (2007). *Evil Genes: Why Rome Fell, Hitler Rose, Enron Failed, and My Sister Stole My Mother's Boyfriend.* New York: Prometheus Books.

hemisphere processes information and aids in the perception of emotional experience.[26]

However, there are some differences in psychopaths.

For instance, this brain region is approximately 23% larger and 7% longer than others. The rate that the psychopath transmits information from one hemisphere to the other was abnormally high which negatively impacted their processing of information.[27]

With information transmitted so fast, it is likely some emotional cues and clues are missed, mistakes are made in reading situations all of which may increase their response rate before thinking. Since psychopaths have an impaired ability for both regions of the brain to send information and respond correctly to the information, the competition between the two hemispheres makes it difficult to understand and produce language.[28] (However, it should be said that psychopaths are also very skilled at picking up on some other types of cues and clues that will be discussed later.)

This is not unlike what happens in severe cases of epilepsy in which this brain region is the area affected by epilepsy. In these severe cases, the corpus callosum is sometimes surgically severed producing what is called 'split-brain patients.' Interestingly, they seem to share similar symptoms with psychopaths who are also 'severed' in some less surgical ways from the information processing of their impaired brains. In some cases of split-brain patients, they develop bizarre pathologies. One is called the Alien Hand Syndrome during which one hand takes on a life of its own. When the patient is shown an object in his left visual field, they can't name the object despite recognizing it. The speech center and visual fields can't communicate or relay this information.

Here's the interesting part—their inability to communicate between the hemispheres of the brain (much like what the psychopath struggles with) causes them to develop what is described as 'a dual personality, one loosely associated with each hemisphere, a sort of Jekyll and Hyde effect.'

---

[26] Oakley, Barbara (2007). *Evil Genes: Why Rome Fell, Hitler Rose, Enron Failed, and My Sister Stole My Mother's Boyfriend.* New York: Prometheus Books.

[27] University of Southern California 224, March 11. USC Study Finds Faulty Wiring In Psychopaths, *Science Daily.*

[28] Chapter 5 is devoted to communication and language.

Interestingly of course, is that the psychopath is continuously referred to as a Jekyll and Hyde who also seems to have a dual personality—perhaps from the lack of information processing between the two hemispheres.

By far the scariest outcomes related to the increased size of the corpus callosum is that it produces less remorse, fewer emotions, less emotional reactions and less social connectedness—also classic hallmarks of a psychopath, according to Raine.

Psychopaths have high reactions to aggression and are likely to quickly become aggressive in relationships. Their faulty 'Stop' light that regulates behavior does not respond well to his own mounting aggression. This factor alone raises the lethality issue in these relationships.

Lastly, the corpus callosum has negatively impacted their ability to regulate other impulsive behaviors which could play out in the relationship as gambling, addictive or sexual compulsivity issues. Let's see how the impulsivity problems are also repeated in the amygdala.

Amygdala

The amygdala portion of the brain also:

o   regulates impulsivity
o   regulates fight-flight responses

...and is shown to be less reactive in psychopaths. This slow reaction is related to their fight-flight responses, causing them to feel the restlessness we saw in a previous chapter associated with their motivational drives.[29]

It produces a need to 'jack up' that excitement-seeking and risk-taking nature of theirs. He can have knee-jerk reactions to any impulse he feels and can go from "0-to-impulsive-behavior" in seconds. Many women said they saw knee-jerk reactions where the ability to 'think through' choices seems to fast-forward to sheer impulsive behavior. Women have come to understand this reactionary action lends itself to incredible impulsive behavior associated with sex, spending, and even substance use.

---

[29] Oakley, Barbara (2007). *Evil Genes: Why Rome Fell, Hitler Rose, Enron Failed, and My Sister Stole My Mother's Boyfriend.* New York: Prometheus Books.

Impulse control in general has an involuntary temperamental response called *Harm Avoidance* which comes from the feeling of fear. Fear controls our impulses and operates the internal '**Stop**' signal more than any other force or feeling. Scientists agree that although psychopaths do at times experience fear and anxiety (although it is much lower than other people's), these emotions don't *influence* their behavior as in non-psychopathic people. The '**Stop**' light doesn't function properly in psychopaths which is why they pursue pleasure without regard for consequences.[30] We'll be talking about his fear response in more detail later on. What I'd like you to recognize, however, is that with his impaired hippocampus and amygdala which regulate impulsivity, we can see *why* impulsivity is always a feature of the low/no conscienced group!

Orbitofrontal

The orbitofrontal portion of the brain:

o   organizes behavior
o   helps learn from punishment
o   related to motivation
o   empathy and insight
o   impulsiveness and irresponsibility

This affected area causes psychopaths to have trouble organizing their behavior, which seems to stay largely unregulated anyway, in the relationships. It reduces the psychopath's ability to control their impulses and motivation. Although not a surprise, it also appears to affect their ability to positively learn from punishment and to gather insight.[31] If you remember, listed in one of The Inabilities is 'the inability to develop insight how their negative behaviors effect others.' Here is a possible biological reason why.

Psychopaths are not highly responsive to punishment, which in the past was thought to be more associated with the 'nurture theory' of social upbringing—willful or sheer dominating behavior. However, the orbitofrontal is obviously a contributing factor to these behaviors.

---

[30] Contributed by Liane J. Leedom, M.D.
[31] Kiehl, K, Bates, A, Laurens, K, Hare, R. & Liddle, Peter F. Clinical Cognitive Neuroscience Labortatory (paper). Brain Potentials Implicate Temporal Lobe Abnormalities in Criminal Psychopaths.

Related to not learning from negative consequences are the multiple brain regions affecting their moral reasoning, and why they act this way.

Multiple Brain Regions Related to Moral Reasoning Affected

It doesn't take women very long to figure out that the psychopath has a broken internal moral compass. There are functional and/or structural impairments which affect moral reasoning in antisocial populations. This impairment is related to the rule-breaking behavior activated in moral judgment. Antisocials have difficulty with the *feeling* of what is moral more than the *knowing* of what is moral. They know right from wrong but the cognitive recognition does not seem to include behavioral inhibition. That is, stopping the behavior. They are still likely to do what is morally wrong.[32] This aspect alone has inevitable harm written all over it for the women in relationships with someone whose moral compass is biologically broken leaving him (and her) predisposed to his sexual, criminal, and illegal behaviors.

Cleckley had previously noted they have excellent moral reasoning ability when discussing *hypothetical* situations but can't apply this excellent moral concept in guiding their behavior.[33] Many espouse ethical theories reflecting what they say is their belief system yet do none of those ethical behaviors themselves and see no contradiction that they believe something they don't do.

It's not just the morality function that was affected. Functional and structural issues related to these various brain regions included reduced glucose metabolism, reduced blood flow in some areas, and reduced gray matter found in aggressive/violent/antisocial individuals.[34]

---

[32] Raine, A and Yang, Yaling (2006). Neural Foundations to Moral Reasoning and Antisocial Behavior. *Social Cognitive Affect Neuroscience Journal,* December, 1(3):203-213.

[33] This is similar to what was mentioned before that they are good with hypothetical ethics but not real behavioral ethics.

[34] Raine, A and Yang, Yaling (2006). Neural Foundations to Moral Reasoning and Antisocial Behavior. *Social Cognitive Affect Neuroscience Journal,* December, 1(3):203-213.

Other studies found that 64% of violent people have abnormal frontal lobes, 50% show levels of brain atrophy, 40% show EEG abnormalities.[35]

Brain regions are not the only affected areas. We're going to look at some other problem areas as well.

Brain Chemistry

Brain region is not the only problem in psychopaths and some personality disorders. Brain chemistry is just as likely to be affected. Serotonin reception 5-HT plays a role in controlling offensive aggression (or not!) and predisposes people *towards* impulsivity and emotional instability which we have seen is abundantly active in these low conscience disorders.[36]

Serotonin is important because it regulates impulse control, alcohol intake, mood, and aggressiveness. When serotonin is too low, we see an increase in impulse problems, violence, hyperactivity, alcoholism, aggression, and drug abuse.[37]

There are some interesting correlations between altered brain enzymes and pathological behavior. The lower the brain MAO, the more they take advantage of others, have a short temper, and prone to vindictiveness. These altered enzymes are associated with the entire gamut of antisocial/aggressive/criminal behavior showing us just one more view of the potential differences in the brains of those affected by pathology.[38]

Genetics

Genetically, there is equally compelling information about these guys being 'born' into a pretty bad pool of pathological genetics. To date, they have located genes on certain chromosomes that create types of mental illness such as bipolar disorder and schizophrenia. Now they are using this

---

[35] *Truthoughts Corrective Thinking Treatment Model* (PowerPoint).

[36] Oakley, Barbara (2007). *Evil Genes: Why Rome Fell, Hitler Rose, Enron Failed, and My Sister Stole My Mother's Boyfriend.* New York: Prometheus Books.

[37] *Truthoughts Corrective Thinking Treatment Model* (PowerPoint).

[38] Oakley, Barbara (2007). *Evil Genes: Why Rome Fell, Hitler Rose, Enron Failed, and My Sister Stole My Mother's Boyfriend.* New York: Prometheus Books.

new research to find out what contributes to the development of genetic pathology. Supporting this, genetic vulnerabilities have already been found that cause differences in the neuro-development of children who have traits related to psychopathic behavior as well as varied genes that are related to behaviors associated with personality disorders.

There have been similar breakthroughs in genetics and the size and shape of the brain related to personality disorders. Genetically, a single trait that can affect many genes seems to underlie personality disorders and the MAO-A gene has been linked to Cluster B personality disorders and also aggression.[39]

The frontier of the biology of personality disorders, pathology, and behavioral genetics is beginning. With each decade we may come to not only understand the mind and how it is impaired in pathology, but the brain and the genetic DNA that make us who and *'what'* we do!

Conclusion

I hope what stands out in this chapter on neuroscience is the constant re-enforcement within the pathological's altered brain system and function related ***to impulsive and aggressive behavior.*** We have seen how many times impulsivity, aggressive behavior and the inability to learn from negative consequences was mentioned regarding brain function. The pathological's biology is wired for it on many different levels from brain region to brain circuitry to brain chemistry.

If women ever wondered what 'she' could do to help him or how she could 'positively' change their relationship I think this chapter has clarified her ability in any of that.

Now I'll look at why communicating about his behavior or the relationship is likely to not produce change in him, but will only produce the feeling she is going crazy. Talking the language of a psychopath is not easy…

---

[39] Oakley, Barbara (2007). *Evil Genes: Why Rome Fell, Hitler Rose, Enron Failed, and My Sister Stole My Mother's Boyfriend.* New York: Prometheus Books.

5 She Says Potato, He Says Po-ta-to

A Guide to Psychopath's Language and Communication Barriers

"You can construct the character of a man and his age not only from what he does and says, but from what he fails to say and do." — Norman Douglas

Another unique trait about psychopaths which is not only frustrating but likely a reason he goes undetected is the devious (yet distorted) way he communicates with others. On one hand, the psychopath appears to be the Master Communicator, seducing anyone within ear range who can become entranced in his storylines, humor, intensity, or charisma. On the other hand, beyond the seduction of his tongue there is a lot about his communicating that isn't 'normal' and is actually confusing and crazy-making.

In the last chapter I looked at brain dysfunction which is critical for understanding the psychopath's behaviors, and which helped us realize that with brain abnormalities this severe, it's no wonder the relationship is fraught with problems. Yet also important to understanding these relationships is what *is* and *isn't* happening in the communication with the psychopath and why.

These problems stem not only from impulsivity and aggression, but inevitably the communication that is generated *from* a brain this disordered. I will look at the communication dynamics in this chapter (and in more detail later in the section on relationships). We'll see why the psychopath's women become confused about:

o   what he's saying

o   why he's saying it

o   how it became convoluted and contradictory

First, let's discuss some of the challenges that she will *not* overcome while attempting to communicate with a psychopath. The psychopath is bad at some communication elements and yet good at others, even if it's for the wrong reason.

Figure 5.1
What the Psychopath is Bad At and Good At

He's Bad At	He's Good At
Abstract language	Concrete language
Unmoved by some emotional concepts	Smooth talking and hiding communication problems
Devious motivation for communication	Semantically changing meaning of words
Language is contradictory	Mimicking and Parroting words/gestures back to her
Lack of emotional processing related to empathy, conscience, remorse, fear, sadness and disgust	Predatory 6th sense for loneliness, grief, vulnerability
Avoidance of communication he doesn't want to have	Non-verbal cues like body language, eye lingo and gestures/movements

Here's how these play out...

Language and Concepts

Abstract Words

Just like brain function is a fact of his biology, language problems are also a fact within pathology. While he has both the brain hard wiring (biology) and the desire to con (motivation) discussed below, there are other dynamics happening while he is trying to 'communicate.' I will start with what can go wrong using language—hers or his.

Communication is comprised of concrete and abstract language, or words. Abstract is anything that is intangible or without a physical form. Most people use both concrete and abstract words in their daily language habits. Psychopaths, however, struggle with the use of abstract language. They are much better at concrete words.[40]

Women eventually recognize this 'master linguist' surprisingly has problems with communication. Frequent clues of his misuse of abstract words include:

o   A blank look on his face when she uses words he apparently does not understand.

o   When responding back to her about the context of a word, he uses the word incorrectly.

o   He changes the subject when words come up he doesn't want to discuss.

o   Abstract words and related subjects are deemed off limits so these words/concepts are no longer discussed.

o   Words and their concepts are degraded and labeled stupid to avoid her ever wanting to discuss 'stupid' concepts.

While his I.Q. is likely to be adequate (if not high), it is the abstractness of language that causes a psychopath to become a deer in the headlights when language moves beyond his emotional comprehension.

In some cases, psychopaths may pretend to misunderstand on purpose in order to upset her. Some psychopaths are sadistic. Her pain is his pleasure, or in some cases even erotic to him. Watching her in pain about the inability to communicate with him is no doubt pleasurable to him.

Abstract Concepts

Abstract words are not their only abstract-oriented problem. They also have difficulty with abstract relational concepts. Psychopaths are unmoved by some emotional concepts which is partially related to the issue of abstract language. She is shocked to be pouring out her heart in an argument to the most unfeeling of persons who is not moved in the least by her pain. (In the luring stages, he is likely to pay much more attention to appearing to understand her emotions.)

---

[40] Kiehl, K., Hare, R, McDonald, J., Brink, J. (1999). Semantic and affective processing in psychopaths: An event-related potential ERP study. *Psychophysiology,* 36, 765-774. Cambridge University Press.

It doesn't make sense to her that someone who uses language like a fine-honed tool is also challenged with it. How can a smooth-tongued 'Satan-snake' speak so well but understand concepts of the relationship so poorly? What she doesn't realize is what he can *smooth talk* and what he can *conceptually understand* may be two different things. She is likely taken off-guard by the contrast between his ability to speak well but relate poorly. She eventually, although not immediately, begins to see what is missing from the language, communication and the meaning *behind it.* Here are some of those slippery abstract words and concepts that psychopaths probably have a hard time grasping:

o accurate	o identification	o peace
o commitment	o interpretation	o poverty
o communication problems	o justice	o principles
	o kind	o real
o compassion	o lessons	o reality
o consensual	o liberty	o sensing
o courage	o love	o sentimental
o democracy	o loyalty	o solutions
o empathy	o mood	o tension
o future	o morals	o tolerance
o healthy	o mutuality	
o humanity		
o idealistic faith		

From this brief list, we can see how a woman using abstract concepts to discuss emotions and relationship traits can't get anywhere in establishing true communication with a psychopath who has only concrete understanding. After the honeymoon phase with him, she comes to believe that to correct what is going wrong in their relationship, she needs to communicate more. Yet communicating more doesn't help.

Semantics & Meaning

Another issue related to language and psychopathy is the noted problem of semantics.[41] Frustrations for women are the psychopath's

---

[41] Semantics is the interpretation of a word or sentence—the 'meaning' behind and in language.

'unique' use and view of language—or the semantics of what a word *means*. We often call the psychopath's abuse of semantics 'using loopholes' or 'word twisting'—finding ways to avoid traditional use of the meaning behind words. What woman hasn't been tangled up in language while trying to get on the same page as the psychopath when defining just what he means?

When normal people communicate we are for the most part, talking apples-to-apples. However with a psychopath:

o   she talks apples and he hears oranges

o   she talks apples and he tries to make an orange an apple

o   she talks apples and he says the apple isn't really an apple

Her language is not his language. So, when the woman says, "Do you love me?" we have to ask what is the psychopath's 'meaning' for the word 'love'? Given what we understand about his difficulty with abstract words, just what does that mean to him? It likely means something different to him. The closest meaning of the word 'love' to him is her act of compliance to his dominance. That is not what she meant (compliance) when she used the word 'love.'

Here's a guide to what common relationship words *might* possibly mean to a psychopath:

Figure 5.2
A Guide to a Normal Person's Language vs.
a Psychopath's Language

Normal Person's Language	Psychopath's Language
Love	Her compliance
Trust	Paranoia
Communication	Opportunity
Bonding	Attachment
I need you	I want you
Lying	This is my truth
Stealing	Borrowing
Cheating	Equalizing the playing field
Monogamy	Monogamy in the moment

Normal Person's Language	Psychopath's Language
Future	Right now
Morals	To each their own
Interpretation	How the psychopath sees it
Problems	Her hassling him
Humanity	Suckers
Courage	The absence of fear
Sentimental	Unsafely soft
Faith	Not fact

With skewed meanings like these how can real communication occur and how can she not be inevitably harmed by this level of language distortion and relationship pathology?

Loop-holing, Word-twisting and Comprehension-dodging

The psychopath's abuse of semantics is often referred to as 'loop-holing' or 'word-twisting,' which is finding ways to avoid the traditional use of word meanings so he can convert language to support his views or manipulative desires. He is only limited by his own imagination of how twisting and dodging can benefit him. For instance, he may:

o   not answer questions
o   answer with something else unrelated
o   redirect the question to her
o   twist one word in the sentence into a fight
o   reference other discussions
o   use phrases that distract her so she has to ask him to clarify thus getting off the original discussion
o   use gaslighting to warp her reality
o   project his behavior onto her
o   go into long storytelling to deflects the original discussion
o   use a word to express an idea, but the normal use of that word expresses something else

This list reflects the ways he distorts and avoids meaning. His fragmented communication is nothing more than deceptive language.

Sam Vaknin in his book *Malignant Self Love* describes pathological language this way:

> *"Language is a weapon of self defense. It's used to fend off, hide and evade, avoid, disguise, shift semantics, say nothing in length, use evasive syntax, disguises the source of information, talk 'at' others and lecture, use his own private language, emphasizes his conspiracy theories, rumors and phobias. Language is not to communicate but to obscure; not to share but to abstain; to disagree without incurring wrath; to criticize without commitment; agree without appearing to do so. Language is a weapon, an asset, a piece of lethal property, a mistress to be gang-raped. Language is a lover, composition but not content."*

Contradictory Language

The psychopath is also contradictory with his language. He will say one thing and within the next sentence will have said the complete opposite, just as passionately as if he had not said the first sentence. Trying to follow his thoughts and statements can give women whiplash. While contradiction could be generated from the misuse of abstract language, his desire to con, or his sadistic enjoyment, there is also a biological reason in the faulty braining wiring why contradictions can happen. He may have a problem between the right and left brain hemisphere related to how the language is (or isn't) processed. His covert communication mishaps and subsequent cover-ups are sometimes associated with what is referred to as 'weak or unusually lateralized cerebral hemispheres.'[42]

New experimental evidence suggests that what is called 'bilateral language processes' are characteristic of psychopaths. These processes produce a tendency for psychopaths to make contradictory statements. Researchers believe the use of contradictory statements is related to each brain hemisphere trying to run the language-show, but producing speech that is poorly integrated.

While it's hard to know *which* reason the psychopath uses to create contradictions, women have said this is one of the defining features of the psychopath that illuminates the Jekyll/Hyde split in him—the

---

[42] Kiehl, K., Hare, R, McDonald, J., Brink, J. (1999). *Society for Psychophysiological Research.*

psychopath's dichotomous and contradictory statements (covered in more detail in later chapters). These severe contradictions contribute to her development of cognitive dissonance which will go on to be one of her biggest aftermath symptoms. These contradictory statements create not only an emotional split in her but total confusion about the relationship stability and challenges the entire communication process.

Lack of Emotional Language Processing

We have already seen that the psychopath has major problems with both abstract words and concepts. He dodges by loop-holing, word-twisting, making up his own meanings, and he even contradicts himself. In addition to those obstacles within *himself*, psychopaths have plenty of problems with *other* people's emotions as well.

Word association tests done with psychopaths reveal that some emotional words are processed the same in his brain as neutral words.

"You have broken my heart and I am crushed by your cheating!" registers similar to "Can you pass the butter?"

This may be somewhat related to their issue with abstract language mentioned above, but it is also connected to their inability to process specific emotional words and feelings. Psychopaths and the low conscienced group have deficits related to feelings they:

o   do not experience
o   experience in such a low degree to make them notably abnormal or neutral
o   experience as highly skewed

These feelings are related to empathy, remorse, and conscience. However, a possibility was raised that psychopaths may additionally have difficulties processing other emotions related to sadness, fear, and disgust.[43]

The psychopath is not totally aware of his lack of emotional connectedness since he has always been this way. Although psychopaths are proud they are not bound by their emotions, they lack insight into how

---

[43] Kosson, Suchy & Mayer, (2002). *Emotion*, Vol 2, No 4, 298-411.

much they are handicapped in their relationships.[44] He does not understand her arguments about his cold and detached responses, except to the extent that these put a 'rift' in the relationship and he must find a way to turn this around on her.

The salesman that he is, will re-label her feelings, put a spin on the situation that benefits him, and throw her words back at her. While he might not genuinely emotionally understand or empathize with her words, he can still distort and recycle them into something else. As she brings up the need to be heard or tries harder to explain her emotions, the psychopath washes her communication through his own 'wounded-ness.' Looking for a trap door that allows him to stop the dialogue about something he can't fake understanding, he will use anything to dismiss the conversation.

Mimicking and Parroting

Mimic *noun* Actor, impersonator, mime, performer, play actor

Mimic *verb* To copy or exaggerate (as manner or gestures), often by way of mockery

Parrot *verb* To imitate someone else's words without understanding them [45]

While he may have difficulty processing specific feelings, the psychopath does learn how she uses the words and her perception of the meaning of the word and parrots it back to her even if he does not understand the meaning. While psychopaths may have problems experiencing emotions, they can certainly use HER emotions to mirror back to her the replication of emotion.

Mirroring is copying someone else while communicating with them. The psychopath can reflect back to her similar postures and gestures, or even voice tonality. It may include subtly mimicking her body language, gestures, movements, breathing, even her choice of words accentuating they are 'on the same page' which increases the sensation of mutual communication.

---

[44] Oakley, Barbara (2007). *Evil Genes: Why Rome Fell, Hitler Rose, Enron Failed, and My Sister Stole My Mother's Boyfriend.* New York: Prometheus Books.

[45] Webster's Collegiate Thesaurus

Natural mirroring happens spontaneously when people are talking. The psychopath, of course, is not using natural mirroring. He's using mirroring deceptively and with devious motivation. He aligns himself with her by reflecting back her own communication. She perceives him as friendly, accepting and deeply invested in communicating with her. The woman thinks since he discusses and uses her words that he understands her. Highly intelligent parrots (the actual birds) like an African Grey Parrot can mimic so perfectly that he can repeat entire conversations or monologues. People in another room who can't see what's going on, often think it's a human talking in depth about a subject. Although the parrot 'sounds' like he knows what he's talking about, he could obviously not answer questions about his 'subject matter'—so it is with a psychopath. He can parrot back the subject matter or parts of what was said, but it doesn't indicate emotional comprehension.

Communication

As seen in Vaknin's portrayal of language, communication is the best weapon in a psychopath's arsenal against others. In a normal relationship, the purpose of communication is to exchange information and opinions that lead to understanding and intimacy between the couple. A unique trait of the psychopath is his communication *motivation.* Most women don't suspect that someone is communicating with them for the art of deliberate deception, but often psychopaths do exactly that. The manipulation and deception of communication can be as much about gaining power through victimization as it is about his problematic language patterns.

Communication *motivation,* according to a psychopath, is often to say nothing and dodge real disclosure. Rieber & Vetter[46] noted that 'words become detached from meaning and serve instead as means of placating or fleeing an unwary victim.' Nowhere else in her professional life could this happen. Only out of the mouth of a salesman-psychopath, could new definitions of truth, words, and language ever be believed. She would come later to understand that the entire *intention* of his communication was to project on a screen the most fine-tuned of lies, deceptions, and deceit, and see if he could make her believe it.

---

[46] (1994). The Language of the Psychopath, *Journal of Psycholinguistic Research*, Vol 23, No 1.

Motivated by dominance and deceit, guided along by skewed brain function, and with abstract words having little meaning to him—is it any wonder that the psychopath is known to 'verbalize so rationally the totally irrational and absurd?'[47]

Language becomes both a gift of verbal stroking he gives her and at the same time a cave he hides in. What he has done is simply to pervert, convert, or subvert meaning and the possibility of true communication from her. His induction into his warped reality using distorted logic, meaning and language has her believing the most unbelievable of lies, all done with a sleight-of-mouth and purposely.

Predatory 6th Sense

Psychopaths have been endowed with what seems to be a 6th sense to hone in on women's feelings of loneliness and grief and use them in the communication process. Her feelings of loneliness and grief turned out to be huge risk factors related to why and how women ended up with psychopaths (or go back to them).

Here is one of the dichotomous examples of psychopaths. He does not recognize some of her emotions and yet highly identifies with other emotions! This uncanny 6th sense ability is mentioned repeatedly by the women as a communication approach and related to his ability to meet her and immediately 'name' what she was going through in regards to:

o   loss

o   grief

o   loneliness

o   overwhelm

o   emotional vulnerability

o   her perception of emotional abandonment by someone else

Women have stated that the psychopath communicates directly to her situation like a carnival psychic, a hand grasping preacher or a deeply contemplative therapist. Psychopaths affirm this:

"I can pick them out of a room full of people. There's just a certain look, an underlying current of vulnerability. Then to check out if I'm right I'll ask a few questions and she begins disclosing

---

[47] Rieber and Vetter

at the speed of light about being lonely or having just lost someone."

A psychopath can quickly become her Resident Therapist or Resident Minister in moments—applying a salve of B.S. to her wounds.

Women are fascinated by the whole idea of a 6th sense in men who 'know' her so completely so early. Internalized as 'soul-mate' status the 6th sense vibe of the psychopath is mysterious, entrancing and indescribable. This is why it's so confusing for women to communicate with psychopaths. There are clearly emotions and corresponding language to those emotions psychopaths do 'get,' which is strengthened, fueled, and mystified by his 6th sense abilities. Yet there are aspects about other feelings they 'don't get.' Undoubtedly, this confusion only fuels his mystique to her.

Not knowing which feelings and the corresponding language he gets, partners are likely to give him the benefit of the doubt. She assumes that because he understands part of it, he understands all of it.

Super Tuned-on Cues and Clues of Non-verbal Language

It's been assumed that if psychopaths had problems processing cues for some emotions then they probably *also* had problems in processing cues for nonverbal messages as well—meaning they didn't do well in reading non-verbal messages. However, this does not seem to be the case. According to some studies, psychopaths can have trouble processing someone else's emotions of sadness, fear, disgust, empathy, conscience and remorse and yet *not* have a deficit in nonverbal emotional processing. They do pretty well in picking up on the nonverbal language such as body language, eye contact, gestures, and responsiveness to touch, etc. No doubt that his ability to cue in on non-verbals increases his 6th sense abilities to her.

Women have confirmed this, saying psychopaths are master interpreters of cues and clues like eye lingo and body language. Psychopaths are not the only deviant types that read body language. In rape prevention, it is often taught that rapists pick out women based on how they hold themselves, how they move, and what kind of direct eye contact they make. These are just a few of many cues rapists may look for. In working with women, I often spend a lot of time about body boundaries and messages she is unconsciously giving out that are hitting a psychopath's radar spot on.

The fact that the psychopath is good at non-verbal cues and clues are likely to send a mixed message to her during the communication process when:

- o he can't understand some of the emotional words such as sadness, fear, disgust, empathy, conscience and remorse
- o he can understand other emotions like loss, grief, loneliness and vulnerability
- o he can understand her body language

...and will undoubtedly manipulate it and use it to steer the communication where he wants it. The psychopath seems to be one big dichotomous contradiction that we will look closer at in later chapters.

Crazy-Making Communication

How does all these communication malfunctions come together as a 'relational cluster butt kick?' How does it affect the actual interactive process of talking? The attempts at communication are crazy-making and will cause her to question her communication skills, how she views her ability to express herself, and eventually her sanity.

The triangle represents the roles the psychopath and her play in the communication process. Each of them moves around the triangle taking on different roles in the interchange. He is the wounded one while she plays the role of either liberating him or tormenting him. He may later shift and take on the role of liberator to her or tormenter to her. She in turn, might switch roles and become the wounded one. When one role shifts, it forces the other person into one of the other two remaining roles. Each shift shifts someone else.

Figure 5.1
Communication Triangle

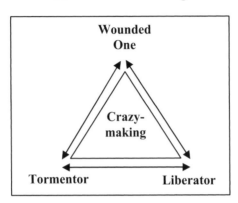

These roles can shift moment by moment, sentence by sentence. One moment he acts as if she is the tormenter and in the next moment expected to liberate him. In the next argument he might aggressively be the tormenter and she, the wounded one. The same argument over the same topic only moments or days later could result in totally different roles by each of them. No consistency whatsoever is held and no resolution reached each time they enter into an attempt at communication.

Nowhere else in her life does she communicate this way. At work, she may hold a highly responsible position and communicate normally, without drama and crazy-making language. However, as soon as she enters into communication with him, the communication lapses into these three well-defined roles. Even when she attempts to communicate normally and utilize the skills she uses in everyday communication with others, the process still pulls her in and she is unable to communicate outside the three roles of Wounded One, Tormentor, or Liberator.

With the psychopath, communication is reduced to a very juvenile emotional age. He brings to this communication process other dysfunctional and aggravating behaviors which contribute to communication problems. For example:

o impulsivity

o splitting one person against the other

o knows-it-all so she can't contribute any new information

o   lying
o   drama
o   manipulation
o   juvenile decision-making skills
o   changing subjects
o   meaning/language differences
o   blaming
o   immature emotional age
o   doesn't take responsibility for his behavior/choices
o   abandonment issues and acts like a victim
o   gaslighting
o   projecting his behavior on others

Conclusion

With biology problems, language differences, deceitful motivation, contradictions, and a crazy-making interactive process, there is no way to make communication with a psychopath work. This chapter helps to identify why feeling crazy while communicating with a psychopath is unfortunately not unusual.

So just how did this psychopathic hook-up happen? I'll discuss that in the next chapter.

6 Her Psychopathic Man

Psychopathic Hook-ups—Why it Happens and Who She's Been With

"The best time to see the light is as soon as you can!" — *Toni R.*

In previous chapters, we discussed characteristics of the psychopath including:

o   his skewed motivational drives
o   his mismatched biological make up
o   possible effects from early childhood 'nurture' issues
o   rampant sexuality
o   extraversion/dominance/status excesses
o   excitement seeking behavior at any cost
o   poor impulse control
o   the inability to sustain positive change
o   the inadequate development of insight about his behavior therefore basically no truly authentic relationships
o   his brain games through communication problems
o   his bent towards spiritual evil

Looking at him from this perspective, no woman in her right mind would want to be with him! So why do women end up with psychopaths?

Contrary to what others may think, she actually began the relationship while impaired. Her impairment came from grief, multiple losses, extended and long term stress, anxiety, or depression. Many women had just gone through extended care giving of a dying parent or multiple events such as deaths, divorce, custody battles, grad school or professional training that just culminated. Most had residual anxiety and/or depression from these circumstances. These risk factors definitely contributed to the women's susceptibility (and the psychopath's '6th sense' picks up on these).

However, these were not the *only* factors. Two additional key contributors that make women vulnerable were *boredom* and *loneliness*.

After all, these are extraverted, active, strong women who enjoy an emotionally, if not physically, active life. Boredom triggered a desire to insert excitement, usually though a relationship, into their lives. Boredom makes highly thrill-seeking, live-wire pathologicals look like just the remedy to a lethargic life while she was 'just looking for a little fun.' As I often say, "If you're not living a big enough life, any psychopath will do!"

The women often perceived loneliness following a grief or loss which was compounded by her boredom. *The Institute's* weekly newsletter reminds women that loneliness is a key risk factor—for hooking-up with, or going back to a pathological. The women's personal stories of their psychopathic hook-up normally revolve around elevated loneliness at the time they met the psychopath. Unmet emotional and social needs are negative contributing factors in psychopathic hook-ups. Sadly, many of the women were not even conscious they were lonely, bored, or living a small confined life. Unfortunately, many predators know or sense these facts.

Women with chronic histories of multiple relationships with psychopaths, however, are sometimes motivated by *different* and *additional factors*. I will refer to these factors as her 'Super Traits' and will discuss them throughout the book.

(A side note: some women said, ironically, they were in a 'great place' emotionally when they met the psychopath. They had worked on themselves in therapy, had been out of a relationship for some time, they were quite content with themselves and feeling very 'open' to what their future held. Some were not looking for anyone at the time they met him, but their sheer lack of expecting a psychopath on their radar landed them one. Most women, however, did not fall in this category.)

Who He Is

Of course, a psychopath doesn't enter a woman's life announcing he is a deceitful, pathologically-disordered, power mongrel incapable of anything more than surface attachment and is so brain-challenged he can't love! Psychopaths present themselves initially as intensely interested in her, passionately loving, abundantly caring, and almost suffocatingly-affectionate men. They have connected-the-dots to design the best approach to get her.

Just 'who' are the women who found their soul-mates in disordered and deceitful psychopaths, and why? Who are the men that these women fell in love with, and how did I know I had *really* surveyed women who love psychopaths?

To answer these questions, I had to find a large group of women to survey. Together Dr. Liane Leedom and I surveyed women who found us and the research project through the web sites:

o   www.saferelationshipsmagazine.com
o   www.womenwholovepsychopaths.com

...and other women's and self-help websites. More than 75 women who had a long-term relationship with a psychopath responded.

To determine if the women were really with men who had at least psychopathic traits, Dr. Leedom and I used two different checklists and the women's stories we received. We created the first checklist from the symptom list for antisocial personality disorder and narcissistic personality disorder in the DSM IV-TR. This is called the ***Partner Rated Assessment of Pathological Men.*** Dr. Robert Hare, known for his work with psychopaths in prison, developed the second checklist. He designed his checklist (called the **P-Scan**) to allow non-clinical people (such as partners) to rate symptoms of psychopathy in another person.

Using these three methods, Dr. Leedom and I were able to determine which women had, in fact, been with men who had significant psychopathic traits. Psychopathic traits, in and of themselves, are dangerous in relationships and often point to various levels of pathology present including full psychopathy.

What we found from the women's stories, the checklists, and the entire surveys was that the men's behavior was *notably abnormal.* The behavior the women described in their stories and checklists in no way resembled normal male behavior. Additionally, the women reported high percentages of ADHD, substance abuse, domestic violence, and arrests in the men. These are also sometimes indicative of psychopathic traits. The percentages of these four issues (ADHD, substance abuse, domestic violence, and arrest) are *identical* to those found in other studies of unsuccessful psychopaths. In my opinion, the women in our survey were with psychopaths and/or those with significant psychopathic traits.

Some people might argue the survey takers were merely 'scorned women' who exaggerated the men's personality traits. The stories and checklists highlighted the typical behavior associated with psychopathic traits and were consistent with the pathological stories I heard for many years in therapy. Over 20 years, I found a consistent thread woven in the stories, behaviors, and aftermath outcomes that begins to build identical backdrops for the pathological love relationships. Identification becomes easier when you have heard the same story with the same outcome for 20 years.

Why is it so easy for me to spot? Healthy men don't engage in the complete and purposeful destruction of women. The men's sheer enjoyment of the destruction is abnormal. While conflict can be part of healthy relationships, healthy men do not destroy women emotionally, psychologically, sexually, financially, and/or physically.

The Partner-Rated Assessment of Pathologic Men (PRA)

We used the assessment below to assess traits often found in pathological men. If you are a woman in a current pathological relationship, feel free to use this checklist below to assess your current situation.

Figure 6.1
The Partner-Rated Assessment of Pathologic Men (PRA) Checklist[48]

Arrogant	Stealing
Charming	Impulsive behavior
Easily bored	Constantly on phone
Thrill seeking	Constantly on Internet
Frequent lying	Always upbeat or angry
Conning for fun	Hyperactive
Conning for profit	Poor sleep
Lacks guilt	Controlling
Lacks remorse	Disrespects authority

---

[48] Compiled by Liane J. Leedom, M.D.

	Lacks empathy		Disappears for hours without explanation
	Irresponsible with money		Disappears for days without explanation
	No realistic life goals		Compulsive shopping/buying
	Sexually unfaithful		Verbally abusive
	Irresponsible parent		Disrespects authority
	Uses friends, family, lovers for money		Physically abusive
	Doesn't own his own behavior		'Knew' organized crime figures
	Childhood behavior problems		Is a name dropper
	Reckless disregard for safety of others/self		Loves competition, but is a poor loser
	Bragged about prior acts of aggression		Has fantasies of doing something great or being famous, and often expects to be treated as if these fantasies had already come true
	Is firmly convinced that he or she is better, smarter, or more talented than other people		Regards anything short of worship to be rejection
	Frequent fights		Becomes irritated when other people don't automatically do what he or she wants them to do, even when they have a good reason for not complying
	Has very little interest in what other people are thinking or feeling, unless he or she wants something from them.		

In addition to this checklist, we also asked the women to write their own stories about their psychopathic partner using the following open ended questions:

1. How did he act when you were ill?
2. How did he treat your family?
3. Did he care for children or pets?
4. Was he friendly with the neighbors?
5. Have you ever talked to any of his other women to corroborate your experiences with him?

These particular questions help further highlight behaviors that are typical in psychopathy regarding interpersonal interactions, a lack of empathy, exploitative relationships, and disregard for others. What is already known about psychopaths is their abject neglect of others in personal relationships after the initial luring and honeymoon phases. Through these stories we were able to see the very similar "up close and personal" relationship behaviors of psychopaths with their intimate others, children, pets, ex-lovers, and neighbors.

The detailed descriptions of the women's observations of their intimate partner's behaviors over the course of the relationship as 'disordered' are remarkably consistent among the entire group and consistent with what has been described to me during 20 years of therapy. These similarities show the consistency of the disorder within relationships. Let's take a look at 'who' the women say they have been involved with.

A Description of Their Men[49]

Race and Education

The average age of the men in the survey was 37 years old. Fifteen per cent were black or Hispanic and 85% were white. One-third of the men had dropped out of high school and only 25% held college degrees.

His Occupation

We were surprised to find that while many of the women in the survey were white collar professionals, the psychopaths they got involved with were far below their level of career status and education. Most women indicated that it was unusual for them to date below their own career status and they did so based on the misrepresentation of himself, his work

---

[49] Compiled by Liane Leedom, M.D.

history, and his financial standings by the psychopath. Many didn't know at the time he was lying about his business history or his current career until well into the relationship.

As previously mentioned many psychopaths do successfully climb the career ladder especially in fields where aggression is rewarded. *Snakes in Suits* by Drs. Paul Babiak and Robert Hare points to growing psychopathy in the higher ranks of the business world, law, politics, medicine, and other areas where business aggression, extraversion, and risk taking are encouraged. So we were surprised to find in this group that we researched that the women were predominantly professional and were with mostly blue collar and uneducated men. According to the women, very few of the psychopaths represented their careers accurately from all angles (given their proclivity for pathological lying, this isn't surprising). Some women began the relationship thinking he was a 'professional' only to find out he worked at KFC. Other women were so taken by his charm that they dismissed his lower career status because they believed in his 'untapped potential.'

While some psychopaths were architects, engineers, accountants, or marketing directors (of a well-known magazine), the overwhelming majority of them were in entry level positions in business, retail sales, or were laborers of some kind. A large number of them had many different careers displaying the frequent job instability common in psychopathy. Psychopaths jump around in jobs looking for an effortless fit, but are easily bored, entitled, and consequently are often fired.

Interestingly, a lot of them were in real estate and several were truck drivers. Some job selections make sense related to pathological disorders. For instance, real estate would seem like a career where a person good in sales (and the 'gift of gab') would find success, or at least be motivated by the hopes of a 'get-rich-quick scheme' of flipping properties or selling quickly to 'easy targets.' Truck driving would appeal to those who hate to be pinned down and love the concept of being 'on the run.' Self-employment often appeals to those who have trouble with authority and bosses.

Others were military men, police officers or security guards. In my previous work with victims, women often mentioned they dated pathologic men from these fields. These careers attract men who enjoy power and the ability to often freely dominate others under the guises of the job description. Furthermore, psychopaths often claim to have done many things in the military they never did. Some weren't even *in* the military. Many psychopaths like to claim they were a mercenary during war, a political hostage, Navy Seal, FBI, or C.I.A. operative—often none of which is true. Interestingly, their claims always portray them in a position of authority or hero-like.

A portion of the women's psychopaths were drifters (initially unbeknownst to her) or chronically unemployed, where the women largely supported them. In these cases, the women indicated she:

o   didn't know initially he was truly and chronically unemployed

o   felt sorry for him

o   thought this was a 'momentary' glitch in his career (according to him) that would be soon corrected

o   thought she would try the 'house husband' role that he offered

Later in the book, you will read about her hyper-empathy and how psychopaths with 'down on the luck stories' were an easy-in with these women. The unequal career and educational status were definitely noteworthy in these relationships.

His Personality

The table on the next page gives a picture of the psychopathic and narcissistic traits the women reported in the men. 100% of the women described their partners as charming, guiltless, and pathological liars. Most of the men were also noted has having arrogance, lack of remorse and lacking in empathy—qualities also associated with pathology, psychopathy and the low conscienced spectrum. Well over 50% of the men were con artists or operating as professional psychopaths (their pathology was undetected). This list of traits left little doubt that the women had indeed been in relationships with highly psychopathic men.

Figure 6.2[50]
Results of the PRA-The Partner-Rated Assessment of
Pathologic Men

% with trait	Personality Traits	% with trait	Personality Traits
95	Little interest in others' feelings/opinions	64	Disappeared for hours at a time
89	No empathy	64	Uses people (parasitic life style)
88	Doesn't own his own behavior	64	Needs worship/adoration
87	Verbally abusive	61	Poor loser
85	Easily irritated	59	Grandiose fantasies
85	Controlling	59	No life goals
82	No remorse	57	Decreased sleep
80	Impulsive	56	Conning for fun
77	Arrogant	50	Physically abusive
74	Easily bored	50	Stealing
74	Believes he is better than anyone else	48	Bragged about past aggression
69	Frequent fights	44	Talks on the phone excessively
69	Reckless	44	Hyperactive
67	Irresponsible parent	38	Compulsive shopping
66	Thrill seeking	36	Disappeared for days at a time
66	Childhood behavior problems	33	Excessive Internet use
66	Conning for profit		

---

[50] Compiled by Liane J. Leedom, M.D.

His Impulsivity

Eighty percent of the women thought their men were 'impulsive.' As shown in previous chapters, impulsivity is one of the leading traits in some personality disorders and psychopathy. Related to lack of impulse control were frequent fights, recklessness, irresponsible parenting, thrill-seeking, irresponsibility with money, and a chronic, angry mood. Between 64%-69% of the men displayed these symptoms of impulsivity. About a third of the men also had compulsive shopping/spending as an impulse control problem. Substance abuse and criminal behavior are also related to impulsivity. Forty percent of the men had a former arrest record including drug offenses and DUIs. Fifty per cent of them had a history of alcohol abuse or alcoholism. The use of other drugs especially marijuana, crack cocaine, and amphetamines were also common.

More on His Addictions, Substance Abuse, Arrest and Violence Record

Addictions in general permeated this group of men, which is common for psychopaths.

"He was a recovering drug addict and alcoholic when I met him, but he's still a heavy smoker, has food issues, sexual addiction problems and is a closet bi-sexual. I can't rule out that he wasn't a child molester... I always wondered if he had molested his children."

Alcoholism is common in psychopaths and of course, alcoholism is commonly associated with illegal behavior and violence.

"He was drinking heavily every weekend and always became abusive and aggressive towards me. He wouldn't admit his alcohol addiction and that he used it to cope with stress."

Substance abuse was very common and is often associated with psychopathy.

"He had drug abuse problems since age 16. Drank the entire time I was with him and he's still drinking and drugging. He was a gambler until 1994 and has had a cocaine addiction from 1995 up until now."

We don't attribute the majority of the relationship problems to the presence of active substance abuse. While substance abuse does impact relationship quality, psychopathy is a bigger disruption to relationship quality and safety than substance abuse alone. Factors of psychopathy almost assuredly add and include factors of substance abuse, emotional/psychological, and sometimes physical violence in relationships.

Although a history of physical aggression was common in the men, pathology always brings its additional levels of complications to existing violence and significantly raises the lethality risk since many of them are impaired in their ability to regulate impulsivity and violent behavior. Fifty percent of the men were violent. While you may have thought that *more* would have been violent, many psychopaths are exceptionally skilled at controlling others without the use of physical violence. For instance, psychopaths in the work place have had to learn how to control others without violence and learned that it's better to control with their mind than with their fists.

Fifty percent of the men also engaged in stealing. Stealing is not based solely on their low career status or even financial constraints, but based on the roots of impulsivity problems and the delight of having power over the environment by taking something. Even wealthy psychopaths steal.

How He Sees Others

Psychopaths are noted for their narcissism, which means they see themselves as superior to others and have little regard for anyone else or other's opinions. Indicators of this narcissism included:

o   disrespect for authority
o   parasitic lifestyle (uses people)
o   is a poor loser
o   cons for fun

"He didn't respect anyone and the farther up they were on a career ladder or in law enforcement, the worse he thought of them. He didn't have anything nice to say about anyone...except to their face. Once they left, the person was completely cut off at the knees verbally by him."

Both lower-achieving and high-achieving psychopaths can be parasites that target women to live off, and not just for the financial benefits. Successful white-collar psychopaths who don't need the income often steal, con others out of money, or live off of others. Other motivational factors for a psychopath's parasitic lifestyle include the power over other people's finances (and thus their futures), the status additional income can bring, and the ability to dominant someone else into giving the money to him.

> *"He had more money than God but still got off on stealing mine or anyone else's. It was a power trip for him to take someone's money. And even better was to con them out of it."*

His Friendliness

"He was charming" was the most common description given by the women. Psychopaths can be very friendly, outgoing, persuasive, persistent, and exceptionally charming in the beginning of the relationship, and especially when she is the target. Psychopaths use their charm to con others into relationships with them, whether romantic or business. As often indicated by the women, he may not have extended his charming style to neighbors and others. Hostile psychopaths use their anger to control women or to isolate them by keeping others around her intimidated.

It's not uncommon for psychopaths to use *both* charm and anger premeditatedly to achieve their goals. The same Dr. Jekyll and Mr. Hyde can use charm one moment and anger the next.

> *"He couldn't remember half of our neighbors' names because they weren't important enough to remember. He would remember those he got something from."*

> *"Charmed some, cussed some."*

His Mental Health

A previous chapter showed that psychopaths almost always have other mental illnesses besides their psychopathy. Over 50% of the women said the psychopath had been previously diagnosed with a mental disorder or the woman came to recognize mental illness symptoms in him. These included prior diagnosing of:

o   Antisocial Personality Disorder
o   Depression
o   Bipolar Disorder

o   Obsessive Compulsive Disorder

o   Post Traumatic Stress Disorder (PTSD)

...or childhood behavioral problems. Twenty-five percent of the men had been diagnosed with ADHD during childhood.

> *"He was hospitalized with bipolar disorder at age 18, was on lots of other psych drugs, too."*

> *"I'm not sure what he was diagnosed, but he spent some time in a mental facility in New Orleans."*

> *"He was evaluated as a child for fire-setting which I now understand is related to psychopathy."*

His Other Biological Issues

Along with personality disorder, psychopaths have other issues in common, including an interesting symptom of a decreased need for sleep. Many of the women arrive for treatment in bodily exhaustion from lack of sleep. The ability to dominate her when she is exhausted is an obvious benefit to the psychopath for keeping her awake, but so is marathon sex or marathon fighting. (This technique of sleep deprivation is often used in hostage-taking and war crimes. I will discuss it further in the chapter on Hypnosis and Trance.) Additionally, one would have to wonder if the psychopath isn't by nature a little 'manic-y,' requiring less sleep. Since a portion of the psychopaths have bipolar disorder, a decreased need of sleep would fit with the diagnosis. Almost half the psychopaths were also hyperactive, which could be the ADHD affecting their sleep. Given the neurological problems reviewed in previous chapters, it may even be related to brain chemistry, brain formation, or brain circuitry problems.

His Other Women

When it came to the women seeking out his previous relationships to check out his stories, lies, or behaviors, two and a half times more women did *not* talk to others, including previous female partners about his behavior than those who did.

> *"He always told me she cheated on him, was crazy and a liar. He said no one could believe anything out of her mouth. So I never thought I'd get the truth. I see now he did that so I wouldn't approach her."*

About 25% of the women successfully contacted prior women who had been with the psychopath. In all but two cases, the prior women told similar stories about his behavior. In cases where prior women refused to discuss the psychopath, children were involved and he was the biological father.

Many of those who did not try to check out his stories said they should have, as the information they would have gotten may have helped them to make a better choice. There were some women in the survey who were told in great detail about his violent and parasitic behavior. The psychopath had his own convincing explanation about every disturbing description of him. *Unfortunately, women don't believe other women when they reveal abuse by the male partner. A lesson learned is that the other woman may have something to say worth hearing and considering.* Ironically, women coming out of the relationships usually have a burning desire to warn other women. As she struggles with her aftermath of symptoms, flashbacks, and obsessions, her greatest desire is that other women not experience him and the aftermath!

> *"How I wish I would have at least tried to contact others. I might not be in the shape I am today trying to recover from what I've been through. If anyone ever contacts me, I'll definitely tell her the truth!"*

> *"I thought she was biased! She was and rightfully so. I needed to hear what she had to say...I wish I had."*

His Treatment of Her Family

Psychopaths live behind a mask—they turn on and off the charm and rage to their benefit. When it benefits them to be charming, they are. When they are not invested in others, they turn the charm off, and sometimes the rage on. Families present unique challenges for the psychopath. Some family members believe his persona so he keeps them close. Others may see him for what he is so he discards them. Overall, the psychopaths remained largely true to their charming demeanor. Many of them were nice or respectful to the women's families; half that many psychopaths were *only* nice in person or they were *only* nice when trying to get something. Not surprisingly, they often talked about the family members negatively and complained about them to her. A number of them were outright mean, aggressive, or violent to her family. Only a handful of women never introduced the psychopath to family members. Here are a few comments from the women:

> *"He always tried to come out like the hero. Whenever he could he always put me down to them but tried to say it in a way that something was wrong with me but he was doing everything in his power to help me."*

> *"One time when my parents wouldn't speak to him he agitated them on purpose. He got a kick out of me crying and begging him not to. He was insulting and belittling to them and did not understand the concept of respecting them because they were my parents (or sisters)."*

> *"He couldn't understand the concept of them not liking what was happening in my life with him hurting me and being abusive and draining our bank account. He didn't understand they were upset because they loved me and their grandchildren and if they were going to be mad at him, he would dislike them more and enjoy upsetting them. I would beg him to make things right with them, apologize to them when he did something wrong. He never would."*

> *"I would try to turn it around and ask how he would feel if I had treated his sister or his mother or grandmother in the same manner but I couldn't ever get him to understand how that would feel. He was totally incapable of trying to put himself in others shoes or understanding what other people's feelings would be in a situation. He eventually would call my older sister and her family and my parents "white trash" even though none of them had ever been arrested or done drugs (as he had). He thought he was better than them."*

His Treatment of Her When She Was Ill

The question that gave the best picture of the psychopath in action was *"How did he act when you were ill?"* Only 20% of women reported any caring response to their illness. Since psychopaths get bored easily, it is easy to anticipate that a psychopath would be 'challenged' to be *consistently* helpful in illness. Couple the sense of being bored with a lack of empathy, compassion, and very low cooperation and you can pretty well guarantee she'll have to take care of herself if she gets sick.

A small portion of the women said that their psychopaths actually helped them when they were ill. However, twice that many women said that the psychopath *only* intermittently helped. He either got bored with helping or he *only* helped when others were around watching. The overwhelming majority of the psychopaths didn't provide care giving when someone needed it. In fact many of the psychopaths ignored serious and life threatening illnesses in their mates. Here are some of the typical answers:

> *"He doesn't show empathy or any kind of support."*
>
> *"Annoyed usually and accused me of making it up."*
>
> *"He didn't offer to help me get better. He would call and **feign** sympathy. But all he really wanted to find out was if I was well enough to come over so he could use me for sex."*

Lethality

There were numerous women that the psychopath actually, overtly or covertly, tried to seriously injure or even kill. Many reported even after 20 years of a violence-free marriage, the psychopath became lethal. Some were assaulted, strangled, poisoned, stabbed, shot, drowning-attempts, brake lines cut, and other equipment tampered with to look like an 'accident.' One client was on life support in a coma for four months after being poisoned with air conditioning fluid. The psychopath worked for an air conditioning company. Others were tormented in ways that implied the psychopath wanted her to commit suicide.

Conclusion

A reoccurring problem in some of the cases is that he did not have a diagnosis. Women felt that since he was not 'diagnosed' something that she was not justified in leaving, or she should work on the relationship. Not all pathologicals get diagnosed, and many dodge diagnosis or lie and conceal prior diagnosis from her. However, the checklist that was developed should help women realize there is no reason to wait for a man to be formally 'diagnosed' to make decisions about whether or not they are in a pathological and dangerous relationship. If a woman is checking off behaviors on that checklist, then she is with someone 'psychopathic enough' to be gravely concerned about and from *The Institute's* stand point, *'inevitable harm.'* If she waits for him to be 'diagnosed something bad enough' she will have already been exposed to trauma through the relationship as will her children.

From the types of behaviors these women reported, it is clear that even *'just'* psychopathic traits (without the full blown diagnosis of psychopath) put women at considerable risk. That is because it doesn't take much deviant, permanent, pathological behavior to greatly affect an intimate relationship. As I often tell clients *'Non-pathological people will* ***always, always, always*** *be negatively affected by someone else's pathology. We aren't wired to be able to sustain extended exposure to this level of pathology.'* It only takes a little pathology to negatively affect others. Men with psychopathic traits are toxic to all those who are close to them.

7 Her Temperament

The Temperament of Women Who Love Psychopaths

"I am what is mine. Personality is the original personal property." — *Norman O. Brown*

Why would a woman be attracted to, tolerate, and love such a highly disordered man? The biggest question others ask is "How could a woman so misread his pathology?" In past chapters, we have looked at how easily he flies under the radar and how normal he can present himself. Now let's discuss the wiring in her temperament that may have predisposed her to him.

Temperament reflects the personality a person is born with and refers to a biological predisposition. To a large degree, temperament is hard-wired—we have what we have as far as temperament traits go. So as a precautionary measure and even an intervention-based step, the women who love psychopaths must come to full self-awareness about their own elevated traits that place them 'at-risk' for predators who target these kinds of traits. Later in the book we will discuss prevention in more detail, but be aware the traits listed in this chapter tell a story about how the psychopath can use the abundant kindness and wonderful traits like a weapon against her.

The survey we administered for this book included a measurement of temperament and character.[51] The TCI provided information about the inner workings of the women's personalities. The results of the TCI as they pertain to the women's trait strengths and weaknesses are covered in this and the following chapter, and were compiled by Liane J. Leedom, M.D.

---

[51] "The Temperament and Character Inventory," or the "TCI" developed by Dr. Robert Cloninger.

The TCI looks at three temperament traits:

1. Excitement-seeking (also called novelty-seeking, sensation-seeking, or exploratory excitability), which refers to the desire to seek exciting people/places/things and avoid boredom.
2. Positive sociability/relationship investment (The TCI calls this reward dependence), which means how easily one does, or does not, respond to the pleasurable rewards in relationships.

and:

3. Harm avoidance, which helps one avoid being hurt.

Our survey found the temperament traits elevated in women who love psychopaths are:

1. Extraversion and excitement-seeking
2. Relationship investment and positive sociability
3. Sentimentality
4. Attachment
5. Competitiveness
6. Concern for having others' high regard
7. Harm avoidance

TCI Temperament Trait - Excitement-seeking

Her Extraversion[52]

The women who love psychopaths overwhelmingly tested as extraverted, which wasn't surprising. Those I have worked with are mostly gregarious and powerful women! Most are highly educated or have done well in their own line of work—successful by anyone's standards. The average woman in the survey had a minimum of a Bachelor's Degree or higher. Many are professionally trained as:

o Attorneys
o Doctors
o Therapists or social workers
o Female clergy
o Nurses or other medical professionals

---

[52] Compiled by Liane J. Leedom, M.D.

o Teachers or professors

o Editors

o CEOs of companies

o Non-profit agency directors

These are a formidable group of women who have knowledge, education, and strength. Before the psychopath landed in their lives, they were financially secure or successful in their field or school, had good self-esteem, goal direction and competitive attitudes. How does the women's own extraversion influence how they ended up in a relationship with a psychopath?

Some of the hook-up factor lies in their extraversion and chasing fun. Pathological and non-pathological extraverts are curious and easily bored, but they are sometimes impulsive.[53] From a negative or pathological standpoint, this impulsivity in extraversion is linked to ADHD, pathological gambling, intermittent explosive disorder, kleptomania, pyromania,[54] and sexual impulsivity. However, on a positive note, the issue of impulsivity in normal extraversion serves to remind us that this same trait 'in moderation' is what our culture associates with ambition. The 'unbridled impulsivity' seen so often in pathology is no longer just ambition. Instead, the impulsivity becomes highly dysfunctional and harmful.

Her Excitement-Seeking

Survey Results
Temperament Trait: Exploratory Excitability
Scores: Her: High Him: High

Some of the magnetism of the hook-up is created because extraverts (both him and her) are 'excitement-seekers' who don't like a boring life. They actively seek others who don't like to be bored either! The more exciting life is the better! Extraverted women are not inclined to be attracted to 'couch-potato' men. They look for partners who are strong and outgoing. However, there are differences between his and her excitement-seeking behaviors and motivations. In

---

[53] Pathological extraverts would obviously be notably *more* impulsive than non-pathological extraverts.

[54] DSM Impulse Control Disorders NOS.

psychopaths, the excitement-seeking is impulsive and manipulative. His excitement-seeking is conning other people, stealing, lying, or participating in daredevil behavior and rooted in his chronic impulsivity problems.

Survey Results
Temperament Trait: Excitement-seeking Total **Scores:** Her: Moderately High Him: High

Her excitement-seeking may be the liking of the 'exciting edgy guy' or maybe just the outgoing, active and exciting lifestyle they both share. She doesn't have to be a sky diver to have excitement-seeking traits. She might simply like a guy who is powerful and dominant (which definitely describes the psychopath) and who is equally as exploratory as she is. The excitement-seeking in him, due to his pathology, may go much further than the excitement-seeking in her. While his may be him riding a speeding motorcycle around curves of a mountain without a helmet just to feel the risk and the wind, hers might be finding that 'Johnny Depp' kind of guy 'exhilarating' because he grabs life and runs with it. Unfortunately, she will also find out his excitement-seeking is often related to how many other relationships with women he can keep hidden and get away with.

"At some level, his false power feels like protection, even though in many ways it is the opposite. It feels like it is the strong protection that I had at home from my father. The fact that he can do actions disregarding rules in society, feels like a strong protective force when it does not work against me or others. It is his nerve and audacity that ends up looking so powerful. For example, when he gets away with something because he is so obstinate or assertive."

Little does she know that his extraversion is not merely 'ediginess' or 'adventurous' but is full blown pathology. *The Institute* developed a seminar on the 'Intensity of Attachment' which discusses why women often misunderstand and mislabel his extraversion issues as 'exciting' or 'soul-mate' status. Look for the audio download on the magazine site.[55]

People who test high in excitement-seeking hate monotony. One thing is for sure in the psychopath's women—just like the psychopath does not

---

[55] www.saferelationshipsmagazine.com

like a boring life, the women do not like boring men, and psychopaths are anything *but* boring. While she may hate monotony, what she has taken on instead is drama with the psychopath.

The extravert's hard-wired reward system is so strongly geared to succeed that she will repeatedly continue a behavior trying to succeed with it even when she fails. Extraverts are competitive, goal-directed, and success-oriented—especially the women in the research. Their strong extraversion covertly encourages reaching their perceived 'reward' or 'succeeding' in the relationship. I have certainly seen this in some of the women who keep trying in a relationship with a psychopath that does nothing *but* fail and will always fail.

While her scores on extraversion put her in the upper range of the trait, ***this doesn't mean the women are psychopathic.*** It means they share the strong and compelling trait of extraversion.

This much extraversion from him *and* her create magnetism. This is important, because the issue of high extraversion in both the psychopath and his woman becomes one of the points of their connection. Extraverts are normally attracted to other extraverts. While there is a cliché that 'opposites attract' which means that extraverts are attracted to introverts, this isn't normally true with psychopaths and their women. This is where 'attraction' and 'similarity' meet up in the dating period. Many women have said when they met the psychopath there was a sense of being 'drawn' to him—an intensity at 'hello' that definitely got her attention.

Repeatedly, women talked about the unusual hooking-up that occurred in this relationship, and how the power of the attraction and hook-up took on a life of its own. This attraction is partially sparked from their shared high extraversion. Psychopaths need (and seek) women who find their dominance and extraversion sexy or desirable—because other women would only sense that level of extraversion as dangerous or overpowering! It takes a strong woman to find this much extraversion in a man non-threatening and even exciting! The pair of extraverts became two powerful magnets pointed towards each other resulting in an undeniably strong pull.[56]

---

[56] More on this in Chapter 9.

This makes extraversion an important concept to remember when tracking pathological love relationships. With two extraverts intensely attracted to one another and who are both action-oriented, they are likely to act on this intense attraction.

Interestingly, this is the only major trait that the psychopath's woman shares with the psychopath—the issue of extraversion and excitement-seeking. The rest of the temperament traits, as you will later see, are almost polar opposite from each other. Only the extraversion and excitement-seeking strongly link the psychopath to his woman.

Her Excitement-Seeking and Extraversion Attraction as Risk Factors

While the trait of extraversion overall can be a positive trait, female extraverts face unique challenges which put them at risk. This type of highly extraverted woman is often a threat to men who are not themselves *equally* extraverted and domineering. This type of extraverted, competent, and competitive woman could easily emotionally overpower a man who wasn't similar in his own extraversion. This is probably why extraverted women are attracted to extraverted men. Consequently, most men interested in a woman with this level of extraversion are *at least* or *more* extraverted than she is.

If she is attracted to dominant, excitement-seeking, extraverted men, then that's her 'bent' and she will always feel a pulling to those types of features. However, by nature of 'who' she is attracted to (the traits in him), she will always be fishing in the 'pathology' pond because psychopaths are mostly dominant, thrill-seeking, extraverted men—exactly who she finds attractive!

Not all dominant men are psychopaths, but most psychopaths are dominant. If she likes dominant men, she'll be more 'at-risk' for hooking-up with a psychopath than a woman who does not find dominant men attractive. She needs to understand her attraction to dominance as an 'attraction risk factor' for her.

Her goal in recovery and prevention is to be able to tell the difference between healthy dominance, extraversion and excitement seeking behaviors and pathological behaviors related to the same traits in men. Since she is not likely to 'do a 180' and not be attracted whatsoever to dominant men, she had better find a way to pick the healthy ones.

The problem the women reported is that they view less dominant men as passive or wimpy. They are more likely to continue to find highly extraverted and equally excitement-seeking mates as a good fit for their own levels of drive. So their challenge is to learn to differentiate between healthy male dominance and the dominance of pathology. Now I will look at other traits associated with extraversion.

Her Extravagance and Disorderliness

Survey Results
Temperament Trait: Extravagance
Scores: Her: Moderately High Him: High

Some women in our survey scored high in disorderliness and extravagance. That means they're a little more 'free spirited' than obsessive about order and routine, and don't feel the need for everything in life to be ordered. Their extravagance may be linked to compulsive shopping, a habit found in some extraverted women. It is hard to know if they were always like this or if this became an issue in the relationship with the psychopath either at his insistence of spending money, or it became this way as a way to manage her mounting anxiety.

Survey Results
Temperament Trait: Disorderliness
Scores: Her: Moderately High Him: High

Her Extravagance and Disorderliness as Risk Factors

This 'free-spirit' part of her that accepts life as it is and is able to go with the flow also has the capacity for accepting the lack of order and routine that is (or becomes a part of) a psychopath's life. These women can easily tolerate the chaos caused by his way of life and pathology and the roller coaster of the inevitable ups and downs. She has an ability to function in chaos, which probably makes her a good manager in her profession. It takes a while with the psychopath before the women tire of the lack of order and constant chaos.

The psychopath is well-known for his own extravagance which is most likely due to his need for status, his possession orientation, his need to avoid boredom, coupled with his impulsivity. Many women in the survey were not overly impulsive[57] so their tendency towards extravagance meshed well with the psychopath's own level of extravagance. Extravagance does seem to go hand-in-hand with a little extraversion and excitement seeking!

Her Competitiveness[58]

Extraverted women tend to be very competitive. Without this competitive and strong spirit, who could even withstand a psychopath's strong dominant demeanor? Her competitiveness enjoys a head-to-head with someone equally as passionate or as headstrong as she is. Non-pathological men likely felt passive, so she doesn't mind a good opinionated discussion (at least before he became verbally degrading every time she tried to talk). Her competitiveness likely made her a leader in school, in her business life or career and competitive in her physical activities such as sports or outdoor pursuits. She's used to being strong, decisive, and proactive. This is why she's confused about how the psychopathy 'swallowed up' a part of her that use to be so strong.

Her Competitiveness as a Risk Factor

As wonderful as competitiveness is in regular life, her competitiveness is a downfall in her relationship with the psychopath. As the relationship begins to become pathologically-driven and his crazy-making increases, instead of running for the hills or making a businesslike decision of 'cutting her losses' she is likely to stay and battle it out. She's not afraid to try to make a point and certainly doesn't want him to 'get one over on her.' Various reasons why women have stayed include:

o   to 'bust him'—such as finding enough information or evidence to confront him or enough info to take to court

o   to be able to break into his car, business, phone, or computer for proof of his infidelity, porn addiction, or the shoveling of money into off-shore accounts

o   to hire private investigators, purchase and place spyware in his car, computer, house, etc.

o   to fight it out about court and custody issues

o   to not vacate (and lose) property

---

[57] Covered in more detail later in the book.
[58] Contributed by Liane J. Leedom, M.D.

Perhaps if they knew they were battling a psychopath, most people would never try to 'fight Hannibal and win.' Many women don't know who they are up against until they are further down the road in the pathology cycle. Her competitiveness in general is going to give him a run come hell or high water.

Her ability to withstand and go head-to-head with a psychopath 'to not take his crap' is dangerous to her mental health. She would rather stay and fight than flee. Her competitiveness is likely to have kept her in the relationship *longer* than if she were less competitive. While competitiveness in business or sports is a bonus trait to have, in relationships with psychopaths it is a pair of handcuffs keeping her attached to a very dangerous relationship. This strong trait of competitiveness keeps her in the ring being battered about by his pathology and mad that she can't continue to hold her own with someone so deviant.

Women get significantly damaged by staying and thinking they can 'outsmart him' or 'give it to him' before they exit. One of *The Institute's* mantras is *'They are sicker than we are smart'*—staying for those reasons will play to the psychopath's benefit. The woman will simply be harmed by exposure to this much pathology. Her normal personality structure and psychology is no match for a psychopath. Normal people are almost always negatively affected by someone else's pathology. People aren't wired to be able to sustain chronic exposure to this level of disorder. He doesn't get hurt by her competitiveness, but she will undoubtedly get hurt by exposure to more psychopathic abuse. So to this end, her competitiveness is a risk factor in these relationships.

Her Impulsiveness

Survey Results
Temperament Trait: Impulsiveness
Scores: Her: Average Him: High

As a group, women who love psychopaths tested as average in impulsiveness. This is because some of the women are impulsive and some of them aren't, so combining those scores together produced a score of average. As I explained previously, most extraverts are somewhat impulsive. Extraverts have differing abilities to stop and think before acting. Obviously, psychopaths in their extreme levels of extraversion don't always stop and think before acting.

In Chapter 4, we talked about which brain regions were affected in psychopaths. Most of those affected brain regions were related to the inability to regulate impulsivity. While the pull to act is very strong for extraverts (even those who are not pathologically disordered), the non-pathologicals are able to moderate this tendency with thoughtfulness. Many of the women in our survey tend to be careful in most aspects of their lives despite their carefree excitement-seeking. This is all the more reason why some are surprised how they could end up with a psychopath when they are normally cautious persons and not prone to impulsively getting involved with someone without careful consideration.

Her lack of impulsiveness is no match for a psychopath, who can easily wait it out with her and masquerade as a good investment for a cautious woman. His persuasive abilities, frank lies, and lightning-speed pacing also move the relationship along faster than she is used to. Her lack of impulsivity can be quickly overcome by a skilled psychopath who spins her cautiousness as 'wisdom' on her part. He simply turns up the attention, the passion, the intensity, the charm and the heat until she forgets why she was taking it slow and being so careful.

Her Non-impulsivity as a Risk Factor

Unfortunately, her break-up will not be impulsive either—she is likely to take her time in reacting to the psychopath's covert displays of pathology. She is not likely to rush into ending the very intense attachment she has with him, no matter how many times he cheats, lies, or misbehaves. Extraverts tend to focus on *rewards* rather than the *punishments.* Interestingly, these extraverted women hyper-focused on the positive rewards and positive memories they experienced with the psychopath to the exclusion of reacting to his negative behavior. Her ability to focus on the positive experiences and rewards and block the growing negative data about him is an unusual factor in these relationships. I will discuss this unusual dynamic later in the book.

Her risk factor in her non-impulsivity may be connected to the excitement-seeking in the psychopath that she *does* find attractive. While she finds excitement-seeking in the psychopath exhilarating, there is a fine line between healthy exuberance in living and out-of-control impulsivity. It's likely that the psychopath has hidden the out of control impulsivity of his real behavior (at least for a while) behind the mask of exuberance—often called 'impression management.' At some point, his hidden life will come out.

She's in an emotional gridlock based on her lack of impulsivity and yet high competitiveness. Whether or not she impulsively entered into the relationship, she will not impulsively end it. Unfortunately, the psychopath will not be harmed in the least by her lower levels of impulsivity. However, she is very likely to be hurt by his out of control impulses which cause him to avail himself of any and every at-risk opportunity. Her lack of impulsivity might just keep her from bolting sooner when she really should have!

In this first segment of the TCI Temperament Traits, we looked in detail at extraversion and specifically at excitement-seeking. Now, we'll take a look at the second group of Temperament Traits measured by the TCI.

TCI Temperament Trait – Positive Sociability/ Relationship Investment

Survey Results
Temperament Trait: Relationship Investment
Scores: Her: High Him: Low

What the TCI calls 'reward dependence' I refer to as 'relationship investment.' This simply means the women are very invested in their relationships. Do not confuse this with what is often called 'codependency.' Psychology lacks a word to describe high relationship reward investment. Many therapists don't even know what that is or recognize it as a temperament trait. Instead, the therapists wrongly label it (especially in these women) as 'codependency.' Codependency has grown into a 'catchall' word that is thrown around to cover a multitude of symptoms—especially those that psychology doesn't have another understanding of, reasoning for, or applicable word. The world has wandered away from the initial meaning of the word 'codependent,' which was related to the field of addictions. The definition of codependent behavior was related to the partners of addicts who enabled continued use of the addict's substance and were controlled by the addict's behavior. While some of the psychopaths *are,* in fact, addicts, and while some of the behaviors of the women that *are* related to his substance use might be codependent, what *ISN'T* codependent is the issue of relationship investment. The women's temperament trait of relationship investment is not the same thing as codependency.

It's normal for humans to want to love and be loved. Wanting love does not make a person pathological or codependent however, there can be excesses in traits related to relational harm. One area of new study in neuro-science is the study of hyper-empathy and its relationship to an almost 'pathological altruism' in which people are harmed by their own levels of high empathy preventing them from exiting highly damaging experiences.[59] It definitely warrants a second look regarding these women considering their involvement with the most dangerous people on the planet.

Her Attachment

> **Survey Results**
>
> **Temperament Trait:**
> Attachment
>
> **Scores:**
> Her: High
> Him: Low

The women in our survey did test very high in relationship investment partly because they attach deeply. Positive sociability and relationship investment are based on the ability to derive positive feelings from relationships. These women find a great deal of pleasure and satisfaction in what they put in, and what they get out, of relationships. These deep attachments are a source of personal satisfaction. While the women may be conservative about attaching (because they may not be highly impulsive) *once they do attach,* it is with great passion and enormous depth. The psychopath *uses* positive rewards such as affection, verbal reinforcements, financial rewards such as gifts or trips to establish his patterns of power and dominance in a woman's life. Each reward trains her to know which behaviors he rewards and which behaviors relieve his punishing acts. She molds herself to maximize the rewards and to avoid the behaviors that set him off.

It becomes simple basic operant or learned conditioning—use behaviors he likes, learn to avoid behaviors that lead to punishment. His punishment can be the withdrawal of attention, pouting or raging, or his

---

[59] Barbara Oakley has a new book coming out in 2010 called *Pathological Altruism.*

imposed aloofness when she doesn't please him. When she does please him, she gets the best of the charming psychopath and the high-excitement from this perceived great relationship. When she thwarts his dominance and displeases/angers him she gets the narcissistic rage, his threatened or implied abandonment of her and the relationship, and anything else he thinks that will tap into her relationship investment.

Due to the depth of their attachment, high competitiveness, excitement-seeking and no real explanation in the DSM for super-elevated traits like theirs in relationship investment, these women are not only wrongly labeled 'codependent' but also wrongly labeled 'dependent personality disorder.' The simplification of these women's behaviors is based on the fact that there are no *other* explanations for their trait combinations. Lack of explanation for a behavior doesn't justify using a wrong explanation in its place. Just like these women were not codependent, they also did not test as dependent.

Remember, these women are often doctors, attorneys, and other high level professionals. These types of job roles don't attract people with Dependent Personality Disorders. The fact is we need another category for their unusual grouping of traits.

For women to safeguard themselves from future psychopaths, they must understand how issues like relationship investment place them at risk with these types of men.

Her Sentimentality

Survey Results

Temperament Trait:
Sentimentality

Scores:
Her: High
Him: Low

Women who are sentimental test high in positive sociability/relationship investment. They are likely to focus on the sweet things of the relationship, remembering the time he brought flowers, was kind to a child or dog, or did something extraordinary on their anniversary. Her ability to hyper-focus on the sentimental aspects of the relationship helps the psychopath camouflage his many other blunders. This issue of sentimentality also seems to be related to her ability to hyper-focus on positive memories and block negative memories. The women needed very few positive sentimental memories to keep them afloat in the relationship. By contrast, there were dozens of negative, even horrible and traumatic memories that were able to be overridden with sentimental remembrances of a more positive time.

The women tested very high in affection, so psychopaths that can pour it on, especially in the beginning, have a good shot with them. If a woman is ending a previous relationship in which she didn't get much affection, hooking-up with a psychopath can feel like she has hit the 'Affection Lotto!' At least in the beginning, many psychopaths know that to give affection is to increase her sense of attachment, and her corresponding loyalty. Violent psychopaths in group have commented "You don't hit them until they have bonded to you. Then if you hit them, they are more likely to stay." Psychopaths see affection as a way of wielding power over both the relationship and the emotions of their partners.

Her Social Sensitivity

These women are also socially sensitive. They are sensitive to the needs of others which explained why they were so sensitive to the needs of a psychopath. They are sensitive to environmental and emotional cues about other people and can pick up when others are hurt or wounded by an act or something said. Many psychopaths play the 'empathy' card early in the luring stage. Picking up on a woman's hyper-empathy, they use their chameleon tendencies to morph into whatever she *is*. If she is hyper-empathic then she needs something to empathize with. Quickly the psychopath has the sad story for her to connect to—his abusive childhood, his wife who runs around, his lost job, his stolen opportunity, his children he never gets to see. Her ability to hyper-focus on the needs of others puts the psychopath dead center as the recipient of her social sensitivity.

Her Concern for Having Others' High Regard

The women are tenderhearted and care deeply how others regard them. This is true for all the people in their lives, whether it is an intimate relationship, work association, or friendship. How others see them, what they think of them, and what they believe about them is immensely important.

Unfortunately, high relationship investment can cause women to have high levels of suggestibility which the psychopath capitalizes on! This suggestibility will also be discussed later in the relationship dynamics as suggestibility may have contributed to the psychopath's ability to exert mind control and brainwashing-like techniques.

Additionally, high relationship investment can cause women to lose objectivity about what is happening in the relationship. With the confusion that psychopaths instill in relationships through gaslighting techniques, it's not hard to imagine how their objectivity about what they were experiencing (versus what the psychopath said they were experiencing) gets skewed.

Her Relationship Investment as a Risk Factor

Women who are not motivated to please others in relationships and aren't high in relationship investment wouldn't last two minutes with a psychopath. Don't we call these women 'Princesses?' He wouldn't want her! Divas and psychopaths don't mix. Understanding that the psychopath's power and dominance needs are largely met through her relationship investment dynamics helps women understand why this trait is a risk factor in the hands of a psychopath.[60]

Her sensitivity to the needs of others makes her the tender-hearted person that she is. In a relationship with a psychopath, however, she is likely to over-sympathize with the psychopath's sad story of woe. She is very tuned in to his emotional needs based on his past history or current stressors, and tries hard to give him what she thinks he needs and what she hopes will stabilize that 'wounded inner little boy.' The psychopath hopes that she will tune in to his every need, because when she sets a boundary he will emotionally punish or remind her why his needs are important and should be met.

Unfortunately, caring deeply how others regard her also includes the psychopath. Amazingly, after all she's been through, she worries about whether or not they can 'still be friends' when the relationship ends. She wants him to like her, and worries he will tell others negative things about her. Women stay in relationships with psychopaths trying to lay the ground work for a 'nice clean breakup,' which of course does not exist with pathologicals. She might also be concerned her friends will think badly of her for 'not making it work' with someone so charming. She

---

[60] *Prevention tip: Be the Princess Diva no psychopath would want!*

cares how family and friends regard her. If others encouraged her to stay with the charming psychopath, how those others would view her and the break up matter greatly to her. Religious concerns may also exist if women are concerned how their church will view this break up. Her largest concern, however, is how the psychopath will regard her.

In many counseling sessions I have said to the women:

"So it's important for you to be liked by the psychopath you are breaking up with, right?"

Said that way, it's easier to see how trapped she gets by wanting others to regard her in a positive light—even him. Women have said this comment helps them see how unbalanced this need to be positively regarded is in them and shines a light on the farce that the highly disordered psychopath's opinions should even matter! As we said earlier, this trait is often confused and labeled as codependency. Labels like this cause women to flee counseling because they are not understood and her temperament traits and attachment intensity are not recognized for the contribution they make in the relationship dynamics.

Unfortunately, the psychopath greatly benefits from the woman's high relationship investment. The more she derives rewards from the relationship, the more invested she is. The more invested she is, the harder it is for her to disengage from her internal relationship reward system and leave the psychopath. Her high relationship investment in a situation like this can do nothing but benefit the psychopath, while his low relationship investment has disaster written all over it for her.

Understanding her own bent toward relationship investment, sentimentality, deep/intense attachments, and caring about how she is regarded could help her safeguard these aspects of her temperament next time around and remind her to move extremely slowly in future relationships.

In this segment, we looked in detail at the trait of relation-ship investment. Next we will look at the last group of Temperament Traits of the TCI.

TCI Temperament Trait – Harm Avoidance

Survey Results
Temperament Trait: Harm Avoidance Total
Scores: Her: Mixed Him: Low

Harm avoidance is related to awareness about potential harm. So women are either very aware of harm or not aware of it enough. Both extremes of harm avoidance can be problematic— those with really high harm avoidance which are strangled with anxiety and those who are totally unaware and then side-swiped by harm because they don't see it coming.

About half the women in our research tested high in harm avoidance and the other half tested average-to-low. The women's harm avoidance scores may have been artificially elevated because many women come out of pathological love relationships with enough symptoms to be diagnosed with Post Traumatic Stress Disorder (PTSD). It was this group of women who had the high harm avoidance scores. People with PTSD, other Anxiety Disorders, and Major Depression have high harm avoidance until these disorders are treated. After treatment they test much lower and are less anxious.

The question that can't be answered definitively is whether or not the women developed harm avoidance traits *because of the pathological relationship.* The reason we wonder is while some of the women tested high in harm avoidance, they didn't test *as high* as other groups of women. For example, those with clinical anxiety disorders tested higher than women who love psychopaths did. We think that the women were not necessarily high in harm avoidance *by nature.* Instead, we believe many developed high harm avoidance *as a reaction to unrelenting exposure to a psychopath.*

Anticipatory Worry

Survey Results
Temperament Trait: Anticipatory Worry **Scores:** Her: Moderately High Him: Low

The high test scores weren't a surprising feature because being in a relationship with a psychopath increases pessimism, worry, and the anticipation of problems because there are so many problems with a psychopath! Increases in worry (since she is worried about the outcome of such an increasingly unstable relationship) and fear (what will she find out next he's done) can plague these women. The fear of the unknown can be a big issue for women who love psychopaths.

Her High Harm Avoidance as a Risk Factor

Harm avoidance is anxiety-driven so if she is high in harm avoidance she most likely has a lot of anxiety. Either she was always prone to worry *or* she developed it in the relationship with the psychopath along with other mood disorder symptoms.

Being high in harm avoidance increases cautiousness and encourages careful planning. However, her lack of impulsivity and her cautiousness which are great traits to have are still not protective *enough* when she is in the path of the psychopath. Her level of mere cautiousness is but a road bump for a psychopath.

Why would exposure to psychopaths increase harm avoidance? Seeking to avoid setting off the psychopath, she may become extremely sensitive to the potential of relational harm through him emotionally punishing her. His gaslighting, her hunches something else is really going on and other red alert behaviors of his are likely to eventually increase her paranoia. If an extraverted woman suddenly stops taking the risks she once took, it is because her self-confidence is damaged from being with the psychopath. To say he 'messes with her mind' isn't a joke—over time her brain chemistry is altered to avoid, rather than to enjoy, risk-taking. Researchers of the TCI test have commented that harm avoidance scores rise when people are significantly stressed.

One aspect of harm avoidance is the 'anticipation of future problems.' PTSD has a similar symptom related to 'worrying about the future' or worrying about being hurt again. Since harm avoidance and PTSD share similar symptoms, her radar for future harm is probably highly activated.

Without treatment, harm avoidance is likely to be a problem in the future if her particular harm avoidance *is* related to PTSD. That's because much of PTSD can be recurring especially when someone is under stress. PTSD can be reactivated or triggered by other stressful or traumatic events producing adrenaline that can become 'autonomic.' When she has a 'feeling' that resembles a feeling she had with the psychopath or she has a flashback, the mind sounds an alarm and the body reactivates with a flood of adrenaline. This adrenaline increases her anxiety which soon becomes a vicious cycle.

While we want women to be cautious, women with super high harm avoidance end up more paranoid than cautious. Women complain a lot about this symptom—that their fear of the future (dating, hooking-up with another psychopath) keeps them from ever *wanting* to date again.

How can this be problematic? Future-oriented worry about being hurt is likely to activate her adrenaline either now or in the future. She is constantly worrying about something negative happening even if it doesn't happen. This adrenaline can put a damper on future relationships as her 'high alert' radar tries to anticipate every possible way she could get hurt in a relationship which causes very high cautiousness. High anxiety can also work against her impairing a woman's ability to leave a pathological relationship because it becomes difficult to concentrate, plan ahead, or find the clear assertion to follow through.

Lastly, being high in harm avoidance is also likely to be damaging to her over the long run. Anxiety takes its toll—mentally and physically. It is one of the symptoms she needs treatment for the most. Her anxiety increases the intrusive thoughts and cognitive dissonance which are hallmark symptoms of the aftermath she struggles with. Her risk factor in harm avoidance is associated with current problems in her mental health. Getting treatment for PTSD or other harm avoidant behaviors will help her towards recovering.

Her Low Harm Avoidance as a Risk Factor

Women who tested lower in harm avoidance can be significantly at risk for involvement with psychopaths. People who are low in harm avoidance are carefree by nature and optimistic in situations that worry others. Women who are low/average in harm avoidance are more relaxed, bold, daring, and dauntless. They don't battle the issue of anxiety the way the women who are high in harm avoidance do. Couple low harm avoidance with extraversion and excitement-seeking traits and we have bold women excitedly seeking new adventures who aren't likely to be on the lookout for ways others can harm them! And even *if* they did get a little peek at the potential danger, things that worry other people don't worry them.

The lack of *enough* harm avoidance clearly keeps them blind to the danger of an oncoming psychopath since they tend to believe the best in others, doesn't expect to be hurt and believes that whatever happens, they can deal with it anyway. Low harm avoidance means the women have low levels of radar detection and aren't looking for ways they might be harmed. Low harm avoidance can lead to becoming a victim (again) because they don't have enough suspicion about getting hurt. Their radar is not finely tuned, but their optimism is!

Some research studies have looked at 'extreme sports' which involve a lot of risk-taking and have noticed low levels of harm avoidance in athletes who participate in these sports. Some scientists believe that certain persons are relatively *unresponsive to danger* or are *unreasonably optimistic* when they are in danger. They seem to have a self-confidence that they can get themselves 'out' of any real danger. This raises the question if low harm avoidance isn't a sort of 'immunity' against the trauma that others would experience in the same situation. However, trauma immunity with a psychopath means her ability to react sooner rather than later is impaired.

Her risk is also increased because she finds the low harm avoidance in the psychopath attractive. Tests have associated low harm avoidance with the carefree attitude and boldness in the psychopath. These traits connect her to the same extraversion and excitement seeking in him that she finds so appealing. Low harm avoidance in her is likely to find low harm avoidance in him an attractive 'vortex.' In her, low harm avoidance may be merely distraction from danger. In him, however, it is utter fearlessness associated with pathology.

While the psychopath is not likely to be affected by her harm avoidance trait, she will definitely be negatively affected by his. What I have seen repeatedly is if someone is going to repeat the pattern with yet another psychopath, it is likely to be the woman with low harm avoidance.

The good news is that anxiety, PTSD, intrusive thoughts, and cognitive dissonance can all be treated with counseling. Women who love psychopaths need to find a balance between the paranoia of high harm avoidance and the 'everyone can be trusted' of low harm avoidance. Whether the women are high or low in harm avoidance, most likely this trait will need counseling focus during recovery.

In this last segment of the TCI Temperament Traits, I looked in detail at harm avoidance which is a significant risk factor in women who love psychopaths.

Conclusion

Temperaments, as we have seen in this chapter, have significant power to make women strong and resilient people or open exposure to their own temperament-driven risky behavior. Hopefully this chapter has helped to understand why temperamental 'super traits' have produced a type of woman who can find a relationship with a psychopath initially exciting, fulfilling and yet un-alarming.

Change is only possible when we recognize a problem starting with the awareness of elevated temperament traits and their affect on patterns of relational selection. Certain temperament traits are excessive in women who love psychopaths, and since temperament is permanent and hard-wired, they must learn how to safeguard these vulnerable aspects of themselves just as they would learn self-care if a medical condition warranted safeguarding their health in particular ways.

A woman's understanding of her own temperament is crucial for her ability to protect herself relationally. Those temperamental traits that are elevated in women who love psychopaths are:

1. Extraversion and excitement-seeking
2. Relationship investment and positive sociability
3. Sentimentality
4. Attachment
5. Competitiveness
6. Concern for having others' high regard
7. Harm avoidance

Those temperament traits that tested in the low range are also important, they also place her at-risk. These included the Low Range Traits of:

1. Low impulsiveness for some
2. Low harm avoidance for others

For one last look at the issue of extreme temperament traits see the chart below. It helps us to view the women's surplus of traits and the psychopath's deficits of traits to understand how this 'excess and deficit' concept of temperament could potentially impact not only the attraction phase of dating, but also affect the dynamics of the entire relationship.

Figure 7.1
Her Temperament Traits vs. His Temperament Traits

Temperament Traits	Typical Psychopath	Women Who Love Psychopaths
Excitement Seeking Total	High	Moderately High
NS1-Exploratory Excitability	High	High
NS2-Impulsiveness	High	Average
NS3-Impulsiveness	High	Average
NS3-Extravagance	High	Moderately High
NS4-Disorderliness	High	Moderately High
Relationship Investment Total	Low	High
RD1-Sentimentality	Low	High
RD3-Attachment	Low	High
RD4-Dependence	Low	High
Harm Avoidance Total	Low	Mixed
HA1-Anticipatory Worry	Low	Moderately High
HA2-Fear of Uncertainty	Low	Average
HA3-Shyness	Very Low	Very Low
HA4-Fatigability	Low	Low

Conclusion

This chapter has given insight into how elevated temperament traits can contribute to the pathological love relationship dynamics and leave her as a target to psychopaths. In the next chapter, I will look at the second half of the results of the TCI traits we examined in women who love psychopaths. These character traits reveal how a woman sees herself, her own specific goals, and her personal values.

8   ᴀAbout Her

Her Character

"Character develops itself in the stream of life." — Goethe

In the last chapter, we talked about the results of the TCI as they related to the **temperament** traits of the women we surveyed. In this chapter, we are going to look at the TCI results as they pertain to the women's **character** traits. Character refers to those aspects of her personality which determine how she sees herself, her goals, and her personal values. While her traits are likely to make her the inspiring woman that she is, they are also a risk factor in attracting psychopaths and can contribute to a woman's *remaining* in a pathological love relationship.

Let's see why…

The Three Categories of Character Traits[61]

Character traits are grouped into three categories. The character categories are:

1. Cooperativeness
2. Self-directedness
3. Self-transcendence/spirituality

Category One - Cooperativeness

The Cooperativeness category consists of:

o   Cooperativeness
o   Empathy
o   Tolerance
o   Friendliness, Compassion, Supportiveness, and Moral Principles

---

[61] Compiled by Liane J. Leedom, M.D.

Additional traits we noticed in the women:

o   Trust

o   Loyalty

Her Cooperativeness

Survey Results
Character Trait: Cooperativeness
Scores: Her: High Him: Low

The women in our survey scored high in cooperativeness. Since the women ranked high in attachment, it didn't surprise us that they also ranked high in cooperativeness. Cooperativeness is related to connectedness within her character traits, just like attachment is related to connectedness within her temperament traits. These traits are at the heart of who she is and what makes her selfless and other-person oriented. These agreeability-based traits are advantageous in teamwork in her career and within social situations. Cooperativeness shows her level of motivation to get along with others and what she brings to the table to accomplish it.

Since many of these women are either in professional caregiving careers or are in the business sector, we would expect them to test high in this trait. Their cooperativeness has helped them succeed in jobs that require a lot of give-and-take interactions with others. Their cooperation is part of the service they give in the relationships they have, both personally and professionally. The trait of cooperation implies that they value getting along with others and when necessary, the women will compromise their own interests to help the group or couple achieve their goals.

The set of cooperation-based traits of the TCI shows us how she sees herself as an integral part of human society. When she is cooperative, she uses:

o   empathy/compassion to understand how someone else feels.

o   tolerance to manage differences.

o   friendliness to be approachable.

o   supportiveness to contribute with helpfulness.

o   moral principles of life to choose between right and wrong, good and bad.

These groups of traits contribute to an altruistic view of others. This means she believes cooperation benefits everyone and will give consideration to the thoughts and needs of others. New studies are emerging about *excessive* altruism and its effect on the person who has it. We eagerly are waiting to see how this applies to women who love psychopaths who show such elevated altruism.

Her Cooperativeness as a Risk Factor

This issue of high cooperativeness is not just a 'small' issue for her—she was *97% more cooperative* than most women! It's these excessive altruistic and cooperation-based traits which make her a flashing billboard for psychopaths. Obviously a psychopath needs to find a woman who is cooperative and a team player when it comes to 'Team Psychopath' and playing out his agenda. He looks for the following traits in his team recruits:

o   Friendly so she is approachable

o   Compassionate so she can connect to his 'struggles in life'

o   Tolerant so she can endure his antics

o   Supportive so she can help to him

o   Empathetic so she never stops listening, helping and hoping

Women who rank high (especially *that* high) in cooperation traits are at significant risk of entering pathological relationships. While psychopaths find extraversion and excitement seeking traits attractive, they *need* their women to be cooperative.

What other woman could maintain her optimism in the face of the psychopath's narcissism if she wasn't cooperative? These cooperation traits are her drawing card to a psychopath. Her overflowing empathy, tolerance, friendliness, compassion, supportiveness and her moral principles are what balance the lopsided scales of the relationship, since he lacks these qualities to a gapping deficient degree. This delicate balance helps camouflage the glaring gaps of the character traits between them. Her cooperativeness helps to smooth out the character he doesn't have and makes the relationship seem more normal—at least in the beginning.

If he won't do his part, she may find his lack of cooperation as a sort of 'I fought the law' desperado. This doesn't register to her as the significant risk factor of psychopathy that it is. She will likely fill in the gaps of his non-cooperation with her extraordinary cooperation so that the relationship still feels like it is effortlessly moving ahead.

Very high cooperativeness is the *most* significant reason these specific women were targeted. Psychopaths instinctively know that women high in cooperativeness will stay in relationships with them longer. That has proven to be true. She indicated that when the psychopath had dated a far less cooperative woman, their dating period was far shorter! This trait of high cooperativeness needs to be therapeutically treated through work on boundary issues. Most assuredly, psychopaths tested her cooperativeness by violating her boundaries early on. He even tested covert and insignificant boundaries that gave him, in his mind's eye, a green light.

"My cooperation was definitely a calling card that I didn't realize at first. Over the years, he has bilked me for close to $100,000 in dribs and drabs. I even refinanced my house to fund his needs, wants, and to cooperate with his career plans of starting his own business. I wanted to be supportive in a way, that he indicated no one in his life had been for him. I'm in my 50's and my life savings is now gone. I am faced with having to actually move to a 3rd world country in order to financially survive and make retirement. Imagine that? Having to live somewhere so extreme because what I did was so extreme and who I gave it all to was so extreme. It's surreal."

Her Empathy

Survey Results
Character Trait: Empathy
Scores: Her: High Him: Low

Empathy is the ability to understand how others feel, experience it from their view point, and in some cases, directly feel the emotion of someone else. Empathy has even been linked with the mastery to 'read' someone else—translating, if you will, the other person's thoughts, feelings and even movements into understandable emotional language. People with this level of empathy are often referred to as 'empaths' who (voluntarily or involuntarily) 'resonate' with the feelings of others by scanning others psyches for thoughts and feelings that run deeper than what is being portrayed on the surface.

The women who have been in pathological relationships have talked about how they feel the emotions of someone else—especially the wounded psychopath. This is one indicator of why they feel so deeply attached to the psyches of the psychopaths—sensing at a deeper level the undiscovered disorder and its brokenness.

Although empaths often talk about a 'knowing' of someone else, interestingly the ever illusive psychopath can fool even the empaths genetic aspects of 'knowing.' This is a testament not to the 'faulty' empaths sensing but to the great power of pathology.

The issue of these women as empaths deserves more attention because it appears that their high levels of empathy may be pointing to something even more intrinsic to their nature. With the new studies emerging around the issue of low and high empathy, 'empaths' may come to be better understood than they are today.

As an example of empaths and their feelings, we have listed some of the traits normally associated with them. Keep in mind the women's temperament traits we have already discussed. We have bolded the words that correspond to the temperament traits we have covered so far. To understand how empathy and empaths are connected, here is a blurb from www.blogxero.com:

*"Empaths are highly sensitive. This is the term commonly used in describing one's abilities to (sense) another's emotions and feelings. Empaths have a deep sense of 'knowing' that accompanies empathy and are often **compassionate, considerate, and understanding of others.** Empaths often possess the ability to sense others on many different levels. From their position of observing what another is saying, feeling and thinking they come to understand the other person. They can become very proficient at reading another person's body language and/or study intently the eye movements. While this in itself is not empathy, it is a side-shoot that comes from being observant of others.[62] Empaths are often **very affectionate in personality and expression,** great listeners and counselors (and not just in the professional area). They will find themselves **helping others and often putting their own needs aside to do so.**

---

[62] Authors Note: Ironically, this seems to be what the psychopath himself can also do—intently study eye movements, body language and can be an intense observer of others, yet he does not have empathy.

*They are **highly expressive in all areas of emotional connection** and talk openly, and, at times, quite frankly about themselves. Empaths have a tendency to openly feel what is outside of them more so than what is inside of them. This can cause empaths to ignore their own needs. If they find themselves in the middle of a confrontation, they will endeavor to settle the situation as quickly as possible, **if not avoid it all together.** If any harsh words are expressed in defending themselves, they will likely resent their lack of self-control and have a preference **to peacefully resolve the problem quickly.** People of all walks of life are attracted to **the warmth and genuine compassion** of empaths. Even complete strangers find it easy to talk to empaths about the most personal things. It is as though the person knows instinctively that empaths would listen with **compassionate understanding.**"*

You can see that many of the other traits the women have seem to fuel the trait of empathy adding to its depth and strength.

Ironically, women who tested this high in empathy may have differing childhood backgrounds that contributed to their hyper-empathy. Empathy is largely genetic. Some may have been raised by other empaths in family systems where highly focusing on other people's feelings was normal. These seemingly 'kind' families are often genetic hotbeds of potential victim-hood when their wonderful qualities meet Dr. Jekyll and Mr. Hyde. These high genetic empathizers were likely to feel below the surface into that wellspring of darkness and brokenness and likely have found the challenge of a lifetime in that pit of pathology.

But on the other hand, these high empathizers could have also been raised by adults or parents who were pathological and/or addicted. Children raised by narcissists and psychopaths learn early on how to cater to the needs of the pathological parent in order to avoid punishment or wrath. As a proclivity to 'avoid punishment' in early childhood a behavioral pattern could have been established. She learned that the wrath of pathologicals was to be avoided at all costs. It would be smart and safer for a child to be highly cooperative in a household that was being run by a pathological parent. The trait and skill of empathy in that environment would be emotionally safeguarding to the child, if the child could figure out how to empathize with the pathological parents instead of hating and fighting with them. If she was raised in a home with an alcoholic, mentally ill, or otherwise pathological parent, her skills in cooperation were probably created at a very early age.

In families like these it is not unusual that pathological family dynamics produce children who run the gamut between their own levels of pathology and high levels of empathizing victims. When viewing the 'Jerry Springer Families' often associated with rampant pathology, you will see personality disorder/psychopathic parents with children who straddle the spectrum between emerging psychopathy themselves to the highly empathic.

Her Empathy as a Risk Factor

Empathy has made her a sensitive partner, a good listener, and yet a target for psychopaths. She has more empathy than almost everyone else! This is not just a tad bit of additional empathy she's toting around—her scores in empathy put her on the highest end of the empathy continuum. Too much of a good thing can still be bad for her.

Just what can too much empathy do in the hands of a psychopath? He can keep her tied to the relationship way past the point of sanity. Add to her empathy some of her other 'super' traits and she has a steadfast connection to the psychopath that is not easily broken. This misread steadfast connection is what confuses her family and even her therapist.

With this much hyper-empathy she can easily put herself in a psychopath's shoes with genuine concern. Her empathy is like a drug that the psychopath uses to feed his *need* for power. Although she may not realize it, the psychopath doesn't need her empathy but uses it to maintain power over her emotions and the relationship. This could really be said for any of her temperament or character traits—they are all tools and weapons in the hand of a psychopath. Any psychopath can use his own sad history to hook her into his long-term plans by playing the empathy card. Feeling for his personal situation and even subconsciously 'sensing' he is disordered pulls her heart strings to keep her there. Not knowing the permanence of pathology can keep her hoping change is on its way. After all, if she leaves, who would want him? If she leaves, who will help him? With all that empathy, she believes she has the best possible chance of reaching him, touching him, and helping him grow into the potential she sees in him. All that empathy is indeed a manipulative tool in the psychopath's hand.

The obvious question is, "If she's empathic, why didn't she know what she was feeling from the psychopath was fake?" The ability to make an empath feel strongly about his false stories is probably no more shocking than how psychopaths con prison psychiatrists and other forensic professionals who are supposed to know what psychopathic behavior is all about. The intensity of attachment and her ability to feel his emotions is often confused as some kind of verifier of 'true' connection.

Her Tolerance

Along with very high scores in empathy, the women scored high in tolerance. Tolerance is the ability to recognize and respect the beliefs or practices of others and the ability to endure hardship or pain—a highly-needed quality in pathological relationships.

The ability to tolerate the 'beliefs or practices of others' is especially essential to a psychopath whose own world view and corresponding practices and ethics are so twisted. Her ability to tolerate verbal abuse, cheating, not working/over working, addictions, physical violence (if applicable), sexual deviancy, and any other negative behavior trait associated with the psychopath of course, benefits the psychopath.

There is much to tolerate in these relationships. The psychopath gets a "feel" for her level of tolerance by starting out with small boundary violations and working up to full fledged relationship transgressions. What is tolerated is then pushed as a limit. Her ability to endure the hardship and pain keeps her telling herself that it isn't that bad. His ability to get her to tolerate more unbelievable behavior from him feeds his sense of entitlement and dominance over her and also power to get her to tolerate *even more the next time from him.*

Her Tolerance as a Risk Factor

What these women *can* tolerate is amazing. The amount of pain and the frequency of pain (emotional, physical, financial, sexual and spiritual) are significantly higher than what other women can tolerate. We are unsure whether this is related to her hyper-empathy. Until his behavior is virtually continual or increases dramatically, many of the women stated they didn't notice the increase in tolerance they were using. Much like turning up the heat on a lobster in the pot, it takes a while until the heat is hot enough for her to know she's only seconds away from being boiled alive!

This high level of tolerance could also be related to her competitiveness as well. "I can wait this out! He won't get to me this time!" Empathy and competitiveness coupled with tolerance can be a critical combination in a relationship with a psychopath.

Other combinations of the TCI traits that are in surplus also create unique and dynamic factors. Think about the issue of:

high tolerance ("I can take it.") +
high empathy ("I understand his behavior.") +
high attachment ("I love him.") +
high relationship investment ("I get satisfaction from the good parts of our relationship.")
= **Inevitable Harm.**

These types of trait combinations are like an emotional deadlock where she is held in the relationship by her surplus of super-traits.

If she has PTSD as well, the symptoms of PTSD related to 'numbing' may increase what she can tolerate. The pain or discomfort she normally would experience with a psychopath may not even be registering. The PTSD can keep her emotions and pain threshold 'numbed out' to the pain of what she is really living.

For the psychopath, this level of tolerance is a pretty good guarantee she'll be around for quite a while…no matter what! Since it is likely that she is a tolerant person in general—with her kids, at work, and with others—her tolerant character was just the breeding ground for the real test of her tolerance in a relationship with a psychopath.

Her Friendliness, Compassion, Supportiveness, and Moral Principles

Survey Results
Temperament Trait: Shyness
Scores: Her: Very Low Him: Very Low

These traits have been coupled together for discussion. These traits are part of the cooperation-based traits which means the women tested very high in these as well. Like the problems associated with being too high in empathy and tolerance, she is *equally strong* in these traits.

Survey Results

Character Trait:
Compassion

Scores:
Her: High
Him: Low

Friendliness is connected to her approachability and lack of shyness. Unfriendly people aren't approachable but her open nature and her extraversion make her an easy person to approach and talk to. Mutually, she is likely to also be an easy talker— quickly surrendering the details of her life and thoughts. Her supportiveness combined with her tolerance keeps her at his side as the cheerleader of his life.

Just what is meant by her moral principles?

Moral principles are a person's sense of right and wrong. The women in our survey had high moral principles and a strong internal moral compass of right and wrong. Their moral sense and its relationship to a psychopath are quite interesting. Although many of the women tested very high in the morality department, they ended up with the immoral and unprincipled psychopath. Many have gone on to remark how their moral principles were severely compromised in this relationship.

Psychopaths, interestingly enough, seem to want women who are highly moral for two reasons:

1. He likes the image and status of himself with a moral person because she makes him appear moral by his affiliation with her.
2. If she is highly moral, she will continue to adhere to her principles despite his behavior. She is not likely to 'do unto him' as he has 'done unto her' when he cheats.

Since psychopaths are chameleons, they pretend to have the same morals as the women. Women in pathological relationships seem to project their normal characteristics including her sense of right and wrong onto the psychopath—endowing him with traits he doesn't have. Her ability to project and his ability to pretend, allow him the stage to mimic her moral principles in his life.

Ironically, many of the women's stories end with the loss of their moral principles in the relationship to a moral monster. This could be through sexual deviance he asked her to participate in, or asking that she lie, steal, cheat, or in some other way violate her own moral code. In the relationship with the psychopath, she was likely to become mortified at the immoral behaviors he engaged in and some she was drug into as well.

Her Friendliness, Compassion, Supportiveness, and Moral Principles as Risk Factors

All of her cooperation-based traits are risk factors:

Supportiveness is likely to keep her hinged to him as she 'waits it out' while he pretends to be working on himself, looking for a job, starting his own business or triumphing over an addiction.

Compassion is likely to keep her helping and supporting, all the way to the bitter end. The psychopath's salesmanship has women believing that "just a little more" support/help/compassion/empathy/tolerance will get him to the place that no other woman was able to help him get to. After all, she's come this far and invested this much if just a *little more* investment will finally get her what she wants with him in the relationship, then it's worth it to just hang in there! Of course, it's down the road that women realize that all the support in the world can't change the incurableness of his pathology.

Moral principles – Many women who have become sexually involved, feel particularly 'invested' morally in the relationship and would rather try to make it work than face starting over elsewhere or struggle with any misgivings they might have had about the sexual element in the relationship.

In addition to the character traits that are covered on the TCI, women who love psychopaths tend to have some additional traits related to cooperativeness that seem to be very strong. These include:

1. Trust
2. Loyalty

Her Trust

Universally, the women who have ended up in relationships with psychopaths or other pathological-types are women who have extremely high degrees of trust. However, the kind of trust the women have would be defined as *'blind trust.'* They give trust freely even when there is no reason to know whether the person can be trusted. These women begin relationships with a full carte blanche of trust even though they may not know him very well or for very long.

New studies on the neurobiology of trust indicate that there are higher levels of oxytocin (a hormone that will be discussed later on in the book) in people who have high trust. These higher levels of hormone can produce a feeling of trust even for complete strangers.

However, the difference is that women who avoid psychopathic relationships approach the issue of trust differently. These women tended to have people earn trust slowly over time through repeated proofs of loyalty. If loyalty was broken, the relationship was broken. But women who love psychopaths didn't wait for trust to be earned. They begin with the philosophy of 'everyone deserves to be trusted until proven otherwise.' This approach is most likely related to low harm avoidance—her ability to believe that people are trust worthy and not be on the lookout for being harmed.

I have noticed in counseling that once women internally think he is ok, whether that is within moments, days, or weeks—the 'declaring it so' to herself that he is 'a nice guy' switches off her red flag signals. Tragically, once she has made the decision that he is ok and can be trusted she stops, blocks or doesn't recognize internal information from her red flag system. This is a critical error that will cost her so much in aftermath symptoms.

Her Trust as a Risk Factor

If her trust issues were only connected to 'everyone deserves to be trusted until proven otherwise,' then the psychopath would quickly be out because he so frequently breaks trust. However, her trust issues aren't simply based on 'until proven otherwise.' She has other generous conditions associated with her blind trust. This includes giving him multiple chances because she is compassionate, tolerant, and deeply believes everyone can change and grow. The psychopath is given dozens of chances…because beneath it all, her deepest desire (related to her relationship investment) is that she is with a man she can trust. Sometimes her desire to believe she is with a man she can trust is more important than the reality that she is with someone who can't be trusted.

If the women had waited for the psychopath to earn trust the long hard way, she may never have been in the relationship at all. Or, if she had broken rank at the time of one of his earlier untrustworthy events, she would have been far less damaged from the relationship.

Just this one issue—how she handles the issue of upfront trust and violated trust separate the women who have been (and are at risk of) future pathological relationships—from those who never have been and probably never will be. You can bet that psychopaths count on her ability to continue to trust even in the face of proof they are not trustworthy.

This highlights another fact about the women we surveyed. When given the choice between trusting what the psychopath *says* he has done/not done/or will do, or trusting what she has caught him actually *doing,* women who love psychopaths will likely choose the words over the actions. She could catch him in bed for the fourth time with someone and he will deny it, gaslight her by saying she's crazy, or say it meant nothing and it will never happen again. He can convince her that what she saw him do he didn't do by massaging her issue of high trust. These high levels of trust accentuate her ability to be gaslighted.

Even if the psychopath has a long history of this behavior in every relationship he's ever been in she will choose to believe his words and not his behavior. This interesting behavior dynamic in her deserves more study so we can understand what is behind her choice of 'what' to believe.

Her Loyalty

Women in the survey have high levels of loyalty. Loyalty is connected to and feeds many of the other complimentary and elevated traits. The women were loyal in their jobs, friendships, and relationships. She is likely to be a consistent and faithful worker, friend, and partner. She will be loyal even when others do not return her intense loyalty. While she's likely to be deeply wounded by others lack of loyalty (because she is highly sensitive and empathetic), her trust, tolerance, and hope will win out keeping her loyal even in the face of betrayal. In a relationship with a psychopath, betrayal will test her loyalty over and over again.

Her Loyalty as a Risk Factor

Loyalty invested in a psychopath is always bad banking for her but a great pay off for the psychopath. Due to her loyalty, intense attachments, and hearty tolerance, the psychopath soon realizes he can count on her devotion to stand with him in the face of great odds. The psychopath realizes even when he is unfaithful, is caught lying, or in other acts of deceit, her loyalty is the consistency he can count on.

Much like the issue of blind trust, women who love psychopaths have unusual systems of loyalty. In recovery circles this is referred to as 'insane loyalty' in which high levels of loyalty in the face of reality are still clung to. Insane loyalty levels are often associated with traumatic and betrayal bonding in reactions such as Stockholm Syndrome and even cult programming. Who can argue that a psychopath is a cult unto himself?

Her loyalty to a psychopath is treacherous for her own emotional health and is likely to be a contributing factor to the pain she feels today. Breaking loyalty ranks even with someone who has betrayed her, cheated, stolen money, abused her children or did other unspeakable acts is still likely to cause guilt feelings. Many women in the survey felt guilty for breaking the promises they made to the psychopath like, "I'll never leave you" even despite his excessive harm to her life. This undying sense of loyalty made it difficult for her to leave the relationship.

Much like the issues of hyper-empathy and hyper-altruism, the insane loyalty of victims to the most disloyal person on the planet (psychopaths) deserves more research by the neuroscientists to make the connections.

In the first segment of the TCI Character Traits, I looked in detail at cooperativeness and its facets including empathy, tolerance, friendliness, compassion, supportiveness and moral principles. In addition to those TCI Traits, I also examined two other components of cooperativeness in the women related to trust and loyalty. Now I'll look at the second group of TCI character traits, those related to self-directedness.

Category Two - Self-Directedness

The Self-Directedness category consists of:

o   Self-directedness
o   Self-acceptance
o   Goal-congruent habits

Her Self-Directedness

Self-directedness measures a person's responsibility, reliability, resourcefulness, goal-orientation and self-confidence. These stellar character traits allow a women to be successful, realistic and effective in making sure her behavior is lined up with her life-long goals.

Survey Results

Character Trait:
Resourcefulness

Scores:
Her: High
Him: No Data

Survey Results

Character Trait:
Responsibility

Scores:
Her: High
Him: No Data

These women use their self-directedness as gifts to others through their own resourcefulness. I reiterate that these are successful women outside of their extremely unsuccessful relationship with a psychopath. Over the years, I've counseled women in pathological relationships who were high achievers as professors, lawyers, an air traffic controller, accountants, financial analyst, surgeons, multi-millionaire business executive, artists, writers, therapists, anesthesiologist, OR nurse, teachers, documentary producer, famous journalist, recording artist, to name a few. They are in careers that require resourcefulness and solid judgment as part of their job functioning. Her skills of responsibility and reliability have helped her to be successful in other parts of her life, like her career. Her goal-directedness assisted her to get into the field she is in, aids her in meeting the objectives she sets in her life, and enables her to succeed in her field. Consequently, with this package of self-directed traits she is self-confident (or at least was before the psychopath).

The question is "If these stellar qualities lead them to occupations where they exercise sound judgment, why don't they apply this judgment to the facts of the psychopath?" In the rest of the book we will address the process and dynamics involved in how pathology alters other people's behavior and beliefs.

Survey Results

Character Trait:
Self-Directedness Total

Scores:
Her: High
Him: Low

Her strong traits of self-directedness related to her responsibility, goal-direction, resourcefulness and goal-congruent habits will greatly influence a significant part of her aftermath symptoms related to cognitive dissonance. Cognitive dissonance is created when behavior does not align with belief systems—when the walk doesn't match the talk. Being strongly self-directed is going to cause her mental distress during the relationship with the psychopath when it becomes impossible for her to align her beliefs with her behaviors.

Her Self-Directedness as a Risk Factor

So how in the world could a psychopath use responsibility, reliability, resourcefulness, and goal directedness to his advantage? How can those traits in her help a psychopath's cause? For those who ended up with psychopaths who were high functioning and highly successful, her responsibility and goal directedness probably mirrored a lot of the traits she *assumed* he had in his own business or career—after all, he looked successful from the outside. These traits were camouflaging traits in his case, in which he used responsibility and goal directedness to mask behaviors of manipulation and coercion. The highly successful psychopath can make her traits seem like a good match for two professional people. While her traits of responsibility, reliability and resourcefulness are authentic, his traits are used in the service of the number one goal in his life: himself and whatever it is he's after. To this degree, he is indeed also resourceful.

For women who ended up with low/lower-functioning or even criminal psychopaths, the women's ability to be reliable and responsible built a structure to his life from which he could appear to function. Many of the lower functioning psychopaths are in and out of jobs, quit because they hate the authority of their boss, or are repeatedly fired. Unemployment or sporadic employment can be an ongoing lifestyle for these types of psychopaths. Her stability in these traits helps to stabilize an otherwise unstable way of life. Many psychopaths like these features in the women because no matter if they are high functioning or low functioning psychopaths, her traits related to her self-directedness benefit his illusion of stability.

Her high functioning ability carried him along and provided structure for him almost like a parenting relationship. Most likely when his functioning level frustrated her, she just did what was needed to move the relationship along and handle the problem at hand. This level of responsibility and reliability covered his lack of functioning or his criminal functioning.

A common thread throughout the stories of the women is the 'professional care-giving career women in a relationship with an emotionally (and sometimes financially) bankrupt psychopath.' From the outside, this appears to be hugely incongruent for her. Yet given her 'super' traits, it is highly congruent with traits so abundantly represented in her:

Occupation...	May...
Accountant	Help him financially restructure
Attorney	Help him beat a 'bad rap'
Child Care Worker	Nurture his abused inner child
Female Clergy Member	Soothe his soul
Nurse	Nurse his emotional wounds
Social Worker	Help him get back on his feet
Teacher	Help him realize the potential she sees

Given the academy award-winning performances that psychopaths are capable of, and women who 'care' for others as a job and career—caring in the intimate confides of her life isn't such a far stretch. I didn't say it was a 'healthy' stretch—just that given her 97% higher than normal empathy and a genetic makeup that drew her into the very career she chose—we can see from afar how this happens.

Her self-directedness, which keeps a psychopath afloat in his own projection of normalcy, will eventually create cognitive dissonance in her. Her strong traits of self-directedness misused and abused for his impression management will eventually start her brain 'ping ponging' wondering why in the world she would use her professional skills to help someone so sick.

Women who are lower in self-directedness/reliability would not have taken on the responsibility of 'caring for' or 'carrying along' the psychopath and his low functionality. Just like a 'Princess-Diva' would not have appealed to him, neither would a woman unwilling to shoulder his pathology. To this degree, her level of self-directedness was a risk factor in the pathological relationship.

Her Self-Acceptance

> **Survey Results**
>
> **Character Trait:**
> Self-Acceptance
>
> **Scores:**
> Her: High
> Him: No Data

Self-acceptance is a person's level of self-acceptance, weaknesses and all. It is a somewhat realistic appraisal of the good and the bad of one's core self and the ability to embrace those aspects. The typical woman in these types of relationships is well-adjusted, realistically able to appraise her strengths and weaknesses and has good self-acceptance. She has the capacity to manage herself, finds self-worth in her own person-hood, has a good level of self-esteem and can validate herself. Society seems to think that these women must have poor self esteem which is why they got involved with psychopaths to begin with. This is one of several ways that these women test differently than other women who have gotten into abusive relationships.

Remember, for the most part, these are professional women. The trait of self-acceptance would be an important asset to a successful woman but later in the book, we will see what happens to this trait of self-acceptance in the hands of a psychopath. This trait will take a terrible beating and will leave her unrecognizable to herself and to others close to her. A psychopath can effortlessly dismantle a lifelong sense of self that was once strong and positive.

Self-Acceptance as a Risk Factor

Women who have solid self-esteem aren't on the lookout for someone as brutal as a psychopath to systematically dismantle the way they see themselves. For the women with low harm-avoidance, she probably isn't *expecting* to be side-swiped by a psychopath. In her own self-confidence (generated by her solid sense of self and her professional accomplishments) she feels the ability to handle whatever life brings her.

Since she has a strong sense of her own strength, she feels at ease with other strong personalities, like the psychopath's. Because she is extraverted she likes other extraverts as well and because she is self-accepting, she is likely to be accepting of others and easily accepts the psychopath for his strengths and weaknesses as she does her own.

Unfortunately, the psychopath only loves himself and will systematically attempt to annihilate her sense of self-esteem, self-validation, and self-worth. Her extraversion has been an overt challenge to his dominance. Much like pack dog mentality, the alpha dog will exert himself, attacking her strengths to reduce them and magnifying her weaknesses as a way of mentally capturing her emotional territory. Many women say he seemed to be initially attracted to her because of her self-acceptance and inner strength and yet it was the very thing he targeted in her to take her down with. This is accurate. Her self-acceptance is a challenge to him or the psychopath would consistently pick emotionally weak and dependent-oriented women, which psychopaths don't tend to pick.

By the end of the relationship, her sense of self is so mangled she can't remember who she was when she was that strong self-confident woman that others remember her as.

Her Goal-Congruent Habits

Survey Results
Character Trait: Congruent Habits
Scores: Her: High Him: No Data

A woman who tests high in goal-congruency will normally act in accordance with her long-term values and goals, is consistent, has rapport with herself, and others think of her as a sincere person. The women in the survey are sure about their priorities and feel self-trusting. These habits in her develop because they are practiced and acquired over time, not from flash-in-the pan short-term behaviors. This is who she really is at her core.

These habits that will be challenged and changed from the relationship with the psychopath also produce high cognitive dissonance in her when her own long term values are not adhered to. Her own inconsistency to act in accordance with her long term values will produce terrible aftermath symptoms.

Goal-Congruent Habits as Risk Factors

Psychopaths have the uncanny ability to stand downwind of someone competent and look competent themselves by mere affiliation. Before these traits and habits are ravished by the psychopath, they will be used by him to further the relationship. Her consistency in moving ahead is likely to hide the psychopath's veiled impulsiveness and inconsistency. Her ability to initially embrace her long-term values and goals sets the firm foundation in the relationship where the psychopath is likely to hide behind her consistency. Her 'certainty' associated with her goal-congruent habits must on many levels challenge the psychopath's dominance. This will spark within him the drive to want to dis-mantle this consistency and strength in her that he feels opposes him. As the relationship continues, her normally goal-congruent habits will become very incongruent, increasing her sense of cognitive dissonance when her strength becomes her weakness. Knowing what she 'should' be doing about him and her inability to do it when she was once so strong, pours gasoline on the fire of her cognitive dissonance.

Category Three – Self-Transcendence and Spirituality

The Self-Transcendence and Spirituality category consists of self-transcendence alone.

Her Self-Transcendence and Spirituality

Survey Results
Character Trait: Self-Transcendence
Scores: Her: Average Him: Low

Psychopaths' women tested average in self-transcendence. This trait is a reflection of spirituality and spiritual principles. Self-transcendence and spirituality determine a woman's ability to see her place in the universe and how all things are connected in the world. Self-transcendence is 'big picture thinking' and people who have this trait are un-pretentious, humble, and fulfilled in life. Self-transcendent people are on a quest to help others find self-fulfillment and to reach their own highest potential. This is the reason why so many of the women are in the professional care-giving jobs—because they enjoy helping other people reach their potential.

Survey Results

Character Trait:
Spiritual Acceptance

Scores:
Her: Moderately High
Him: Low

Due to this trait, she is able to deal with the difficult things in life like suffering and illness, and can find meaning in these concepts and experiences. She is likely to try to help others do the same thing. She is less focused on the acquisition of wealth, power and the material pleasures that life can bring and more focused on the intrinsic meaning of life.

The women scored average in self-transcendence primarily because they scored high in one trait and yet low in one aspect causing a combined score of average. Without the one low score, we can see that these women have a lot of the traits of self-transcendence.

Interesting, the women scored high in the trait that indicates a tendency to 'believe in miracles'—which makes sense considering it is certainly a necessary trait in a relationship with a psychopath. She must believe he can be different in order to stay—on some level this would have to be a miracle!

Self-Transcendence and Spirituality as Risk Factors

Self-transcendent women like to encourage others to self-transcend. Her ability to want to *help* the psychopath on his journey to reach his highest potential in his career, self-understanding, and self-actualization is probably a driving force for her in the relationship. Of course there was no way in the beginning that she could know that he was a psychopath and can't self-actualize, can't reach his highest potential due to the hardwiring of his personality disorder or pathology. Many psychopaths have some brilliant and fascinating qualities that women see 'great potential' in. However, a psychopath has no ability to embrace that potential, except as a way to manipulate others. Nonetheless, an unknowing and highly empathetic, tolerant and supportive woman will spend enormous amounts of time trying to steer the psychopath on the path of self-fulfillment, real success, or further his existing success. Some of the women had put their psychopaths through medical or law school only to be dumped afterwards.

Her lack of interest in the acquisition of wealth and power fits nicely with a psychopath, who is hyper-fixated on more power and who will help himself to any wealth she may have acquired. Her trait of not being highly fixated on wealth (even hers) is probably related to why so many women have lost great deals of money to the psychopath.

Conclusion

The excessive amount of temperament and character traits possessed by women who love psychopaths balances the horrendous deficits the psychopath has in many of the same traits. This balance creates, at least in the beginning, a counterpoise relationship. It's the only way that the relationship could ever mimic something that resembled viable. Her excesses diminish the significance of his deficits. Without the softening of his glaring absence of many of the traits that lovers look for in each other, these hook-ups simply wouldn't have happened. No one has on their date wish list 'Satan—can't wait to meet him and see his total package of awfulness.' If there wasn't some camouflage to his emotional bankruptcy, few women would willingly sign up. That he hid it well and her 'super' traits balanced the toppling scales is what kept this relationship in the fast lane. The symbiotic-ness that he needs what she has in her excessive traits and she wants what he brings to the fantasy relationship, works—at least initially. The psychopath brings to this fantasy his fair share of unusual approach, elixir-like intensity and a vortex-sucking draw that can cause even the most well-grounded women to lose their focus and follow the cult leader right into 'drinking the kool-aid' and her own emotional doom.

In the last few chapters, I looked at her traits and how they create risk factors for her in the relationship with a psychopath. If you review those traits on the charts on the previous pages you will see how the psychopath is likely to be perceived using the same trait list. Looking at her traits compared to his traits we can begin to understand this 'trait dynamic' that has fueled the pathological love relationship.

The charts on the next two pages summarize the TCI findings for the women in our study compared with the "typical psychopath" scores on the same TCI.

Figure 8.1
Temperament Traits of the Psychopath and His Women

Temperament Traits	Typical Psychopath	Women Who Love Psychopaths
Excitement Seeking Total	High	Moderately High
NS1-Exploratory Excitability	High	High
NS2-Impulsiveness	High	Average
NS3-Extravagance	High	Moderately High
NS4-Disorderliness	High	Moderately High
Relationship Investment Total	Low	High
RD1-Sentamentality	Low	High
RD3-Attachment	Low	High
RD4-Dependence	Low	High
Harm Avoidance Total	Low	Mixed
HA1-Anticipatory Worry	Low	Moderately High
HA2-Fear of Uncertainty	Low	Average
HA3-Shyness	Very Low	Very Low
HA4-Fatigability	Low	Low

Figure 8.2
Character Traits of the Psychopath and His Women

Character Traits	Typical Psychopath	Women Who Love Psychopaths
Cooperativeness (C) Total	Low	High
C1-Social Acceptance	Low	High
C2-Empathy	Low	High
C3-Helpfulness	Low	High
C4-Compassion	Low	High
C5-Integrated Conscience	Low	Moderately High
Self-Directedness (SD) Total	Low	High
SD1-Responsibility	No Data	High
SD2-Purposefulness	No Data	High
SD3-Resourcefulness	No Data	High
SD-4 Self-Acceptance	No Data	High

Character Traits	Typical Psychopath	Women Who Love Psychopaths
SD-5 Congruent Habits	No Data	High
Self-Transcendence (ST) Total	Low	Average
ST-1 Self-Forgetfulness	Low	Low Average
ST-2 Transpersonal Identification	Low	Low Average
ST-3 Spiritual Acceptance	Low	Moderately High

9 The Intense Attraction, Attachment, and Bonding[63]

"What you have become is the price you paid to get what you used to want." — *Mignon McLaughlin*

"Repeatedly women told me about the unusual bonding experience they had with psychopaths. I found it curious that many of the women had identical stories of a 'mystical-type' union they described that was electrified by a vibe-like intensity. Identified as some of the reasons she felt gorilla-glued to the psychopath and why he was hard to leave included the extraordinary sex, the deep bond, 'intense' attachment, and a soul-mate experience of being completely 'known' by him. It led me to investigate the nature of attachment in these love relationships and to explore how these pathological relationships might indeed be different." — *Sandra L. Brown, M.A.*

Women were confused even early on about the unusual feelings she felt towards the psychopath. What she remembers is the instant fierce flame of attraction, the rapid onset of psychological attachment, and a mystical process of soul-bonding that she can't explain. Women described their emotions at that time as irrational, frantic, and out of control almost from the moment the relationship started (and sometimes for years after when she thinks of him). The women's conclusion is this desperate sensation of an almost addiction-like-feeling must have been soul-mate status. Consequently, she believes what she is feeling now in aftermath symptoms is simply the loss of her once-in-a-lifetime-soul-mate. Let's take a look at this process of attraction, attachment and bonding and see what happens in, to her, and why.

Attraction—The Heat

Social psychology describes attraction as the 'appealing to another person's desires.' This happens not only naturally through the relationship

---

[63] Contributions by Liane Leedom, M.D.

development, because this is how relationships progress, but also manipulatively because the psychopath finds out what her desires are and morphs himself into what she is attracted to. Women have stated the 'mystical-ness' of attraction with the psychopath happens on an *undescribable super-natural plane* grossly heightening her sense of uncontrollable attraction.

Attraction may not be mystical after all and might be quite understandable not only given a psychopath's make up, but our natural chemistry as well. Attraction has at its core some very scientific (although unromantic) reasons *how* it works.

To begin with, women are most attracted to masculine characteristics that are indicators of high testosterone 'advertised' through virile appearance and dominant behavior. Testosterone motivates his sex drive and psychopaths as hyper-sexual, intensely seek many sex partners, often of both sexes.

With all this overt virility, women indicated they registered their level of attraction for the psychopath sometimes *within seconds* of meeting him creating a high risk situation. A few fleeting, yet intense, seconds or minutes are not enough to screen out dangerous but highly attractive psychopaths. These women, who are conservative by temperament and responsible by character, have confessed to having been so uniquely attracted that they had sex within minutes or only an hour of meeting him. Nowhere in their own sexual histories had they ever responded so 'primitively' to the sense of attraction.

One client told me she met the psychopath in a parking lot. He threw her against her car and said in a sultry Chilean accent "I muuuustttt havvvee you! Meet me here at 5 p.m." She did, even though she had been happily married for more than 25 years. This started a pattern of degrading sex for her that lasted for years simply because the attraction that was fueled in that moment was so primitive and vortex-like.

Why? Attraction can feel primitive and sort of wild and 'driven' and is often subconscious. Attraction with its 'out of control' magic feels like it gets whatever it wants. Attraction can be subtle—like the unconscious erotic imprinting that causes women to select men based on physical, emotional or behavioral attributes. Early erotic imprinting 'imprints' their minds with their own attraction 'guidelines' to the opposite sex when they are adolescents. Although these traits might guide our relationships selection, this is not the foundation of love. It's the foundation of selection.

For many women, attraction is so unconscious that when they feel a stirring, they don't give much thought to whether their attraction feelings are reasonable, healthy, normal, or even safe. Due to these unsafe selections (especially with pathologicals) *The Institute* created a workbook[64] to help women dig deeply into their issues of subconscious attraction, heighten her awareness of her patterns of selection, and help her look for traits she subconsciously chooses over and over again. This subconscious attraction and subsequent choosing could be:

o   largely physical—for instance tall, dark and handsome men

o   emotional—funny, emotionally sensitive or even aloof men

o   a traumatic replay—she keeps picking dad all over again in many different forms, trying to fix the relationship she never had with him

o   a dozen other well hidden reasons why she is attracted to someone

Attraction of course can lead to selection. When women look over their history they may see some remote linkage for instance, they 'always pick alcoholics' but most women don't see the subtle connections in their patterns of selection. Until she understands what traits she is *subconsciously* selecting and reselecting, she is likely to continue to do so.

Sometimes the dynamic is Traumatic Attraction that seems to drive her patterns of selection. People who have been abused or are from dysfunctional homes can have unusual and destructive patterns of selection. While this may seem contrary to what one would expect, these patterns are largely driven by unresolved trauma and these people repeat those exact patterns in their selection of a partner. They often select individuals who have similar 'characteristics' to the abusive/neglectful/addicted adult they grew up with or were exposed to. The unresolved trauma drives them to select abusers or pathologicals for relationships. Today, they are mystified as to why they keep picking pathologicals for relationship partners.

That which remains unresolved, revolves—around and around through their lives until it is resolved. When she has no idea that attraction

---

[64] *How to Spot a Dangerous Man Workbook*

(good, bad, or dysfunctional) is guiding her selections, she just keeps picking the same way and getting the same thing. Yet because the world (and the psychopath) keeps using the word 'love' she uses it too and labels her pathological attraction-based-choices as 'love.' Her attraction is NOT love. It is merely traumatic attraction. What DOES or DOES NOT happen IN the relationship is more an indicator if it was 'love' than attraction based on unresolved trauma.

Attachment—The Magnet

After attraction, the early stages of what she *thinks* is intimacy building occur while they are communicating about feelings, mutual histories, and life aspirations. These moments of 'deep sharing' lay the foundation of the intensity of attachment she will experience. Although psychopaths do attach, their attachment is a superficial 'tie,' not a 'love connection.' Attachment, in its most surface state, can be a tie without love. People have ties to others that they don't necessarily 'love.' This is certainly exceptionally true in psychopaths. In fact, the psychopath has been referred to as the ultimate attachment *disorder* because he has never truly 'bonded' (thus loved in a healthy sense) other people. Attachment disorders, often seen in rageful and out of control children, are sometimes a pre-cursor for adult psychopathy.

So within the attachment phase of this relationship, we have a woman who tests 97% higher in attachment than other people and who tends to trust automatically, and her partner, the psychopath, who has the equivalent of an adult attachment disorder who is trying to camouflage it by masquerading enormous amounts of zealous affection. Although, attachment precedes bonding in the female, not by much! The rapid pace that psychopaths are known to have in relationship skill building will move her quickly from attachment into gorilla-glue bonding at lightning speed. Moving from attraction-to-attachment-to-bonding is likely to be much faster because of her traits and also because the psychopath puts the relationship on the fast track.

Psychopaths are known for their charm and charisma and are skilled in getting women talking about the 3 P's—her:

o past
o pains
o perceptions

...as a way to get info to sculpt his persona and increase attachment. I refer to this process of rapid disclosing from the women as 'verbal bulimia.' It's a flashing red light for a psychopath trying to get her emotional DNA to replicate in himself.

It's Not Just Great Sex

Attachment is increased through sex. Sex with the psychopath happens much earlier in the relationship for her than with other men she has been with. She is hard-wired to be trusting and to deeply attach. Add to that a little known biology fact about the hormone oxytocin and you have a love cocktail that is going to knock her off her feet.

Oxytocin is a sex hormone. Emotionally, the hormone is referred to as the 'love' 'cuddle' or 'bonding' hormone. It's released into the blood stream by:

o   snuggling and cuddling
o   hugging and kissing
o   childbirth and labor
o   sex and orgasm
o   and especially in breast-feeding which induces the feeling of 'bonding' that a woman has with her baby

It increases the feelings of love, well-being, peace, affection, nurturing, security and attachment and causes humans to want to 'stay together' and organize as family units. It's the glue of the family structure.

Physically, the hormone also:

o   increases heart rate
o   sensitivity of nerve endings in various locations (which is why cuddling feels good)
o   is released in women during orgasm and increases her sense of attachment to him
o   is also released during pregnancy

Oxytocin is found in men's semen which is yet another way that women have oxytocin in their body—through his ejaculate. He is hyper-sexual, there is lots of sex, lots of oxytocin from her and from him!

Recently, oxytocin has also been associated with another of her super-traits—her trust. It's not only known as the bonding hormone, it's also known as the 'too trusting' hormone.

In recent studies the act of trusting someone correlated with elevated levels of oxytocin. Zak indicated:[65]

"It literally feels good to cooperate."

...and we know how much cooperation she has! Further:

"As the hormone level rose, people were more likely to reciprocate trust. The stronger the trust, the more the oxtyocin went up. Interestingly, they were unable to articulate why they behaved the way they did."

Even when there was no reason to trust someone, they did.

Blind trust might just be chemical! Here's how it works—oxytocin only occurs in people who have *received* a trust signal from someone else which normally occurs during social interactions (even by complete strangers!). When oxytocin is increased in the brain, the person feels more trustworthy. In the relationship, sometime during the hook-up the interaction with the psychopath sent a trust signal to her. Most likely it was when he was acting like he 'trusted her with his deepest feelings or traumatic story' increasing her oxytocin production resulting in her feeling 'trustworthy.' Extending trust to her is like switching the oxytocin to an 'on' position reinforcing to her 'this is someone safe to interact with.' She in turn then trusts the person who has shown her trust (and who has upped her oxytocin production that she isn't even aware of!).

---

[65] The Neurobiology of Trust, Scientific American, Inc, June 2009, Zak, Paul.

Figure 9.1
Cycle of Trust

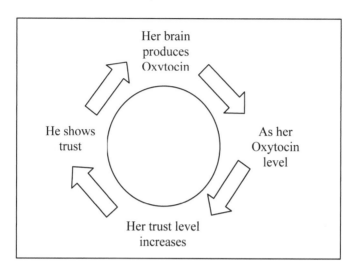

This is a cycle—the more he shows trust, the more her brain produces that cuddling, trusting, wellbeing feeling hormone. The higher the level of oxytocin goes, the higher the level of trust. So while she may already be high in trust because of her super-traits, after the relationship is in full swing and more trusting is occurring and more sex is occurring, her trust is likely to be through the roof. Trust underlies the issue for emotional closeness, or in effect, attachment and bonding.

Yet oxytocin is also negatively affected by stress, uncertainty and isolation all which erode the sense of trust and deplete oxytocin. As the relationship wears on and when the psychopath's behavior is disclosed, the once abundant sense of trust will turn to the dichotomy of distrust.

More Chemical Cocktails

Other brain chemicals also play cupid during this time period. Chemistry sure takes the wind out of the sails of love when we are looking at science instead of libido. Whether we like it or not, neurotransmitters are highly involved in anyone's sex life and our romantic passion is largely a function of our own endocrinology.

Not very romantic is it? When she was feeling hot and lusty? It wasn't his cologne, it was mostly testosterone. When her thinking about the psychopath was a full time job and obsession—she was soaked in serotonin, dopamine and norepinephrine—more potent than a martini but also a similar chemical combo as what is found in obsessive-compulsive disorder. 'Intoxicated' by him—drunk on love? Um…probably not. Just a jigger full of dopamine—the same high people get from alcohol and drugs.[66]

Dr. Helen Fisher[67] indicates that having sex, drives up the dopamine and can push her over the threshold *towards* falling in love. Adding orgasm to that, gives the sensation of attachment. When she was high on the energy and exhilaration of new love with him, PEA was cranking through her body (phenyl ethylamine—the chemicals that are released when she meets someone she is attracted to). We already know that the snuggly cuddly feeling of her 'can't-get-enough-of-him' was the oxytocin. So while she thinks it's just a 'whole lotta lovin' going on'—what is building is a chemical connection with the emotional g-force of an atomic bomb. The chemical portion alone is enough to super glue this new attachment she is feeling, and we haven't even gotten to some of the other factors involved in what Dr. Fisher calls:

"the truly intense and insane attachments that produce the crazy energy drive, emotional elation, mood swings, emotional craving, separation anxiety, childlike possessiveness and total madness."[68]

When skeptics scoff that she 'surely knew all along what he was doing and just didn't want to see it,' they haven't learned the lesson of what oxytocin and its cousins of other brain chemicals can do to a biological trust system.

Bonding—The Glue

Beyond the beginning phases of mere attraction and attachment is the stage (at least for her) of bonding. The psychopath is no doubt 'working it' to assure the deep connection. Women talk about the bonding phases with fond, if not, gazing kinds of far away looks. The psychopath is doing his best (with the limited emotional repertoire he has) to show attention in every way possible. The bonding phase may include love bombing—the intense focus on her, sending gifts, texts, phone calls hourly/daily/multiple

---

[66] www.molly.kalafut.org
[67] www.helenfisher.com
[68] www.helenfisher.com

times a week. Traveling, spending 24/7 with each other, and gradual isolation through the guise of 'love' is also part of this bonding time. As she is becoming 'swept off her feet' she loses contact with who she was, what she use to do, and those she spent time with. Gradually there is nothing else she wants then to be 'lost' in this mystical connection.

"I loved him so much I just wanted to crawl up inside of him."

As the relationship builds, sharing of feelings, talking, and eye-gazing are phases of creating the woman's love bond. Once a love bond is formed, it does not necessarily depend on pleasure to be maintained.[69] Her loyalty in and of itself can probably carry her in the relationship for a long time. In fact, it is very possible for a woman to be bonded to a man she comes to 'hates.' That's because it's not merely her emotions that have bonded with the psychopath. It's also her brain pathways and hormonal chemistry that have responded and bonded to him. Since she is high in relationship investment and is predisposed to being highly responsive to relationship rewards, sex and bonding are perceived by her to be her reward. When she thinks of the psychopath, her body remembers the pleasure reward she has experienced with him *even if* her mind remembers his cheating ways. Women often attest to this horrid bond that keeps them attached to the predator they have come to loathe.

The women become most aware of the 'feel' of the love bond when it's threatened—such as in a break up or infidelity. Threats to the love bond create feelings of depression, stress, anxiety and the sheer 'panic' of losing the one she loves/hates. With a psychopath, the women perceive there are constant threats to the love bond—as in each time they suspect he is cheating, each time he threatens to abandon the relationship, or when he disconnects and is distant and aloof. For instance, she doesn't want him but she doesn't want anyone else to have him either. She feels 'strong' leaving the relationship until he finds someone else. Then she wants him back. The fear itself can increase the desire and feeling of attachment even if she wants it to be over. The roller coaster of the pathological love relationship is sure to be fraught with threats to the love bond. Since pathology's theme is 'inconsistency,' this inconsistency will also be perceived by women as threatening the relationship connection.

---

[69] Contributed by Liane J. Leedom, M.D.

Anxiety Bonding

These threats to the love bond, increases anxiety and stress hormone levels. During the relationship, the psychopath isolates his woman from the rest of the world and her social network under the guise of 'being into her.' She has little emotional support from others that would normally serve to help her reduce or manage her anxiety effectively. In fact, the loss of these emotional support systems has probably increased her anxiety. He either encouraged her to cut ties or her support system was on to him and confronted her. With her level of loyalty, she is not likely to break the love bond now.

Being with a psychopath is anxiety-producing. The psychopath fights with her, raising her level of anxiety. She thinks about leaving or takes steps to leave the relationship and that triggers profound anxiety in her. Without friends and family as support to help her manage her anxiety, she is in need of anxiety relief. She turns to the psychopath himself—both the creator and reliever of stress. He gratefully relieves her anxiety through sex, she feels closer to him during sex, hormones are released, and afterwards she is indeed, momentarily less anxious. With her hyper-hopefulness, she believes they will reconnect during sex and it will heal the current conflict. The psychopath as both the creator of her anxiety and the reliever of it as well is part of the trauma bonding and betrayal bonding patterns[70] that produce the well known dichotomies we will later look at in the relationship.

Nearly all the women in the survey made reference to 'make-up sex' which is extremely powerful in strengthening a love bond. The psychopath creates anxiety, she seeks him for anxiety relief, sex relieves her anxiety and makes her feel 'bonded' again to him, and then he recreates another anxiety event so this sequence continues.

---

[70] Carnes, Patrick J. (1997). *The Betrayal Bond.* HCI.

Figure 9.1
The Anxiety/Sex/Bonding Cycle

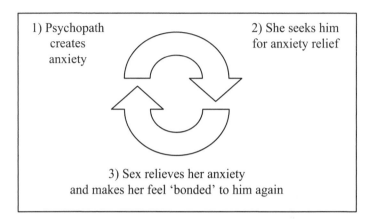

1) Psychopath creates anxiety

2) She seeks him for anxiety relief

3) Sex relieves her anxiety and makes her feel 'bonded' to him again

Each cycle is constantly reinforced and strengthened through anxiety and sex. The pathological bond can actually be a stronger bond than that is formed in normal relationships.

The frequency of sex with the highly sexual psychopath creates bond, after bond, after bond. This is why women describe attachments and bonds with psychopaths as 'the most intense types of attachments' they have ever experienced. Repeatedly, women have stated that this attachment with the psychopath is not like attachments with non-pathological men. Misunderstanding what this intensity is, they say "I thought it meant we were right for each other and just really into each other." Or they ask, "It feels like a drug. Am I addicted to him?"

Intensity of Attachment in Pathological Relationships

Throughout all the phases of attraction, attachment and bonding, the women experience an unprecedented intensity that remains 'undefined' and not understood. Just what causes this unusual level of intensity? Why are these gorilla-glue relationships misunderstood as 'soul-mate' status?

o   **Pathology as Intensity.** The low conscienced disorders are, by their nature, intense to experience by others. These people are often referred to by these phrases:

Positively	Negatively
o edgy	o draining
o something different about them	o exhausting
o interesting	o sucks the life out of you
o exciting	o high maintenance
o always has something going on	
o mysterious	
o unachievable	
o can't quite figure them out which is intriguing...	

Whatever you call it, the disorder is intense to experience to those around them including family, friends and therapists. I don't know anyone who would say narcissism or an antisocial is not intense! What society doesn't realize is that this intensity is often covert pathology.

o **A Quality/Trait within the Disorder.** The intensity within the relationship she is experiencing is *often a quality or trait within the disorder.* She could be reacting to the impulsivity, the emotional roller coaster of non-regulated emotions, or grandiosity that she is experiencing as 'intense.' Any number of the traits in the low conscienced disorders could be a trait of the disorder causing the intensity. Additionally, NPD and APD have qualities that 'draw people in' which feels like an 'emotional vortex' or a 'magnetic pull.' The intensity of the 'draw' can definitely be misunderstood or even increase her sense of his mystique.

o **High-risk Behavior as Intensity.** The disorder itself is drawn to high-risk behaviors which lead to:

   o physical illness (additions)

   o self-destructive and reckless behaviors (arrests, jail, prison)

   o out-of-control sexual behavior (finding out about infidelity, breaking up) o   bucking the laws and society (always fighting or in conflict with someone)

With these types of pathologies that are motivated by risk/reward and not by punishment/guilt, they create drama through flings, affairs, prostitutes, porn addictions, and other behaviors often associated with sexual deviancy. Problems = drama. Drama and deviancy increases intensity.

o   **Mental Illness and Addiction as Intensity.** Related to many personality disorders and pathology in general is the existence of other mental health and addictive disorders. Chronic un-stabilization of the mental disorders (not taking meds, not staying in treatment, not getting help, or treatment truly isn't helping) increases intensity. Relapsing within addictions as well (whether she overtly knows he has relapsed or is just experiencing the unspoken fallout from it) increases intensity.

o   **Confusing Bonding with Intense Attachment.** Women confuse her authentic bonding with his surface attachment. Bonding and attachment are different processes and reflect different depths. Since pathologicals intensely pursue, she is likely to confuse the intensity of the pursuit with true intimacy. Normal people bond, but pathologicals merely attach which is why they can quickly move on to the next person.

o   **Betrayal & Trauma Bonding as Intensity.** Exploitive relationships can create trauma bonds that link a victim to someone who is dangerous to them. These situations of exploitation are incredibly intense and increase the sensation of (pseudo) bonding.

o   **Fear as Intensity.** Fear INCREASES the sense of bonding and vicariously then increases intensity. Fear and intensity are used in coercion, hostage taking, Stockholm syndrome and war. Pathological Love Relationships use varying levels of fear (of violence, of abandoning the relationship, of being unfaithful) for increased fear effect which causes the person to feel it as an intense attachment. Fear is experienced as intensity. The higher and more frequent emotion of fear, the stronger the attachment and intensity will be perceived.

o   **Attraction and Early Erotic Imprinting as Intensity.** She confuses attraction with the emotion of love. Pathologicals are more likely to pursue intensely. Intense pursuit is perceived by her as 'I must be the one because he's working so hard to get me.' The heat of her physical attraction to him is experienced as intensity. Additionally, early erotic imprint that is subconscious and remains largely unnoticed becomes mystique. Mystique is experienced as intensity.

o   **Traumatic Attraction as Intensity.** She engages in trauma-repetition or trauma replay by re-engaging in situations that replicate an authentic wounding that she is trying to heal. Each re-engagement is experienced (subconsciously) as a way to resolve the trauma, relationship, or wounding. The more times this is repeated, the more engrained the pattern is to be drawn to it. The more she is drawn to it, the more it feels as if it has a 'life of its own' and the less control she has over it. Feeling 'out of control' has a level of intensity associated with it.

o   **Sexual Bonding as Intensity.** Hormones increase the sensation of attachment. Hyper-sex creates more hormones which increases the sensation of 'bonding.' Sex is experienced as intense.

o   **Temperament Traits as Intensity.** The women's super-traits that were 80-97% HIGHER than other women's: Relationship Investment, Tolerance, Attachment/Bonding, Loyalty, Trust. With personality traits this high, all of these emotions are intensely experienced by her within the pathological relationship. High levels of relationship investment set up an entrapping cycle which is experienced as intensity.

o   **Trance States as Intensity.** Intensity of attachment can also be increased through casual trance states that are natural body rhythms. The women had higher susceptibility to trance and suggestibility.

With all the multiple levels of woven intensity factors and the 'buzz' of the bonding hormones, this 'mystical union' with her soul-mate is not likely to be seen for the pathology pot it really is. She will continue to ride the high of intensity believing that this really is the stamp of 'love.'

The Psychopath and Bonding

While she has gone through an intense emotional, sexual, and hormonal bonding process with the psychopath, this in no way means he has gone through the same process with her. In fact, he hasn't. Psychopaths don't have the same experience regarding bonding that non-pathologicals do. Almost all the literature discusses the psychopath's inability to attach or bond. I agree with other researchers that the psychopath *does not bond,* however I believe the psychopath *does attach.* True bonding would require the full spectrum of emotions which the psychopath does not have.

However, he does have the ability to 'attach.' That level of attachment only requires desire, such as the desire to possess something or someone. Attachments between things and people are not that different to a psychopath. Psychopaths seek others because it is through human contact that they get to experience dominance. Relationships are the only avenues from which they obtain the control and satisfaction from harming others. Attachments also help the psychopath overcome his boredom, which is why they have many relationships with many women. *If psychopaths didn't attach, they also wouldn't stalk which we know they often do.*

Normal-ites attach too. We might be attached to our comfortable recliner, our well-worn slippers or our plasma TV. For psychopaths, intense attachment to a TV or a person is similar. That's why it's so easy for them to leave relationships as if they are hauling off the recliner to the dump and going to the furniture store to get another. It's a surface attachment capable of being replaced with something or someone else.

None of the attachment has anything to do with emotional intimacy or bonding. Sex is ejaculation and hopefully for the psychopath, dominance of the woman in some manner (whether it is just in his mind or he really does get to control her during sex). Sex is just one more activity (in addition to many others) where he can enjoy his dominance and experience the height of his rewards.

Like many other ways that the woman projects her emotions and experiences on the psychopath, this is another projection. She may confuse emotional intimacy with sex because of the bonding *she* experiences and assumes he is experiencing too. It is the bonding that produces the feeling of emotional intimacy but since the psychopath doesn't have the brain wiring emotional intimacy depends on, he doesn't bond. Her experience of bonding is not shared by him.

Figure 9.2
Imitation of Bonding

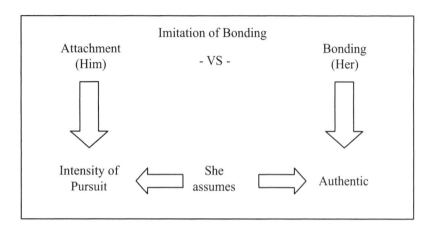

While attachment is clearly not bonding by the time a woman gets an inkling that she is bonded and he is not, her sexual experiences and emotional connections with him have already set the cement of the relationship. She's hooked.

What is Sex with a Psychopath Like?

The experiences of sex with the psychopath varied widely. Consistently though, women alluded to some similarities which included the bonding they thought occurred, the intensity, frequency, deviancy, and either the best or worst sex they had ever had. The sexual aftermath of symptoms contributed to what the women struggled to recover from. Much of what they experienced became recognized as emotional, psychological, physical or sexual abuse or manipulation. Almost none of the women, in retrospect, felt like their relationships were 'normal' or they emerged 'untainted' or 'unharmed.' While they recognized the sex was good, over time things changed in the relationship that affected their overall relationship.

Assumed Bonding

"Sex with him was the best part of my life. I bonded more with him than any other human being on this planet. We fit together so

right. We merged together as one. I have never had this before. I know he felt it too."

"He was so completely captivated by how our sex drives were identical. He said he had never felt that about anybody and how we were completely different from anything he had experienced."

"We had a great sex life. It was much more emotionally intimate than it's been with anyone else. He was always all there—in the moment. His mind didn't seem to wander or his moods ever seem to affect this part of our relationship. He was very focused that way. It was exciting to feel so wanted."

"We were so connected, uninhibited, sensual and completely in tune with one another."

Intensity

"He was always very demanding, intense, and sexually voracious which I found wonderful in the beginning. But it quickly became the most disturbing thing I'd ever experienced."

"We both have had orgasms just thinking about each other from afar. And sometimes it happened when we looked into each others' eyes before any foreplay had begun. I could feel his body jerk, and mine too, and we would both feel the energy come up our spines and be like two spastic people."

"Sex was amazing and intense from the beginning. He acted as though he was quite shy and how sex was sacred to him. I don't believe that—it was at odds with his gangsta behavior!"

Hyper-Sexuality/Good Sex

"We have a great sex life. After we have sex, he asks when we can have it again. Sometimes he says we've never had it—I'm not sure if he's trying to play with my head, or what."

"I couldn't get enough of him and the passion was electrifying. He was a very giving lover. He was a favorite lover of mine and only comparable to the other (psychopath) I was with!"

"The sex was very good and we both wanted it even if we were in an argument—we'd just have sex. It makes no sense unless it was a mutual addiction."

"He was the best lover I ever had. It was if he knew my body better than I did, and was very intent on pleasing me but would never let me please him."

No Emotional Connection

"It was great animal sex. Just sex. No feelings."

"He was considerate sexually, in some ways he was always concerned about me having an orgasm... and one thing and probably the only thing he didn't criticize me about was my body... I felt that he desired me that he liked my body. I never felt that we made love as there was no feeling or emotion. It was just sex. There was no emotional connection or intimacy, no sharing of feelings, just the physical act."

"The last time we had sex I burst into hysterical tears because he was just so detached without feelings at all. He carried on and then rolled off of me after he had orgasmed. I couldn't let him near me after that."

Demeaning/Traumatic Sex

"He would speak to me disgustingly like, "Come here and suck my dick." He would put me down sexually. He couldn't see how his treatment of me led to my lack of desire for him. He told me he didn't have to put up with me—that other women wanted him."

"He made me feel like a piece of meat and sometimes treated me like a whore. He could be totally disrespectful and hostile. He used locker-room language about sex around me and make juvenile references to body parts and sexual acts."

"He held my head there and forced me to swallow his ejaculate. I almost threw up. I was a virgin...to this day I've never had sex with anyone else."

Narcissistic Sexual Demands

The psychopaths often demanded their women express admiration for their special sexual abilities.

"He would force me to talk about how good he was."

"I would have to measure his penis regularly with a tape measure and tell him how nice it was to know I was sleeping with a man so well equipped and that his penis was attractive."

"But it was still always his call, anytime, anywhere, and I had better comply with gratifying his needs or expect to be punished."

Power and Control

Although psychopaths want adoration for their sexual abilities, they do not necessarily like it when women 'come on' to them sexually. A woman who initiates sex may detract from his experience of power.

"I found that if I wore nice lingerie or tried to seduce him, he would ignore my attempts and turn me down no matter what. I realized that it was a control issue for him. If I could turn him on and seduce him then that gave me some sort of power. He did not want that, so we only had sex when he instigated it and I didn't dare turn him down."

Sadistic/Deviant/Dark

"He enjoyed spanking, giving and receiving pain, and anal sex which I couldn't participate in. He wanted sex 2-3 times a day and had an erection all the time."

"It was quite energetic. I'd have to say that the sex was probably the best I'd had in any relationship—although there was a twisted, dark aspect to it. "

"I never felt totally comfortable with him sexually. I always felt like he was a pedophile."

"It was dark...something wasn't right with it—him, or me. I'm not sure who or what was right...but it wasn't."

Other sadistic behaviors reported:

1. Was forced into anal sex against her will.
2. Forced anal sex at 39 weeks pregnant.
3. He refused to use a condom when he had Hepatitis C.
4. Forced her into sex during an argument.
5. Made her perform oral sex on him when he came home drunk.
6. Tore her vagina with his fist.
7. Because he had prematurely ejaculated he turned around and defecated on her.
8. Spit on her as he was having sex with her.
9. Threw a bucket of cold water on her during sex.
10. Smeared ejaculate in her hair.

11. Gave her STDs.
12. Drugged her to have sex with her.
13. Coerced her into making porn and then he reproduced the tapes and gave them out without her permission.
14. Criticized her sexual performance.
15. Called her frigid or prudish if she didn't want to do an act.
16. Talked about his sex lives with other women to increase insecurity, low self esteem, and fear of leaving the relationship.

Conclusion

By far, the female victims are the best people to listen to about the intensity of attraction, attachment and bonding with psychopaths. They were in fact, correct that many factors contributed to the red hot attraction, the magnet of attachment and the super-glue of bonding. They were also correct that these relationships were in fact, different than other relationships and the intensity was fueled by many pathological influences.

Unfortunately, by the time she may have realized her out-of-control feelings were a premonition of his pathology, she was harmed. Let's take a look at some of the stages of the relationship dynamics.

10 The Use of Trance, Hypnosis, and Suggestibility

"An illusion is responsible for the voluntary selection of a path that leads to sorrow." — The Soul Illusion

Luring Through Trance and Hypnosis

Attraction, attachment and bonding were definite hook-up and intensity factors in the pathological love relationship. Also increasing the intensity sensation and affecting the relationship dynamics were the hypno-powers of the psychopath. In fact, the hypnotic qualities are likely to be one of the strongest factors of intensity within her entire relationship dynamic. It may have been the attraction heat, the attachment magnet and the bonding glue. Given how quickly people can be induced into hypnosis, the luring that happens may be highly hypnotic. The way that she comes into the relationship with a psychopath, given her super trait proclivity, may be primarily through the vortex of hypnosis.

Women question whether the psychopath was in fact inducing trance, hypnosis, mind control, or used other forms of subconscious coercion. Women ask because they acted contrary to their own relational histories with other men. Some say they felt heavily emotionally overpowered, trance-like, or spaced out through much of the relationship. Does the psychopath have the ability to induce trance? The answer is yes.

We should not be surprised that the skillful psychopath finds many methods for luring women and keeping emotional control over them including using hypnosis, trance, and capitalizing on her suggestibility. Although he likely introduced these methods in the early stages of luring and attraction, they are also likely to remain or reappear throughout the relationship. Once hypnosis is in play, it is likely to stay in play through the relationship and even beyond. After all, if it works, why would the psychopath stop using it?

The psychopath, like anyone else, can induce trance in others. Just surf the net under 'seduction techniques' and you will see a hundred websites teaching men how to use covert hypnotic and Neuro-linguistic Programming techniques to bypass a woman's cognitive resistance to being 'picked up' or 'seduced.' If these techniques didn't work, there wouldn't be so many men using these techniques and it wouldn't be a million-dollar-a-year industry.

However, psychopaths are different from these mere 'seduction students' because most psychopaths don't have to be taught to use trance states, hypnosis, and suggestion. They are naturals at using these techniques.

What Are Trance and Hypnotic States?

Why does trance or hypnosis work? It works because it is how the mind works. Trance is a natural mind state involving the way the mind tunes in and tunes out. It is also related to what happens with, and to, information while in these states of 'tuning.' There's no hocus pocus to it—it is simply a psychological mechanism used by the mind.

Tuning Out & Hyper-Focusing

'Highway hypnosis' is one form of tuning out. You experience it while getting sleepy watching the double-yellow lines on the highway. Before long, you have arrived at your exit and you don't remember the last few miles of driving. During the driving, your mind was tuning out. By the time you tuned back in, things had happened—time had lapsed, you were back into awareness, and at your destination. For a few minutes, though, you were in a trance.

Trance may be another reason why women who love psychopaths have such a high tolerance for emotional pain. This may be due to their pain threshold being tuned out, squelched, or numbed by trance states. Their ability to eliminate perceptions of emotional or physical pain or even bodily exhaustion may allow them to stay in unbelievable circumstances.

Another form of tuning out is connected to our natural bodily biorhythms, like metabolism, blood sugar and sleep. Check in with most people around 2:00 p.m. after lunch and you'll see sleepy and trance induced people at their desks fighting to stay 'focused.'

Although trance is sometimes associated with the tuning out process, it is most associated with hyper-focused attention which is how hypnotists use it in formal hypnosis (and how the psychopath uses it). The only difference between trance and formal hypnosis is that formal hypnosis is a *focused and controlled trance.* That's why the hypnotist says, "Stare into my eyes"—because staring forces attentional focus.

Hypnosis and trance both involve the ability to heavily-focus on one thing while blocking out others. If you're staring at the highway or listening intently to a lecture, you are entering a trance state. While in this state, you don't notice other things happening around you. If you're listening to a lecture, you might not notice if someone leaves the room and closes the door. In highway hypnosis, you might drive right past your exit. This extremely focused attention on a single thing is essentially a trance state. Trance states of hyper-focus produce a loss of awareness of time. Many women allude to how much time was spent with the psychopath and how 'time flew by,' or months peeled off the calendar before they realized how much of their life was being spent moment-by-moment with only him. When people are 'rapt' in focusing on each other, they lose track of time. Repeated time loss is indicative of trance states.

The women are likely candidates for trance because those with the ability to give something their 'total attention' are more likely candidates to be easily induced in hypnosis. It is likely that when they are really concentrating on that project or person, they are already in some level of a trance or flow state. Given that the women are successful, they have learned how to concentrate well and 'focus.'

Let's not overlook that psychopaths can be initially entertaining and electrifying, giving women a lot to focus on. The more motivating, arousing, and rewarding a situation is, the more highly absorbed a person can become in it, especially if she is highly hypnotizable.

How He Does It

There are many 'ways' to go into a trance, such as tuning in or hyper-focusing, so inducing trance in someone else is not that difficult since it is just helping someone get focused.

How could a psychopath put a woman in a trance state without her realizing it? The psychopath, who has abundant intensity, can easily use that intensity to encourage hyper-focus. The enormous amount of time he is spending with her allows him to get her to hyper-focus on 'them.' All the eye-gazing so known for early romantic stages of relationships is fertile ground for the 'look into my eyes' trance induction technique.

A psychopath does not have to necessarily formally understand the mechanics of trance in order to use it. He is a master of watching what works and doesn't work in controlling others, and has been so since childhood, when he began watching. Stumbling across 'intensity' or any other technique that works in a relationship is all he needs to get to work using it to his advantage.

There are hypnotic techniques that trained hypnotherapists regularly use. The psychopath no doubt uses these as well in the relationship dynamics—glazing their entire relationship during attraction/luring, attachment/honeymoon and deepening/bonding with the power of the subconscious mind. Here are more techniques used mutually by hypnotherapists and psychopaths:

Acknowledging Resistance

The women's initial resistance to him is easily overcome as attested to by the women. With women wanting to trust and be trusted, the psychopath simply remarks on her resistance which is often enough to move through it.

> *"To defuse resistance…remark that resistance is normal and even to be desired."*[71]

Uses Imagery

The subconscious mind thinks and relates through imagery. It is why most religious texts are written with imagery, metaphors or parables. (Think how often Jesus talked in mostly parables). Women noted how often the psychopath used imagery. (Remember, he isn't good with abstract language, but imagery can be used concretely).

> *"Find out about the persons preferred imagery."*[72]

---

[71] Hunter, Marlene E. M.D. *Creative Scripts for Hypnotherapy.* New York: Brunner/Mazel, 1994.
[72] Hunter, Marlene E. M.D. *Creative Scripts for Hypnotherapy.* New York: Brunner/Mazel, 1994.

This is much like 'talking her language'—a form of mirroring and parroting by finding out what images she prefers and using those to sculpt her reality.

Invites

Even the snake in the Garden of Eden invited Eve to partake of the Tree of Good and Evil. The psychopath invites the woman to:

o   emotionally share with him
o   remember her past
o   talk about her pain
o   plan for their relationship together,
o   contemplate the future (although he might actually not contemplate it much).

> *"Use a soft inviting voice even if the direction is a command disguised as an invitation."*[73]

Encourages Remembering Which Produces Hypnotic Deepening

Having women talk about their pasts is helpful to the psychopath in various ways. He is able to find out her history to morph into, gives him the opportunity to mimic and parrot, and to increase her sense of attachment. Also, talking about her past is a natural hypnotic induction. It does so not only through the feelings it brings up (covered below), but through the process of remembering, which is an invitation to hypnotic regression.

> *"Remembering the past experience is an altered state through regression."*[74]
>
> *"Exploring, searching the past and into the present (sometimes into the future) crosses time spans and is a confusion technique that increases hypnotizability."*[75]

---

[73] Hunter, Marlene E. M.D. *Creative Scripts for Hypnotherapy.* New York: Brunner/Mazel, 1994.
[74] Hunter, Marlene E. M.D. *Creative Scripts for Hypnotherapy.* New York: Brunner/Mazel, 1994.

(The women have attested to how often they felt 'confused' during conversation with him. The psychopath may have not only been trying to con them, but she might have also been slipping in and out of trance, tripping up between the conversations and feelings of the past, present, and future.)

> *"Regression to childhood is a deepening technique."* [76]

The psychopath uses a deepening technique which has her both remember *and* feel at the same time. Each of these reconnect her to a time she may have been in trance (and oxytocin!) and enhance or deepen the hypnotic experience.

> *"Reorienting back to a previous hypnotic experience is a deepening technique—remember when we _____ or felt _____ or how wonderful it was when _____"* [77]
>
> *"For deepening: go in and out of hypnosis by talking about and using imagination or thinking about when...(past or future)."* [78]

Feeling and Emotional States

Feeling states are prime ground for induction into, and deepening of trance and are associated with certain emotional states. Words can be used to describe emotional conditions related to actual trance states such as 'enamored,' 'raptured,' 'ecstasy,' and 'absorbed in rapt attention.'

> *"To deepen hypnosis, inwardly focus which is attributed to altered states."* [79]
>
> *"Create an emotional bridge—be aware of the feelings that come with that experience and the feelings that may almost overwhelm at times."* [80]

---

[75] Hunter, Marlene E. M.D. *Creative Scripts for Hypnotherapy.* New York: Brunner/Mazel, 1994.

[76] Hunter, Marlene E. M.D. *Creative Scripts for Hypnotherapy.* New York: Brunner/Mazel, 1994.

[77] CSH

[78] CSH

[79] CSH

[80] CSH

Reframing

The psychopath is a natural at reframing. He takes his bad behavior and reframes his motives, often gaslighting entirely by reframing what he just did. When people are in trance or under hypnosis, it is very easy to reframe what they have, or are, experiencing. Is it any wonder she can't hold on to the concepts of his bad behavior when they have been reframed under trance?

Reframing is reorganizing a new context for the situation. The psychopath didn't change—we know that. But he or his behavior can look differently when reframed. His behavior can be more tolerated and less offensive when reframed under trance.

> *"The picture did not change it just looks entirely different in its new frame."*[81]

He is also talented at what is called 'spontaneously reframing' his behavior. This occurs when something she has thought negatively about previously is being considered differently after talking to him. He is likely to tell her that it is more helpful to think about it like *'this.'* Quickly, the emotions attached to his bad behavior are shifted when he reframed it spontaneously for her. If he does this often enough, it will soon become automatic and she will spontaneously reframe his behavior as well. Suggestive reframing allows her subconscious to reevaluate old things from the past that are interfering with the present. Since she has invested so much in the relationship, she looks for reasons to reframe and excuse his old behavior so it doesn't interfere with her present desire for the relationship.

Neuro-linguistic Programming (NLP)

Neuro-linguistic Programming (NLP) which is a 'cousin' to formal hypnosis, induces trance by preoccupying the mind with statements like, "You're so wonderful and beautiful," then targeting other messages straight to the subconscious mind through short story telling. Psychopaths are master storytellers—inducing her belief system in his virtues while she is in a trance state. One of the main techniques in NLP is story telling—creating belief through building a storyline. NLP is now taught to sales

---

[81] CSH

and marketing people so they learn the most effective way to penetrate into someone's subconscious to close the 'deal.' Who is a better salesman or storyteller than a psychopath?

With storytelling, is it any wonder fairytales worked the same way on us as children?

Absorption into Trance and Fascination

Psychopaths also use fascination. Her ability to be 'absorbed' into the experience with him is related to the level of fascination she experiences. The luring/attraction and honeymoon/attachment phase is all about fascination. She experiences absorption into the trance state as 'effortless' while the loss of control into the hypnotic experience happens outside of her awareness. This is the power of the gentle hypnotic experience….a gentle lulling into a state of fascination where reality begins to fade out.

Women described the general reality of their lives as fading into the background, while they remained in the foreground, experiencing only him. When women ask, "What happened to my life? Where is all the stuff I use to be involved with?" the answer is 'life fading.' As they become less focused on their previous lives, the memory of everything else fades while she is highly fascinated with him. Since intense focus can be fixed on only one thing at a time, the fascinating relationship preoccupies attention, and previous experiences are relegated to the background.

Trance and State-Dependent Learning

State-dependent learning is how what is learned previously influences how someone behaves in the present, including what is learned 'in' trance. Symbolic language and meaning are perceived differently and yet strongly under hypnosis and in trance. When the psychopath talks about symbols ("I have you locked in my heart") the symbols are stored as strong messages. An internal image of being 'locked' and unable to escape can be created in the subconscious mind all under the guise of love and being 'in his heart.' That's why the psychopath's messages have such staying power and emotional strength long after women discover his true nature. Therapists that try to 'rationally' discuss the women's perceptions of him quickly come across these strongholds in their emotional memories that are related to symbols.

Trance produces perceptual biases. That means if the psychopath is telling her wonderful things and she is euphoric with him, she tends to associate wonderful and euphoric things with the memory of him...even after he's turned into a monster. While in trance, a woman tends to 'cement' what she felt or learned in that state. That's why it's so difficult for women to believe he's a liar, swindler, or cheater because she learned all the wonderful things about him in trance states that have been 'cemented' in her memory. If you ask her which sense of him feels 'stronger' inside:

the memory of herself intensely bonded to him

or

his cheating

she will say, 'the memory of the bonding.' State-dependent learning has caused learned conditioning in her, in which euphoria as a reward is connected to him and not his pre-existing negative behavior.

What is learned in one state (euphoria, happiness, intense sexuality and bonding) may have little influence on the behavior exhibited in a different state. When the woman catches him stealing her life's savings, the fact of his stealing has little influence on the state-dependent learning of him as her lover, the one she bonded with, the one who brings her to euphoria—the feelings she still has about him.

State-dependent learning influences motivation and performance. When we wonder why it is difficult for women to leave psychopaths, the difficulty is connected, at least in part, to how trance has affected her state-dependent learning of motivation to leave and her actual performance *of* leaving. This isn't what she chooses to feel, this is the nature of state-dependent learning that often happens in trance states.

A recurring theme in the women's recovery is related to state-dependent learning. Women get stuck because it is easier to remember the good memories than the bad. The bad memories become distant or murky when she thinks about him, and the good stuff pops up, which makes it hard to remember why she's disbelieving him or wants to leave him.

Layers of Trance

Trance can also be induced in other ways, which helps us see how many layers of trance could be occurring in any given pathological relationship such as:

1. Sexual intensity
2. Breathing and heart rate becoming in sync through sex
3. Music
4. Dancing
5. Fasting
6. Sleep deprivation
7. Euphoria—feelings of bondedness and the effects of sex hormones
8. Flickering lights—like candlelight
9. Kinesthetic—through the sense of touch, feeling, or emotions
10. Intense playing or enjoyment
11. Prayer and meditation—which is why cults use it
12. Neuro-feedback—also referred to as Biofeedback—which changes brain waves and alters your state of consciousness
13. Peak experiences or flow states—where heavy concentration produces a sense of harmonization and interconnectedness

These examples are found in literature and scientific studies as ways that trance can be induced. Most of these are normal parts of any early relationship—but added to the issue that it is occurring within a relationship with a pathologically disordered person adds to the inevitable harm as an outcome.

Her Suggestibility & Hypnotizability

Conditions Which Increase Hypnotizability

Personality traits and conditions can cause some women to be more highly hypnotizable than others. Women who dissociate because of a dissociative disorder, experiences of previous emotional trauma, and those who have Post Traumatic Stress Disorder are more hypnotizable. In part, some of the symptoms of trauma and these disorders are trance states. Other conditions that cause women to be easily hypnotized include:

o   histories of abuse or neglect

o   extensive dependency, vulnerability or incompetency issues

o   excessive self-sacrificing, perfectionistic attitudes, or high levels of self-expectations

o   high persistence

The women who love psychopaths are very resourceful and goal-directed, which means they are persistent and probably easier to hypnotize than other women.

Do Psychopaths Capitalize on Suggestibility?

Suggestibility is how easily someone will accept, or act on a suggestion by another person. Suggestibility is also related to hypnotizability. In order to be hypnotized you have to accept the suggestion that is given you.

The women in this survey would be considered to be highly suggestible because they rated extremely high in cooperation on the TCI. Cooperation skills assist them in easily accepting suggestions while her helpfulness and acceptance of others also create suggestibility. Let's not overlook the salesmanship of a psychopath and his ability to 'sell' her the suggestions he wants her to accept.

Suggestibility is also associated with social desirability, another trait the TCI measures as part of relationship investment and positive sociability. These women do care about how others perceive them— even the psychopath. Their social (and relational) desirability is likely to be important enough to them to take suggestions about it, even from him. The psychopath can play this up or down, telling her how desirable she is, increasing her relationship investment, or how others don't like her or don't find her appealing, decreasing herself worth and raising her concerns about relationship failure.

Suggestibility is related to poor memory recall, which in the women is likely to begin happening in the relationship due to stress, fatigue, and trance. Almost all the women who come into treatment say their memory has become seriously affected. The higher her level of sleep deprivation, the higher will be her level of suggestibility. This is why sleep deprivation is also used by cults and in psychological warfare.

Most of the women reported sleep deprivation from marathon sex, fighting, or worry. The women are likely to become more suggestible as the relationship continues because of the confusion created by the psychopath's lying, cheating, gaslighting, and the dichotomous behavior. The more she thinks her mind is beginning to play tricks on her (as the psychopath encourages her to believe), the more suggestible she will become. When he gaslights her by saying she didn't see, hear, or experience something, she will likely believe it.

People who have high levels of suggestibility also have less accurate event recall. Women who have state-dependent learning are prone to remembering the good things in the relationship rather than the bad. They may actually have less accurate recall of the bad memories due to suggestibility. State-dependent learning and suggestibility, then, may serve as a double whammy against her ability to hold tight to the true abusive memories of the psychopath's behavior. Holding on to memories of betrayal and abuse is important, because these enable leaving and later recovery. As part of treatment for this, we weave in journaling exercises that help move the traumatic memories 'up front' so they are more easily retained and used in emotionally distancing from the relationship.

Do Psychopaths Really Do This on Purpose?

Come on now…you probably already know the answer to that one. It is hard to imagine that psychopaths actually 'try' to use trance and suggestibility to get what they want—but these are the same guys whose motivation for communication is to deceive!

Psychopaths are natural human behaviorists from childhood—studying what works in motivating, conning, or hoodwinking others. It would be natural for them to gather a knowledge base of effective techniques. Therefore, it is not a far-fetched idea that psychopaths would induce trance if it worked. However, what about 'other less pathological people'—do they try to mind-control others?

Pathologicals Who Teach NLP, Trance and Hypnosis to Others

This book has been about the entire spectrum of psychopathy, from mere traits all the way up to the extreme psychopaths. Psychopathic traits are found in many people not just diagnosed psychopaths. The web sites devoted to 'seduction techniques' are an example of varying levels of psychopathy and are now being taught online to others. Anyone wanting to do this to another person, by definition is high in psychopathic traits. Here is a list of examples of what is taught on just one website I pulled information from:

1. Pacing for profound rapport
2. Mirroring her
3. Maximum-speed seduction
4. Personality trait exploitation
5. Covert hypnotic commands
6. Sleight-of-Mouth expressions
7. Subliminal arousal techniques
8. Sensual domination
9. Allure

The difference between students of seduction and the professional psychopath is that most psychopaths know these techniques instinctively. In fact, the worst psychopaths are probably the ones teaching others and making a fortune from the new hot seduction online communities.

The Psychopath's Hypnotic Stare

The psychopath's stare has its own allure and may be effective in inducing hypnosis. Many women, before they knew he was a psychopath, thought it was sexy or intense. There really is something extra powerful to the psychopath's stare. Dr. Reid Melloy, in his book, *Violent Attachments* says that women and men have noted the psychopath's unusual and unnerving stare. He referred to the stare as a "relentless gaze that seems to preclude the psychopath's destruction of his victim or target." It is also often referred to as 'The Reptilian Gaze' because of its primitive predatory look.

Robert Hare referred to the psychopath's gaze as 'intense eye contact and piercing eyes' and even suggested that people avoid having consistent eye contact with them—which of course the women did the opposite getting lost in lovers eye gazing. Other writers refer to it as a 'laser-beam stare' or an 'empty hypnotic look.' Our women labeled the gaze:

o intense
o sensual

o   disturbing

o   intrusive

They said,

"He stared me down in the bar until I couldn't stand it anymore."

"He looked at me like I was the most delicious thing!"

"He looked right through me like he could see everything in me. I didn't know what that was...I never had that experience before and I'll never forget it."

"I thought he could have eaten me alive."

Women have described his look as invasive, intimidating... looking them up and down like an animal. Women mistook it for a sexual once-over when in all likelihood it was more predatory than that.

Eye-gazing as trance induction means that the words that follow the induction are seared into her mind with much more meaning and lasting power. Eye-to-eye locks, in which the psychopath strokes her face and leads her into a slight trance state saying, "You are the most giving woman...you have given me what no one else has given. I know that you will always give to me this way and that we will be together forever. I know you would never hurt me, or leave me, or lie to me, or cheat..." are the hypnotic handcuffs that keep her locked to him.

Women reported that certain phrases play repetitiously in their minds long after he is gone. This is probably due to trance states and state-dependent learning building off of each other and increasing the strength of the induction.

Conclusion

The more we study his use of language, trance, and state-dependent learning, the more we will be able to help women break the spell binding dialogue in their heads. One thing is for sure, the issue of the use of hypnosis, trance, and state-dependent learning by psychopaths needs to be further studied.

11 Deceive and Believe: the Luring and Honeymoon Stage

"Deceiving others. This is what the world calls a romance."

—Oscar Wilde

The entire book so far has laid the ground work for understanding how the early phases of the relationship began and why. We have looked extensively at the psychopath—his brain, his motivations, his behaviors and communication, why he flies under her radar, and the hypnotic lure. We have looked at her super-traits, what makes her a target and so appealing to a psychopath, and how she is likely to respond to the charming psychopath during luring. She has no idea what is about to be unleashed into her life through this shark-like predator. The 'dun-na dun-na dun-na' of the Jaws theme song is playing in the background....

Question: Where do you encounter a psychopath?

Answer: Everywhere.

The majority of the women in our survey met their psychopathic man at:

o   work
o   through a work colleague
o   at a bar or other public location
o   online
o   through friends

Those who met him at work, through a work colleague or through friends never suspected that someone they know would be hooking them up with a dangerous pathological. Most felt it was a safer way to actually meet someone—by having someone they already knew introduce them. This helps to illuminate that not only does she not recognize him as a pathologically disordered, but neither did the people who fixed her up.

The beginning of the pathological love relationship is such a crucial time in the dynamics. He needs to set the 'tone' for the luring of her into the relationship. Psychopaths don't show up announcing their covert disorder to women—"Hi, I'm Ed, I'm a psychopath." Encounters with psychopaths don't begin like the opening statements in a 12 Step meeting. They begin with the only thing he knows how to do—deceive and make her believe.

Through inquisitive questioning by him, she reveals what she is *seeking* in a relationship. **Almost all the women indicated they told the psychopath upfront who and what they were looking for in a person.** This happens frequently in online relationships since so much of that information is already shared through the profiles people give of their 'dream' person. Yet these women were just as likely to tell the psychopath in person all of their hopes and dreams, not realizing these disclosures would eventually be used against them, either as information for him to morph into, or later in the relationship when he uses her true confessions as emotional weapons against her.

Since psychopaths rarely behave in the beginning how they are going to behave later on, psychopaths use the charm they've learned 'works' up front when luring women into a new relationship. Some psychopaths say they have learned how to lure by watching romantic movies or eavesdropping on other relationships so they understand the linguistics (what to say to her), behaviors (how to act), and romantic gestures (what women like). Then he adds his own irresistibility and a frenetic pursuit to draw her in.

Of course psychopaths also learn by trial and error, tweaking their relationship skills in each relationship. It is how many psychopaths become such a 'pro' at dating—no blunders, just smooth.

Methods He Used

His Personality

The early days of being wooed and lured by a psychopath are the most exciting times that women remember. The psychopath uses his personality as a drawing card and has been consistently described as:

o   charming and engaging conversationalist

o   agreeable

o   seemingly insightful

o   sweet

o   twinkling eyes

o   a compelling talker

o   funny

o   a great storyteller

o   fun to be with

o   delightful

o   exciting

o   companionable

o   loyal and protective

o   enthusiastic and upbeat

o   sensitive

From this list of traits, it's easy to see why women are enamored with his personality. From this list of A+ qualities what's not to like?

Complimentary, Flattery & Attention

During this stage, he is highly complimentary, effusive with flattery, and almost suffocating attention. While she might be inclined to feel uneasy about his demands of seeing her 24/7 she is bowled over by his generosity of attention or romancing with gifts.

> *"He drew me pictures, gave me flowers, took me to dinner, complimented me, and attended to my every need. He made me feel wanted and told me how special I was. He was accepting, helpful, kind and complimentary, gentle and understanding of me. He romanced me like no one ever had."*

Appeal to Family Desires

Women who want children or a blended family often find themselves lured by the implication that he too wants a family—hers, theirs or her as a mother to his children. He's in a hurry to 'start their family' in whatever format he can sell. Some actually never do have the children she wanted, while other psychopaths don't mind cranking out kids they will never care for. Especially if that means he gets to move in with her, tap into her financial resources, or otherwise benefit from having children/family ties with her.

"He praised me, flattered me, adored me, and practically worshipped me. He thanked me for doing work on myself to make myself available for a long term commitment. He said I would make an excellent mother."

Supporting Her Dreams and Desires

The psychopath feigns seeming support. He hones in on her desires for her career or wanting to expand herself in the arts or education. He encourages her to 'find herself,' 'take risks,' and 'get that graduate degree.' This is all the more reason she is shocked when he later turns the support into deliberate sabotage. He makes her drop out of school, gets her fired, or guilts her into giving up hobbies and dreams.

So Into You, I Can't Wait

To keep women from being able to think things through or to respond to red flags, the psychopath induces fast-paced relationships, whirlwinds of dating intensity, and uses emotional suffocation techniques often referred to as love bombing. The psychopath was so persistent (if not forceful) in his pursuit of her that women found themselves unable to slow down the race to the altar, to their beds, or into their homes.

A hallmark sign of the fast paced relationship is to sweep her off her feet and overwhelm her emotionally so that she moves quickly into a permanent or committed relationship all under the guise of "I'm so into you, I've never felt this way before." Psychopaths imply immediate emotional intimacy of 'knowing' her even though they just met, wanting 24/7 within the first few days and breathing her exhaled air. It's the oldest line in book for a psychopath with an agenda. Claiming to be 'addicted to her laughter' and 'melted by the sound of her voice,' he also finds her to be 'witty, funny, brilliant, or irresistible' and 'his soul-mate.' The psychopath quickly wants to move in or marry usually within weeks or months.

Her temperament trait of relationship investment means she values behaviors that indicate he is equally invested and committed. This is a red flag—I don't know many normal men that *want* to get married within days, weeks or even just a few months!

"He told me he loved me within two dates, asked me to marry him within two weeks of meeting him and we moved in together within two months of meeting."

"He really pursued me and spent heaps of time with me—every night of the week and all weekends. The courtship was very short. Whirlwind trips, gifts and early on started calling me pet names as if we had been together forever. He picked me up from work every day, called me constantly, texted me, had almost every meal with me, sent flowers to home and work, constant emails."

While this may seem just 'dream-like' to her, it's pure manipulation and planning on his part.

"He stuck to me like glue. He came over and just kept coming over. It was smothering at times and good at times as well. He would swarm me with emails, music CD's, gifts, cards, singing phone grams."

"He rushed the romance and within five months we were married. He used gifts, attention, threats of removing his attention, and said "I need you sooooo much."

Many women realized in retrospect that there was a 'reason' the relationship was on the fast-track. The psychopath had a 'need' to be filled whether that was a place to live, a business partner, or a sex partner— **there was an agenda as to why the pacing of the relationship was so fast.**

"He pursued me relentlessly, always showing up where I was. The relationship escalated rapidly and before I knew it he was basically living with me."

"He sent me flowers, cards, wooed me with wine, dinner and trips. He was aggressive yet gentle in his pursuit of me. He promised me the world and told me he was dying so I succumbed to his request to marry him—I knew it was too soon but he was dying..."

Some psychopaths hid the motivation behind their fast paced relationship for other reasons:

"He was my boss and I worked with him but when it finally started, he kissed me on Thursday and took me to a motel on Friday. The following week we went to the motel twice and he told me he loved me."

"What I thought was a coincidental dating was really him having stalked me for years so he could meet me."

Even her red flags often were not enough to put the brakes on the forceful momentum the psychopath had going:

"He wanted to spend a lot of time with me from the start. He constantly called me. I felt very much pursued without being able to take a breath inbetween to think. I really enjoyed all the attention but there was a red flag that I ignored that said, 'Doesn't this guy have a life outside of me?'"

The 'so-into-you-line' was delivered by the ultimate actor with an academy award performance.

"He looked at me like I was the most delicious thing! He seemed obsessed with me...he called it 'enthralled' and said he had never felt this way for anyone before. He couldn't keep his hands off of me and seemed so innocently emotionally attached—like I was all he could see. He told me how wonderful, sexy, attractive, and desirable I was."

"He stared me down in the bar like he was so intrigued with me and wanted so badly to get to know me. He said we were soulmates. He would look into my eyes and make me feel I was the one and only woman in the world. He poured on so much attention that I was breathless."

Helpful

Many women found the psychopath to be initially helpful—whether it was around the house, in her business, helping with the kids, or just listening to her problems. He was interested in portraying himself as caring and helpful—that combination between her resident therapist, pastor or handyman.

"He would do anything to help me out—run errands, buy me things, take care of my kids. He made himself indispensable to me."

She also has very high helpfulness traits. His acts of helpfulness resonated with her helpful personality which gave her a sense he had 'good values' and wanted to be a helpmate to her.

Tapping into Her Empathy and Compassion

Psychopaths expose their wounded side to engage her empathy and get her invested in healing him. It taps into the high compassion/empathy trait of the women. Psychopaths tell sad stories (true or untrue) about their lives, prior relationships, and 'little boy' stories of their bumps and bruises in life. Since women don't normally fear what they feel sorry for, fear and compassion aren't normally associated in their minds.

"He said he was dying and of course, he never died!"

"I was the one that could keep him from doing crack and booze he said."

Some used stories about their children:

"He aroused my sympathy early on with stories about how he had a son he wanted to see but could not get access to and how heartbroken he was."

"He was homeless and missing his daughter."

Others told stories about their own childhoods or their abusive parents:

"He told me about being abandoned by his mother, the death of his dad, childhood abuse and being sexually abused. I actually cried for the little boy he had been that wanted love and care but didn't get it and I held him. He was very sensitive, childlike—a quiet woundedness to him."

"He told me his father was distant, how he hated men who cheated because it had happened to his mother."

Still others used the girlfriend or wife storylines:

"He told me his girlfriend had died suddenly and he was obviously grieving. I listened to his story and he told me he never knew anyone as understanding as I was."

"He told me how mentally ill his wife was, how she took all the money, cheated, and abused his children."

"He was a poor divorced dad."

Whatever story 'hook' was used, it capitalized on the women's empathy, compassion and supportive nature. And with that much empathy, she needed something to empathize with.

Chemistry

The women were most likely referencing both the intensity of the relationship and the different 'feel' that pathologicals have to them when they were referring to their "chemistry." The psychopath in all his hyper sexuality and 'mystique' sends off the most sensual vibe. However, what women think is chemistry is really the intensity of the pathological attachment. It piques women's curiosity to understand how and why this guy is different from the rest. If they only knew! Almost all of the women described the unusual bond they felt that they didn't really understand. Some felt it instantly:

"We seemed to have this incredible immediate chemistry."

"He had me at hello..."

"It was instant chemistry. It was the way he looked at me. He had such an energy. "

"We had an instant bond. He was just like me."

Others felt the chemistry was trance-inducing or magical:

"I thought he was odd but unique. It felt different."

"He would tell me that I worked magic over him as if he was acting against his own will."

"He told me I had him under my spell, which the truth is it felt like I was the one under some kind of spell."

Still others used eye gazing:

"He had the most intense eye contact and bonding."

Some used the general public to validate their strong connection:

"He told me that when he walked into a room with me, everyone was jealous of our connection."

While some used sexual seduction techniques:

"He teased me sexually at first and withheld so I would feel amorous towards him. He was quite charming and his seduction was a very strong drug that got me hooked instantly."

A portion of women noticed the intensity of the attraction or chemistry:

"We had this incredible attraction to each other. It was horrible and wonderful all at the same time."

"We just seemed to connect."

"I found him so attractive in many ways. He knew that and exploited it."

"I tried to stay away from him but…"

"I thought he was the man of my dreams—we had so much in common, hit it off right away and just felt really connected to him."

Communication

To seal the deal in the luring stage, the psychopath uses his best listening and whatever communication skills he can muster. He's respectful, encourages her independence and strengths, and seems to be invested in problem solving together.

"Quite easy from the start—it felt like he was my twin. We could talk for hours. We would finish each other's sentences."

"In the beginning of the relationship communication was exceptionally wonderful. He was so in tune to my morals and beliefs. There wasn't anything that we couldn't discuss. Once he had me where he wanted me, the information he was gathering was turned against me."

"In the beginning he was charming, engaging and funny. Seemed very invested in communicating. He loved to talk so there was lots of conversation. "

"It was completely different in the beginning than it was at the end. At first he was understanding and sympathetic, very agreeable. He appeared to hang on my every word, interested in my ideas and opinions, happy and thrilled to be with me. We had perfect understanding of each other and he enjoyed intellectual discussions."

"Initially I thought he was a good communicator because he would phone me a lot. We seemed to have a lot in common. Now I realize he was mirroring me."

Respect and Truth

To build a connection, he replicates respect and there is sometimes even a level of truth to what he says! Psychopaths 'talk' about the concepts of respect and or truth yet can't live them. Some psychopaths did indeed discuss respect:

"In the beginning he talked about equality, women's rights, and respect for women. I really believed he had esteem for women."

"He thought if he told other people he respected my efforts and work success that it was the same as respecting me. What I learned from him is you can treat someone respectfully without really respecting them deep down."

"He had long rambling lectures about respect. He could lecture about it but he didn't do it or understand it."

Other psychopaths feigned or tried to feign respect:

"He was respectful up front until the day we got married. And then it was gone."

Psychopaths distort the truth so easily because they don't have a conscience about lying. They are *pathological liars*—this means they will lie about anything even things that won't result in negative consequences to them. Psychopaths also lie as a form of dominance. They enjoy controlling the reality of truth or not-truth that they give to women. Part of the psychopath's pathology is his 'pathological world view' which includes how he sees himself, others, and the world. His world view dictates his perception of the truth.

"His interpretation of events was always the truth. I don't think he knew what was true and what was really false. Because he believed it, it was hard to tell that he wasn't telling the truth."

Psychopaths tend to 'mix it up' and combine truth with lies, or truth with distortions. Or as we say, "If his lips are moving, he's lying."

"Looking back, there was a lot of fiction mixed in with facts."

"It was always distorted. He thought his truth was above others because he had this spiritual experience with God."

"He doesn't like the real world. He makes up his own reality and then asks me to live the lie with him."

"There was usually some element of truth in what he said—but you had to dig for it. It left you with more questions than the facts."

Accomplices

Some psychopaths con and lure alone. Yet a number of them have accumulated accomplices along the way that help him in the luring phases of the relationship. It's easy to get accomplices because psychopaths are often engaging and convincing. Their pathological world view is contagious and others begin to come on board with his philosophy of the fun life or the con life.

Family Members

Many of the psychopath's accomplices are his own family members which may also be pathological and adhere to his pathological world view. Some family members may not be pathological but 'defend' the psychopath to the end, as a poor 'misunderstood' eccentric.

"His mother and siblings came to our wedding knowing he was already married and continued to keep that secret from me."

"His whole family used to spy on me and report back to him what I was doing."

"He used his mother and sisters to try to convince me to go back with him. They would tell me stories that he obviously told them to say to me. They were trying to sell me on his virtues."

"His family told me he was a brilliant business man. He was really a dead beat dad!"

His Friends

"There was a network of men keeping his game in play. Some lied for him to protect the secret that his business was going down the tubes and to portray him to me in a good light so I didn't suspect anything."

Other Pathologicals

Psychopaths use other narcissists and psychopaths. Many psychopath's have friends just as disordered as they are, who have the same pathology and have no problems assisting the psychopath in his games and cons especially related to 'love.' Much like the outlaws of the gun-slinging days, the outlaws covered each other's backs but then turned around and shot each other. So can be the assistance that psychopaths receive from other pathologicals.

Normal People

The psychopath also uses normal people, the people he works with, the people the women work with, or mutual friends as a means to deceive the woman. They unknowingly filter his lies and stories to her, or cover for him when he's got a second life going on.

Non-existent People

He even uses 'invisible' accomplices who supposedly deliver notes, cards, or leave messages for her that support the psychopath's storyline. Psychopaths have made up imaginary people who increase their intrigue, add dimension to their storyline about themselves and use non-existent people as covers when they have a hidden life going.

People He Could Manipulate

"He said she was his secretary but really was a prostitute. He used other women by offering to help them and then they were indebted to him so they did his dirty work. He often used them by giving them places to live. In exchange, they would tell me whatever he wanted me to believe about him. Anyone would lie to me for him."

"Sometimes I felt he used other women to hurt me and control me. He so subtly had contact with other women and would have them call him so I would see him talking to them on the phone. I know he told them what to tell me and what not to tell me in the beginning."

Some accomplices willingly help the psychopath. Others are totally unaware they are being 'used' in ways to further the psychopath's lies, life, income, or sex life. Accomplices help the psychopath keep the image alive that he is trying to project early on, help hide his true pathology, cover for his other relationships or addictions, and otherwise convince the woman that she is with a healthy and desirable guy.

All Tools in the Hand of a Psychopath

These techniques are used to deceive and lure her into the relationship. Due to his ability to fly under the radar he will hide well. Some hide for decades while living a complete hidden life full of other women, children, diseases, and overt or covert criminality. She is likely not the only one in the luring phase of a relationship with him. Most psychopaths have many relationships in early, mid or ending phases with him. She is just one face in a wave of humanity being taken in by him.

Figure 11.1
Relationships Timeline

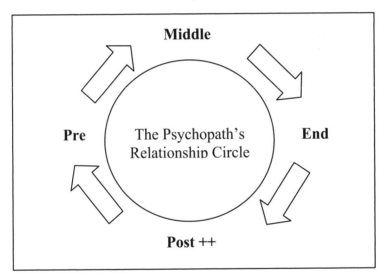

While she is having the romance of her life, the psychopath is in various phases of contact and relationship with a multitude of others. Even if she does not find out about others, it doesn't mean they don't exist. Sometimes, it years later that women come across the evidence of what he was really doing.

Given his extraversion, dominance, brain malfunctions, lack of moral reasoning, and hyper-sexuality, most psychopaths don't even know the true meaning of monogamy. We sarcastically refer to their concept as 'serial monogamy'—they are monogamous in many relationships at one time! Since they hate to be alone or bored and can't say no to a perceived reward of extra-curricular sex, infidelity is imminent even in the beginning of the relationship.

The stages of the relationship time line listed below are multiple stages existing at one time with multiple people. The women in our survey were just ONE of many that were involved in these stages of relationship with the psychopath.

The **Pre-Stage:** He is trolling—online, out in the physical world, at work, in the neighborhood, anywhere. He is looking and testing the waters of connection with other women and men. He measures his possibilities by eye contact, boundary violations, and other cues and clues that hint to him someone is an open target. He could have many women and men that he is in this testing phase with—trying out the waters before he moves in to lure.

The **Early Stage:** He moves in to make more contact with those he has his eye on. He may have multiple cell phones, multiple email accounts or a dozen other ways that he keeps himself available for contact with other male and female potential sex partners. (Even psychopaths who allege they are not gay may engage in same-sex activity.) In the early stage partners are ruled in and out by their levels of availability. He will only troll for so long and will then look for those who are willing to take it to the next level.

The **Middle Stage:** He is having regular contact and sex with numerous partners which can include another semi-full life with these other sexual partners. The woman who is in his life may begin to find unusual behaviors while in their 'romancing' stage. He may be 24/7 with her and then she will not have contact with him for days. 'Plausible' excuses he gives cover for where he was, but texts, pages, phone calls, emails and other suspicious behaviors from others can begin even as early as the honeymoon phase with her. That's because he has multiple relationships that he has been in for quite some time probably before her.

The **End Stage:** He is constantly ending the relationship with someone at some time. The end of the relationship comes for various reasons—some are on to him and confront, others won't give him money or sex any longer, or he has enough other relationships going and needs to cut some off. Various reasons can exist why someone gets the relationship axe from the psychopath.

The Post ++ Stage: This is a time period extending after the formal 'end' of the relationship with her or with others. Those that the psychopath has broken up with are never off the speed dial and never out of the Relationship Circle even if he hasn't contacted them in years! Women in current relationships who find out about his affairs often feel that if he says he has 'stopped' fooling around than he has stopped contact with others. While he may take a hiatus to try to win back one of the women's loyalty, no one ever really leaves a psychopath's life.

Women have said they have heard from him 'out of the blue' 6 months-10 years *LATER* after the break up. He calls as if nothing has happened, says she popped into his mind and he wanted to check on her to tell her how much he always cared for her. Given both his boredom and excitement seeking, women must know that they, nor any other lover, ever really flies off his radar—for long.

Conclusion

The relationships circle exemplifies the strategic targeting that psychopaths use of multiple relationships at one time. While woman #1 is basking in the hyper focus of his attention, he is trolling, in the middle of, and ending, multiple other relationships with men and women. His multiple relationships that are beginning, enduring, and ending no doubt play into her relationship dynamics with the psychopath. Of course, woman #1 is high on oxytocin and can't believe she just met her soulmate!

12 Grieve and Cleave
Mid-relationship Dynamics as the Mask is Slipping

"Just because everything is different doesn't mean anything has changed." — Irene Peter

Just what is the relationship like as the couple heads into the middle portion of their time together? The psychopath:

o　successfully lured her into the relationship with excessive use of attention, flattery, intensity, and mirroring of her values and interests.

o　portrayed himself as helpful and indispensable

o　showed interest in her

o　applauded her virtues and strength

o　showed his exciting and fun side

o　probably isolated her from family and friends

o　told her he found her desirable

o　had a lot of sex with her that promoted her deep bonding and attachment

o　has multiple other relationships that are beginning, in the midst of, and/or ending all the while their relationship is building.

While he worked hard to win her in the luring stage and to woo her during the honeymoon phase, during the mid-relationship stage he will begin the bait and switch and see how attached, tolerant and invested she really is. The mid-relationship dynamics can begin within a few months or as far into the relationship as 20 years or more. Women may not have hit the mid-relationship point with the psychopath for years, even decades. How long this relationship lasts will depend on how good he is at covering up his hidden life. Other women hit this stage quickly because their overall relationship with the psychopath was relatively short. No matter when she hits the mid-point, when his mask slips, she realizes who she thought she got is not who she really got.

What's Behind the Mask?

Pathology, of course! She begins to see inklings of the dark side of his personality. Maybe she becomes aware of, or suspicious of, prostitutes, porn (even pedophilia), crime, embezzlement, the use and misuse of other relationships, abuse, drug/alcohol problems, sexual addiction, his parasitic lifestyle, or his other relationships through unusual texts, calls or emails. What she finds on the other side of the mask brings great grieving.

o   Grieving for the relationship she thought she had.

o   Grieving for the exciting side of the psychopath.

o   Grieving a future she wonders if she will have with him.

o   Grieving a past of wasted time and who knows how much risky exposure for herself?

o   Grieving the reality that he might not be who she thinks he was.

This is why the mid-relationship dynamics are marked by grieving. What she becomes acutely aware of is that her grieving is caused by a unique feature of the psychopath. This unique feature is the unbelievable contradictions, opposites, and dichotomies that mark this man as the disordered person he is. This is what separates pathological love relationships from other merely 'bad break ups.' These dichotomies not only mark these relationships as the pathological pot of misery they are, but will deeply impact her by the creation of cognitive dissonance.

The Dichotomies of a Pathological Love Relationship

Dichotomy *noun*   the division into two contradictory parts or opinions

The dichotomies are the positive traits he exhibited in the beginning and the negative traits he reveals later in the relationship. The existence of both the good and bad behaviors is shown at different times. The two contradictory parts are what comprise the Jekyll/Hyde personality of the psychopath (which is why *The Institute's* logo is a black and white mask representing the good and the bad). These inconsistent and totally contradictory statements, behaviors, and beliefs cause women to feel like they are 'going crazy' in the relationship.

The exposure of his dichotomous beliefs and behaviors begins when he can no longer completely function in the mirage he first created. They signal the end of the 'bait' and the beginning of the 'switch.' According to some of the women, nothing prepares a woman for a relationship with a psychopathic man, where underneath none of the elements of a healthy relationship are present. Instead, the elements are the opposite (or dichotomous) of what a woman usually thinks makes a healthy relationship and what she has experienced in the past. Her frame of reference for 'what makes a relationship' is largely related to what she has experienced in prior relationships. She then brings those beliefs and thoughts into the relationship with the psychopath only to find that everything she ever believed, according to him, is wrong.

She begins to question her own experiences, beliefs, and thoughts. The more he insists that that their relationship is normal, not the other ones she has had, the more she begins to think she is 'crazy' or something is wrong with her that she doesn't understand the basics of what makes a good relationship. Once he convinces her that their relationship is normal, he can start to shift her reality off-base. He sets up a double-bind where she begins to work harder at the pathological relationship (based on her high relationship investment) while he is telling her she just isn't measuring up and 'no wonder she hasn't had successful relationships.' The double-bind keeps her jumping through his hoops while he sits on the sidelines telling her to jump even higher. The harder she works, the more she fails.

All she can remember is that up to this point she has gone through an extraordinary early courtship in which the charming, exciting, and attentive psychopath has idealized and worshipped her and portrayed himself as the ultimate catch and partner. The last thing she expected is her charmer has turned into a viper and that everything she lived was a lie.

She doesn't expect that:

o   every sensitive thing he said about her is going to become horrible things said about her;

o   everything he has told her about himself, his history, or other details is a lie;

o   that his purpose in the relationship is not to love but to dominate and gaslight getting his deviant needs met through any means he can;

o   that everything she told him in confidence about herself will be later used against her;

o   that all his pontificating about life, relationships, love, community, family, children, God, or anything else was not at all what he believed.

As the women try to align themselves with his belief system, it shifts. As they try to align with his behaviors or promises, these shift. This constant shifting and moving keeps women off-balance. It's like trying to straddle a fault line of an earthquake. She spends most of her emotional energy striving to stabilize the relationship with an extremely unstable person.

Before she accepts his new startling opposite attitude and behavior, these dichotomies are first sifted through her temperament and personality traits. Long before there is an 'aha!' moment for her that she isn't crazy, her personality in all its super-traits is looking at and loving the psychopath:

	Her Super-Trait	Her Thought
1.	High empathy	"He's this way because he's been hurt."
2.	Low impulsiveness	"I'm not going to just run away."
3.	High sentimentality	"He can be sweet—like when he …"
4.	High attachment	"I love him like I've never loved anyone else—I feel so connected to him."
5.	High relationship investment	"I've poured my soul in this relationship. I know we can make it work."
6.	High regard	"I want him to think well of me. What am I doing wrong?"
7.	High harm avoidance	"Would I ever find anyone else if I left him?"
8.	Low harm avoidance	"He's not that bad. I'm sure he can turn this around."
9.	High resourcefulness	"I could find a counselor for him and we could get couples counseling."

The Opposites That Produce Cognitive Dissonance

Normal people bring to the relationship a core self that is not highly dichotomized. They are not fragmented into the extreme of good/bad behaviors that are so representative of pathology. Normal-ites are not use to trying to line up with a person who has such opposite thinking, feeling, relating, and behaving. These extremes in his behavior require that she too split, in some ways, to develop a coping strategy for being in a relationship with the good and the bad in him. In essence, she has two relationships going at one time, and she must bring to it skills acquired for both. Her alignment to both parts of him creates, and over time, increases her cognitive dissonance.

The left column of the figure below is an example of feelings she has from the good side of the Jekyll/Hyde psychopath. It most likely represents how she was treated in the luring or honeymoon stage. She may still carry those feelings and remembrances of when the relationship was so wonderful and he was so magnetic. The right column of the figure lists her feelings and his behaviors when the honeymoon is over and his pathological behavior has come to light.

Figure 12.1
The Relationship Dichotomies

She feels extreme bonding...	...and yet expects probable abandonment.
She feels high levels of protection by him...	...and yet extremely exposed and at-risk because of him.
She feels a lot of trust for him...	...and yet red flags of distrust are building.
She is worshipped as a sexual madonna...	...and yet often treated like a whore.
She feels an intense amount of loving towards him...	...and yet intense amounts of loathing him at the same time.
She thinks he is the most excitement she has experienced...	...and yet she is exhausted by him.

She senses his child-like vulnerability or woundedness...	...and yet his adult mystique under which he hides his life is very intriguing.
She hears him say he supports her...	...and yet watches him sabotage her.
She's had the most fun with him...	...and yet in the midst of fun he will often rage.
She thinks he is a wonderful soul-mate...	...and yet the sickest person on the planet.
He acts as her rescuer...	...and yet he is her tormenter.
He can be very calculated in what he does...	...and yet be impulsive and knee-jerk.
He is frequently hyper-sexual...	...and yet often non-sexual/refuses her sexually.
He idealizes her...	...and yet will totally devalue her.
He is super-connected, inhaling her exhaled air...	...and yet totally aloof.
He acts as if he totally understands her...	...and yet is clueless about her feelings and motives.
He is the kindest of people...	...and yet can be the most sadistic.
He is overtly generous...	...and yet incredibly cheap and selfish.
He is attractively 'macho'...	...and yet wimpy and needy.

While it is not necessary for me to explain every item on the dichotomy list, I will cover a few to give an example of how these opposite beliefs and behaviors are exhibited in pathological love relationships.

The Dichotomy of Bonding and Yet Abandonment

She feels as if she has bonded more with this person than anyone else in her life. He too has mirrored back this incredible sense of 'soul-mate' status and yet he has not had that experience of bonding. However as the mask slips, and the bait and switch begins, she becomes more aware that at any moment she could be abandoned or left behind in the relationship. While she once felt he was the one she most bonded with and the one that would spend a lifetime with her, her other set of feelings and beliefs is that she has never been more at risk of being broken up with, cheated on, abandoned or emotionally devastated.

"Our intimacy and high emotions exploded rather than evolved. He seemed to want and need so much from me. But it was a smoke screen—he could also be gone in a flash."

In one sentence he is likely to say how attached and bonded he is, and in the next sentence remind her how disposable she is or how he will leave her. Some psychopaths don't say it outright but 'hint' or leave clues lying about that they are thinking of leaving, or they become aloof, detached, disinterested, and distant.

"He would draw me in and then push me away with various methods. I was constantly perplexed about why it seemed that he wanted a relationship with me on some levels but not on others. He was committed at times but not entirely. I've never been so confused about how someone really felt about me."

This leaves her feeling unstable in the relationship. The psychopath is likely to tell her that she's crazy and the relationship is the same as it has always been, making her question her own perception. Alternately, he may tell her that something she has done has caused him to want to abandon the relationship (such as questioning him, challenging him, catching him in lies, or asking him to perform adult duties). This attaching and rejecting builds the internal reaction in her of constantly ping ponging back and forth between the old childhood game "He loves me, He loves me not, He loves me, He loves me not."

"The intensity—the changeability—how one minute it could all seem good and normal and I would forget the craziness and then suddenly the tables turned and the monster I was living with re-appeared."

The Dichotomy of Idealizing and Yet Devaluing Her

The women have never felt such adulation before. He has told her he sees her as 'the most incredible person, brilliant, loving, sexy.' Idealizing speeds up the sensation of attachment often called 'profound rapport building.' Yet, by mid-relationship, he is devaluing her—because that is what pathology does—it lives out of both sides of the mask. Devaluing her also increases his sense of power over the relationship. The days of compliments may be gone. This leaves her feeling she needs to do something to get him to feel how he previously felt about her. She can spend an enormous amount of emotional energy trying to figure out how to shift the relationship back to the previous dynamics in which the good side of the psychopath was experienced.

"He could be so awful and degrading to me and not even seem aware that what he was saying was horrendous. It was as if he thought it was normal to relate like that. He used to call it normal fighting. There was nothing normal about what he did and what he said."

The Dichotomy of His Perceived Protection and Yet Created Dependency

A woman has never felt more protected than the beginning stages of the relationship. He may have even talked about this protective feeling he has towards her. Since pathologicals are extraverted and dominant, they do have a protective 'feel' to them. While she may be cuddling up to his super-powers of keeping harm away from her, the other side of her inklings are growing. In many ways she has never felt more exposed or at-risk. She's right. Protection by a psychopath is an illusion. Her exposure to disease, financial ruin, emotional devastation, and his impulsive behavior has indeed put her at-risk.

"I wanted the security of a relationship, a father for my children. I was invested in an illusion. He wasn't any of that—although he always pretended to protect."

The Dichotomy of the Pursued Madonna and Yet the Alleged Whore

The experience of the psychopath's high sexuality draws her in through the deepening emotional powers of the sexual connection. The psychopath is highly sensual and she is intensely sexually pursued. The psychopath is likely to describe their sexual relationship as 'unique' or 'deep and meaningful' or simply 'really great sex.' Whichever way the psychopath spins the lingo about the sexual relationship, she most assuredly feels special and pursued as the Madonna. But eventually to humiliate her, the title of Madonna will be dropped and he will allege her as a whore.

The dichotomy of having experienced this intense sexual bonding with him and being rejected (as a whore or simply as a sex partner) sets up pursuit/rejection dynamics in their sex life. Many women talked about feeling humiliated to have to beg for sex not merely for the sexual experience but to try to emotionally reconnect with him and have him experience the 'bonding' that they thought the relationship was based on.

"I don't know what it was that we had. I use to think I knew. I thought he was as connected as I was. In the beginning, he couldn't get enough of me. But halfway through the relationship he withheld sex and acted as if I was repugnant. He called me horrible sexual names...even used the 'c' word. How could I have dropped that low in his eyes?"

Psychopaths will often:

o accuse their women of infidelity so they can label them as whores and reject them

o or they will introduce her to deviant sexual practices she has never done before and tell her no one else will ever want her because of her participation in them

o or they will compare her to other sex partners in an attempt to coerce her into more unwanted sexual acts and so the cycle repeats itself

All this leaves her feeling inadequate and striving to please him sexually so she performs more sexual acts that she finds degrading. He degrades her for doing them, and yet demands them.

"I am repulsed by my own sexual behavior. I allowed so many things that were against who I am as a person—my own personal values. I will never be the same sexually...I feel so dirty and violated. Of course, that's what he wanted all along. He reminds me of every horrible sexual act I performed and how normal men would find me to be a whore. Since I'm so disgusting he thinks I should just stay with him—since we are alike and understand each other sexually."

The Dichotomy of Trust and Yet Distrust

The psychopath spent a lot of time in the luring phase establishing trust with her. That's not hard to do because the women are prone to trusting before it is earned or validated. He may have told stories about his own trustworthiness or performed trustworthy actions to cement her trust in him early on. This became the foundation off which he could constantly refer to himself as trustworthy while doing everything that proves he is untrustworthy.

"Half of being a con man is the challenge. When I score, I get more kick out of that than anything; to score is the biggest kick of my whole life."[82]

Although she may have a nagging feeling he is violating her trust in some area, the psychopath will likely spin it as a problem with her paranoia, her own emotional issues, or another reason he uses to abandon the relationship. The dichotomy produces in her a conflict between trusting her gut or trusting her memories. In the early part of the relationship, she will trust her memories of him. Only *much* later will she begin to trust her gut. Interestingly, because of the woman's high trust trait, she will even trust the psychopath's explanation when she has caught him red-handed. 'What' she catches him at could be in bed with someone else, swindling her money, or another horrendous lie.

When prompted to choose between trusting what she just found out, or trusting the explanation given by the psychopath, many of the women trust the psychopath and discount the truth of what they learned.

*"I opened the door and saw him in bed with another woman. By the end of the evening, I wasn't sure I had seen it at all! He didn't convince me that it meant nothing—he convinced me it **didn't happen** and there was no one in the bed with him! It took me forever to learn to trust my own perceptions. When you think you are going crazy, it's easy to rely on someone else's version of reality. It wasn't the issue of reality I now see…it was the issue of truth."*

This conflict between trusting what she uncovers or trusting his explanations will be repeated many times before the end of the relationship. Even if she catches him, he is likely to allege she didn't see what she saw, didn't read what she read, and didn't hear what she heard. Blatant attempts at gaslighting her reality are not beyond the psychopath, and is a well-used method by him. Overtime, this erodes her ability to do her own reality testing, and plays with her mind in ways that makes her think she is losing her mind. As a last ditch pitch, the psychopath will also threaten that if she can't trust him (even in the face of catching him red-handed) then he might as well pack up and go. His convenient threat of abandoning is always present.

---

[82] Blum, R.H. (1972). *Deceivers and Deceived.* Springfield IL: Charles C. Thomas.

The Dichotomy of Excitement and Yet Exhaustion

The excitement-seeking in her that found the psychopath's extraversion attractive is now causing extreme emotional exhaustion. The adrenaline rush she used to have at his 'edginess,' 'risk-taking behavior,' or just his extraverted dominance is beginning to burn itself out. The drama, the highs and lows, the daily power struggles, the weekly uncovering of some new lie and the constant fear of being abandoned are all now producing fatigue.

"I kept thinking—if this is the most exciting man I have ever been with, why am I so exhausted in every way—emotionally, physically and even financially. If this is so much fun why do I feel like THIS?"

The Dichotomy of His Child-like Vulnerability and Yet His Adult Mystique

The psychopath invested a lot in portraying himself to her as 'wounded.' Psychopaths have no problem simultaneously playing both dominant and doomed personas. Likely, he acted as if the disclosure of his hidden pain was only to her. She was the only one who 'understood him' or he felt 'safe enough' to share his pain with. Women stated that he had a 'child-like quality to him' or he seemed 'vulnerable' or 'emotionally wounded.' The dichotomy of his vulnerability through wounding meets up with his aloofness which casts a 'mystique' on the psychopath. Women define him as 'different,' 'unique,' 'eccentric' or 'electrifying.' Some women mistake his hidden life and sneakiness for mystique.

A conflict exists for her when she gets an inkling to leave. She feels like she is abandoning a wounded child who needs her. She also wants to stay because he is so baffling that she wants to figure him out before she exits. The psychopath is likely to play both ends of the spectrum.

"Was he a child or a man? Was he a power hungry psycho or a knee clinging toddler? I don't know...he was both. I couldn't put my finger on what it was in him that pulled from both sides of me—the part that saw him as powerful and mysterious and the part that saw him as damaged and in need of me."

The Dichotomy of Loving and Yet Loathing

She feels the magnetic pull into an emotional and sexual vortex that she can't free herself from. She mistakes intensity for love and passion for bonding. It doesn't take the psychopath long to test the depths of her love (and tolerance) and to figure out he has a lot of wiggle room in the relationship to abuse.

As the women begin to see the other side of the psychopath's mask, this recognition causes her to loath him. She loathes his lies, his deviancy, his disorder, and she may loath herself for loving him, even in the midst of everything she finds out.

"It's to the point now that I cringe when I am around him. I used to feel sorry for how sick he obviously is. Now I feel repulsed. He is revolting."

Crimes of passion occur this way when the pathological love attachment is fierce and the betrayal is equally as fierce. Unfortunately, the love bond transcends hate, so she remains bonded in spite of her loathing.

Other Occurrences

By the mid-part of the relationship a woman who is normally dominant and resourceful may for the first time in her life feel 'fragile' or even 'mentally ill.' She may seek counseling fearing she is the one who is 'sick' or 'disordered.' Not only has the psychopath repeatedly told her that, but she is also shaken by the incongruencies in the relationship and in her own emotions. The roller coaster of the ups-and-downs and the enormous attempts at pleasing him and stabilizing the relationship have taken their toll.

"You feel trapped constantly in some weird kind of game that you didn't ever want to play in the first place. You know you'll never be the same again. You see who you were just evaporate."

When the dichotomies become apparent to her and start to cause psychological reactions in her, she is well into the pathological relationship dynamics. Similarly, how long it will take to transition into the ending phase of the relationship is different for each woman.

One Woman's Dichotomies

"I felt all the above but also thought I was less than a woman for feeling these things. I felt I just didn't know how to be in a relationship and blamed myself. He made me feel all his previous relationships worked well, so it must be me. These are the same relationships in which he claimed the women were being

dishonest, cheating and crazy. It was as if he was setting out to prove that all women were crazy and the men were saints for putting up with them. He believed all women were sexually manipulative and all could be manipulated and used because they were stupid and needy. He proved this to himself by manipulating women to send in photos of themselves half dressed to his internet site. He thought it was fun at first to make money from it and then got more interested in the sex-industry. To him this proved that all women could be bought because they all wanted to prove they were sexually attractive. He couldn't see how he was manipulating them. He couldn't see how he was being seduced and manipulated by the sex industry himself. He thought he was in control. I felt it was a form of escapism for him and helped him to distance himself from me. He made me feel inadequate compared to these women who appeared happy to know him and made him feel attractive and powerful while using him to advertise themselves on his site. He would show me pictures of the half dressed women looking more sleazy than sexy and become frustrated that I didn't share his enthusiasm for making money from them. I began to hate him and didn't like how the future was panning out. He seemed like a frustrated wanna-be porn star who needed acceptance from shallow porn women to feel sexually powerful and masterful. It left me feeling that all his passionate declarations of wanting a relationship based on honesty, fidelity, and trust were not in line with his actions and true feelings of sexual inadequacy."

Figure 12.1
Dichotomies Summary – Percent of Women Endorsing

% of Women Endorsing	Relationship Dynamic
92%	Acting out then playing the victim
89%	Creating bonding yet denying woman is bonded
88%	His childlike vulnerability and his adult power/mystique
82%	Idealization and devaluation
80%	Bonding and abandonment
73%	Respected competent woman & incompetent female
63%	Safety and un-safety
55%	Pursued madonna and alleged whore
50%	Wealthy man who asks for money

Figure 12.2
Dichotomies Summary – Percent of Women Deeply Affected

% Women Deeply Affected	Relationship Dynamic
89%	Acting out then playing the victim
76%	Creating bonding yet denying woman is bonded
76%	His childlike vulnerability and his adult power/mystique
75%	Idealization and devaluation
59%	Bonding and abandonment
53%	Respected competent woman & incompetent female
59%	Safety and un-safety
49%	Pursued madonna and alleged whore
43%	Wealthy man who asks for money

As the dichotomies slowly tear away at the fabric of her stability, it increases her sensation of cognitive dissonance—the inability to hold a consistent view of him as wonderful or horrible. It also affects her ability to hold a consistent behavior with him—leave or stay. Instead she makes up and breaks up repeatedly, each act increasing the disorienting symptoms of cognitive dissonance. This produces what women refer to as 'ping ponging' in her mind where his good traits parade through her mind and then her mind is pulled to the other dynamic of his bad traits. She has internal whiplash from being pulled back and forth between good and bad memories and good and back concepts of him.

By the middle of the relationships when the mask has slipped and she has seen the dark side of the psychopath, the peacefulness of his previous mimicking is quickly replaced with marathon fighting. Each event of fighting with him produces a 'cycle' of behaviors and attempts he uses to get her back, or at least, get the power back in his court. Shifting the power back to him, like a volley in a tennis match, may result in him immediately wanting to break up with her. He may have pursued her to come back to him so he could then end it. Many of the dichotomies of the relationship are played out in the cycles of fighting.

On the next page is what I call a Relationship Event Cycle that helps to see the franticness and the extent that pathologicals will go through during an argument, discussion or break up. It exemplifies why communicating is hard with them, why there is such emotional exhaustion in the relationship, and the drastic means they will go to, to recapture the dominance in the relationship. Being right is preferable to being happy for them.

Figure 12.3
Relationship Event Cycle

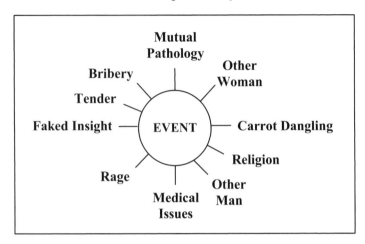

When an argument or threatened break up occurs:

o   He rages.

o   When that doesn't work, he is tender.

o   When that doesn't work, he says she is just as sick as he is so they might as well stay together.

o   When that doesn't work he threatens to find another woman.

o   When that doesn't work he fakes insight that she was probably right all along about what's wrong with him and is the only one who understands him.

o   When that doesn't work, he bribes—he'll tell her family, work, children, etc. something negative about her.

o   When that doesn't work he carrot dangles with something she has wanted—to get married, have a child, buy a new house.

o   When that doesn't work, he says she must have another man which is why she is not making up with him.

o   When that doesn't work, he'll go to church.

o   When that doesn't work he claims he has serious medical conditions like cancer to bring her back to him.

These events listed in no way cover all the excuses he will have during an event. It is only limited by his creativity.

Conclusion

This is a difficult turning point in the pathological relationship. It brings much grief to her when she realizes the honeymoon is over and he stops idealizing her. There is enormous grief in recognizing in him the disordered dichotomous behaviors. Yet, given her super-traits of empathy, bonding, tolerance, and relationship investment, she will cleave—not leave during this portion of the relationship. This is why this stage of the relationship is called Grieving and Cleaving. The more he pulls away increasing her fear, the more attached she will become. The cycles of break up and make up are just increasing her cleaving to him and the relationship while the entire time, she is loathing the dark side of the psychopath which is becoming more easily identified.

13 Perceive and Leave

End Relationship Dynamics as She and the Relationship are Disintegrated

"And the day came when the risk it took to remain tight in the bud was more painful than the risk it took to blossom." — *Anais Nin*

Disintegrate   *verb*   to decay, break down, crumble, decompose, rot

Perceiving

The path to her perceiving his disorder in all its destruction is littered with the remains of her mind and soul. The Jekyll/Hyde personification through his good/bad traits are constantly playing hide and seek. Yet her grief of previously glimpsing the dark side of the mask is giving way to a lot of current reality. She gathers perceptions of him and the relationship that point to the severity of their problems.

Her attempted communication about his impulsive and erratic behaviors:

o   goes through the crazy-making triangulation process resolving nothing

o   his language is contradictory

o   his words have different meaning

o   he doesn't appear to understand her

o   he is gas lighting

Every day is dread because she knows there will be a new discovery of:

o   other women/escorts/prostitutes

o   porn

o   spending

o   lying/hiding another life

o   devaluing/degradation

o   violence (when applicable)

o   him being nothing like he use to be

"He mocked my feelings so much that I really began to question my own being and my own perception of things. He was so convincing . He could make me do anything. I have never been so vulnerable, so trusting, or so willing to go along with any idea he had. It's like I lost my internal compass of who I was. I don't know where 'I' went."

Gut wrenching reality is creeping in that the end, in some form, is near. Women vacillate between ending the relationship with someone they loathe and staying to understand who he is, why he did this, and what just happened. She doesn't know whether to hope he leaves or to hope she can muster the emotional clarity to leave herself. Everything that pathology is works against her clear comprehension of his disorder. Everything that her super-traits are works against her voluntary emotional disengagement. Everything that the intensity of attachment generates works to keep her hand cuffed to her relationship fantasy without her psychological approval. There is not much that is cooperating with her dire need to leave.

Leaving—Getting out of Hell

His Leaving

If the psychopath has enough new emerging relationships in the pipeline of his girlfriends/sex partner cycles, he might be done with her. Since most of his behavior is based on power and dominating, he won't mind leaving if it entails a power play on his part. His power plays are always based on levels of destruction or deviancy. How he ends the relationship is just as indicative of pathology as his behavior in the relationship. Some pathologicals will:

o   do things that make her think she is having a nervous breakdown/gaslighting her

o   set her up by using information against her to bribe her into signing over money, property, or custody before leaving or making it a condition of his leaving

o   tries to get her fired/gets family and friends out of relationship with her to push her over the edge o flaunt relationships in her face, have fake phone conversations so she hears his plans, feelings, thoughts that he doesn't want her anymore

o leave a phone message, text, or email breaking up with her with no other explanation

o disappear and she has no idea why he left, worries he was killed and doesn't hear from him for months or even years

In other cases, he will not merely go away without leaving his final calling card of his impact on her, he will also:

o threaten to kill her, children, family or pets

o have final acts of physical abuse against her or others (even if he was never violent before)

o do covert actions to make it look like an accident occurred (cuts brake lines, tampers with other equipment, etc.)

o actually try to kill her

o stalk her

Breaking up with a psychopath is not like leaving any other relationship—whether it is his choosing or hers. This can't be emphasized enough—psychopaths rarely:

o walk away without a power play

o leave and don't come back

o exit without leaving one more mark upon her soul

Psychopaths are boomerangs. Even when they are thrown 'out there' they still swivel back around. If the women are not looking, the psychopaths will surprise the women as they ricochet back into their world. Psychopaths and other pathologicals don't disappear from her radar for long, even if they remove themselves from her life.

How do we think those who are psychopathic break up? How did Scott Peterson leave his relationship? What about O.J. and all the endings of his relationships? What about the nightly news filled with the same stories of psychopaths leaving their mark upon the relationship? If we really paid attention to how pathologicals end their relationships, we would know that all endings are on their terms and often with dire, if not fatal, circumstances. Given his brain, impulse problems, and grandiosity, why are we surprised? For survivors reading this book, take note.

Psychopaths rarely yield their power and control without a fight—including the power of ending relationships. This is all the more reason to have support, safety planning, law enforcement protection, and all the services you can muster or accept.

When She Can't Leave

Too often, she has disintegrated so much that she cannot initiate the disconnection. This can happen due to several reasons. One is that the intensity of attachment is so strong that even with all the evidence of his behavior and pathology, her 'entrancement' in the relationship keeps her tied to him. In other relationships, the women are too impacted by Post Traumatic Stress Disorder, depression, and other symptoms to be able to initiate and carry out the disengagement process which requires a level of functioning she does not currently have. For others, contemplating leaving triggers anxiety which also triggers remembering the solace experienced from him. This sets off the dynamics of Betrayal/Trauma Bonding which increases attachment when fear is experienced. For some women, there may be other financial, social, career, familial, or religious reasons why she isn't leaving. Because of her super traits related to self reliance and resourcefulness, these are the women unfortunately, most likely to NOT seek shelter support or care. They may also be less inclined to get restraining orders, notify their job of the need for protection, or devise a safety plan.

With her emotionally frozen inability to leave, she becomes a toy that the psychopath bats around at will, tearing at the fabric of her soul like she is prey. Despite her ravaged psychological condition and the depth of depravity they experienced at the psychopath's hands, the women still described the decision to disconnect as 'excruciatingly difficult.'

Competent women who are CEO's of companies become paranoid and believe that the psychopath will know when she attempts to leave—even if he is out of town. Powerful female attorneys can't remember how to file a restraining order for themselves. Life saving doctors can't remember how to give themselves care. Insightful therapists can't identify the symptoms they are having and most of the women can't figure out how to leave or remain safe after they have left. This is not a testimony to her indecisiveness but a testimony to the power of a psychopath's influence to immobilize others ability to combat his evil in strategic ways.

"I can't believe the amount of abuse and hurt I put up with. I think it's because he would start to cry and use emotional blackmail so I would stay. I never saw myself as the kind of person who would put up with this hurt and pain. I am angry at myself for putting up with this when it was so obviously wrong for so long."

When She Can Leave

In the instances in which she can initiate the break up, she is sure to have triggered the pathological's narcissistic rage and dominance that will fight back with everything that is vile in him. It is *these* men with multiple disorders, poor impulse control, high dominance drives, and little response to fear of punishment that are the most lethal—physically and emotionally. Psychopaths with their poor impulse control and low reactions to punishment are not motivated by verbal boundaries or even restraining orders. Women do have an incredibly difficult time leaving these relationships due to not only her exhaustion but also because of his perceived 'lethality.' Women think there is a safer way to leave Hannibal, that there is a way to smooth the exit, to let him down gently, to reason with him so he lets her go. Others think if he hooks up with someone else that it will be an open door. Unfortunately, psychopaths with their ability to multi-task and micro- manage multiple relationships at once, won't always see it that way. For general power purposes, they aren't likely to look the other way while she steals his power by walking out on him.

Detailed safety planning is required because the women are most at-risk while leaving or shortly after having left the psychopath. This is problematic because she isn't likely to want to set up safety planning. She may not also realistically appraise what he is capable of, or likely to attempt with her. In fact, we know she isn't likely to be realistic about it given her super traits. Likewise, therapists who don't understand psychopathy may have a difficult time 'predicting' the psychopath's next move against her during disengagement and may have as little realistic ideas about his capabilities when provoked as she does.

Lethality

The psychopath's faux-crying and his elaborate promises to change are likely to begin, especially if he did not initiate the break up. Refer back to the Relationship Event Cycle in the previous chapter for a review of all the behaviors that go along with the drama of the break up. Stalking is more likely to occur in men who have psychopathic traits than in men without those traits so it is likely to begin or continue if it had already started. This raises the lethality risk of her break up. Add to this his lack of respect for authority or laws, his frantic feelings over losing control, his need for dominance, and any weapons he may have access to, and you have a high lethality risk. Women often hope that if he goes to jail or prison that this will be helpful in the disengagement process. Psychopaths who end up in prison rarely see prison as disengagement. After all, they always have accomplices on the outside and he eventually gets out of jail.

Some of the psychopaths will:

o   stalk and cyber-stalk relentlessly

o   ignore restraining orders

o   try to get her fired

o   abduct children

o   hire people to spy, harm, or hurt her

o   attempt to kill

o   court stalk through chronic law suits against her

"He was always spying on me and keeping tabs on other people. What kind of person needs to do that? And why?"

Psychopaths are vindictive and will spend enormous amounts of time, energy, and money to assure she is hurt *further.* He may hurt her further by not allowing her to know why he left, will stalk, or harass her or use the kids during the break up. He will flaunt his life with other women while stalking her because she is dating someone else. Clearly, his dichotomous behavior does not stop because they are not together.

Breaking Up and Using the Law Against Her

For those women who go on to court cases with pathologicals, there are legal dichotomies as well. He will spend more in attorney fees than what she is seeking, stay in court for years no matter the cost in order to have access to her emotions, and will fail mediation, counseling, family co-parenting classes because all the information and education falls on pathological ears. Even the courts identify these cases as 'High Conflict' because nothing ever gets resolved because his motivation is to deter.

Women feel like they never get through the break up because they never get out of court.

Unrecognizable To Herself and Others

Women describe the disengagement like they have crawled out of a grave, heaving themselves onto safe ground—gasping for air that is not filled with the pathology and dichotomies of him. There is so much to heal from after the phony moral monster—after the 'Don Juan of Con' got her. Her symptoms increase almost daily making her appear mentally ill or obsessed with understanding what is wrong with her, him or them. Some of the women are falsely diagnosed as paranoid or borderline personality disordered, neurotic, or delusional. In fact, many of the women have the same symptoms seen in other types of conditions associated with emotional manipulation or psychological torture such as:

o   Stockholm Syndrome
o   cult programming
o   psychological warfare
o   coercion
o   mind control
o   trance logic thinking

As she psychologically de-compensates, she experiences (and has already experienced), the same four dynamics seen in the Stockholm Syndrome:

1. She *perceives* (and has already experienced) a threat to her physical or psychological survival and believes he can carry out his threats. She has already lived months and maybe years of him carrying out his ability to harm her through the use of his dichotomies, and maybe even violently.

2. *Perceived* small kindnesses from him set the emotional tone for her repeatedly letting down her guard and seeing him as human or kind. This repeating kindness increases her relationship investment and hope in him.

3. Isolation from outside *perspectives* other than his is indoctrination into his pathological world view. He begins to control her perception of reality by actions that create near delusional experiences of reality.

4. A *perceived* inability to leave. The psychopath has already trained her that he will find her or that he has special abilities to know when she is leaving or where she will go.

Her symptoms are highly reflective of a warped perception of how she has come to perceive herself, him, the relationship, and what she just experienced. Unfortunately, her symptoms are rarely recognized by others (including her therapist, attorney or family) as psychological terror because the psychopath looks normal. How could she be terrorized by a normal person?

On the occasion when others really do *get* that he is pathological and she is damaged, they are still likely to not understand the severity of her symptoms. Friends and family say "We've all been through bad break ups. Just move on. Get back out there and date. Don't think about it!" They remember who she was before she was shattered and expect that the strong persona is still within her. When her symptoms increase instead of decrease, they think she is malingering, wallowing in it, trying to not get over it, histrionic, or a drama queen. Her reduced functioning could be effecting her job performance, her ability to parent, or her other relationships with family and friends. There is almost no area of her life or functioning that hasn't been disintegrated.

Actually, there aren't many minds that can take this kind of torture and stress and not disintegrate. Her symptoms are indicative of, and point to, abnormal exposure to emotional and psychological torture and are likely to be somewhere along the stress disorder continuum of various stress related disorders. These can range from moderate to severe, including Post Traumatic Stress Disorder (PTSD). Other women have Major Depression and other forms of anxiety or panic disorders. Some have developed substance abuse from trying to medicate the symptoms of disorders they did not know they have.

By the time women arrive at *The Institute*, very few have been formally diagnosed or treated for their severe symptoms of PTSD, major depression, panic, emerging sleep disorders, or substance abuse. While the women may not know 'what' the disorder is that they have, they do know they no longer resemble the strong, confident, professional woman they use to be. They no longer recognize the passive, distracted and fearful person they have become. The consummate assured attorney, doctor, artist, therapist, or teacher that these women represent in their careers, now becomes the walking dead. Her symptoms include:

o   glassy-eyed
o   dissociated
o   overweight or underweight/eating disorders
o   sleep deprived, over sleeping, or vacillating between the two
o   hyper vigilant with exaggerated startle reflex
o   chronic adrenaline pumping through their body
o   their brain sucked dry of serotonin and/or dopamine
o   attention-deficit type focus problems
o   paranoid and highly harm avoidant
o   alternating between hyper vigilance and lethargy
o   intrusive thoughts
o   flashbacks
o   relationship obsessions
o   cognitive dissonance
o   onset of auto immune disorders
o   other medical problems like migraines, TMJ, gastric issues
o   substance abuse (including prescriptions)

Conclusion

This comprehensive list of serious emotional disruptions shows the real snap shot of who she was with. If she was a soldier coming home from the front lines of battle in Iraq, we would expect the person would have some of these symptoms from unrelenting exposure to abnormal war events. And yet she has been at the front lines with a terrorist for many months or years with unrelenting exposure to abnormal pathology. This list of aftermath symptoms shows the power of pathology, the real proclivity of psychopathy to damage at the same level as war or torture.

To some degree, this is the ultimate power play for a pathological to take someone strong and slam them to the mat emotionally. This is the totality of psychological triumphing for the psychopath. Victimizing the weak does not parade his psychological strength, deviancy, or manipulation the way destroying the strong does. These were, and are, the strongest women I have ever met.

14 Reprieve and Achieve
Recovering from the Aftermath

"It is the wounded oyster who mends its shell with pearl."

— *Emerson*

In the years of treating the women and their aftermath, I have come to a new and haunting awareness of not only the similarities among them but the severity as well. This book has laid the ground work for understanding why they were *all* harmed—from his brain functioning to her super traits, from the communication and intensity dynamics to her PTSD. Her aftermath is a complex manifestation of several contributing factors. The end result is that these women are perhaps the most damaged victim group from exposure to the most toxic (and often lethal) pathology. It reminds us why Public Psychopathy Education is so important in the world today because of toxic inevitable harm. This chapter will help focus on what we have discovered about the women and what they need in order to recover well.

Let's look specifically at the types of victimizations that the women reported in our survey.

Inevitable Harm: Every Woman Was Harmed

First and foremost, all of the women reported that they were harmed by the relationship with the psychopath. Stated another way, 0% reported 0 harm. That alone should alert courts, custody evaluators, judges, attorneys, mediators, batterer intervention programs, anger management classes, and others who have interaction with and decision making power over, psychopaths and pathologicals that someone is *always* harmed by them. My mantra about pathological behavior is:

Perceived management by trying to reduce a psychopath's behavior and it's affect on others, is an illusion.

Pathology Proclamation

If we ever *really* got that mantra:

Abuser programs would screen out abusers who can't change.

They would test more to know who these untreatable are and they would offer ineffective 'treatment' less.

They would tell the women the truth about his ability to sustain positive change.

Custody would be handled differently and children wouldn't be forced into mind control by a pathological's distorted world view.

Instead, taxpayers' money would go more towards treating the abusers who *have* the capacity to change and far less to those who are pathological and can't change.

Sentencing would be different and reflect whether there was 'proclivity to sustain positive change and insight about how his behavior has affected others.'

Parole and probation would be tied to the real roots of recidivism.

Fewer women would be harmed, less would die, and more children would not be harmed by exposure to psychopaths.

There would be a funded national awareness campaign for Public Psychopathy Education, just like there is for Cancer or Depression.

We would recognize that the outcome for all is inevitable harm because no one walks free of his devastation—not her or her children.

So many things could change if we really only believed that one concept: no matter what, pathology is inevitable harm.

Here are some of the aftermath affects of the inevitable harm she experienced:

Percent with Symptom Type of Harm Reported

o   95% said they were harmed emotionally
o   85% said they were harmed psychologically
o   71% said they were harmed financially
o   67% said they were harmed in their careers
o   51% said they were harmed sexually

o 51% said they were harmed physically

o 26% said they had other types of harm as well

Many women feel that their ability to be in another relationship is permanently damaged.

"I don't ever want to date again. I cannot trust. I can't trust myself to be wise enough to know when I'm being played or used...and I can't trust that there are actually men worthy of my trust out there."

"It has been over four years since our relationship ended and I still get anxiety attacks at the thought of dating. I am still single and have adopted a hermit lifestyle to make sure I never go through anything like this again."

Emotional and Psychological Harm

"I am mainly numb right now. He has affected my energy level and ability to focus. I am just drained by trying to process all of this."

"Emotionally draining, I had never been a drinker in my life. He is an alcoholic and I became one trying to hide from myself, my feelings of hopelessness and powerlessness and to emotionally stay no matter what happened or what I knew."

"The biggest impact was the guilt feeling I had all the time. He managed to manipulate me and I always ended up feeling sorry for him. I always had guilt feelings."

"It really destroyed my self-esteem. My emotional and mental energy has been consumed by trying to make sense of it all and figure out how to heal from it."

"Finding out the man you loved did not exist...that the single man who was pursuing you with an 'honorable' intent was actually married. That type of betrayal messes with your heart, mind and spirit."

Financial and Career Harm

Many of the men entered these relationships expressly for the purpose of financially harming their partners. This is especially tragic given that single mothers are already at risk for financial hardship. Friends and other family members had to step up to the plate to assist her. Some women who were previously productive workers ended up on government assistance. The financial toll a psychopath costs individuals and society is staggering.

"I lost my home because of all the refinances we did to tide us over while we waited for his purported funds to appear. He took a loan out in my name on my solely owned personal property by having a neighbor pretend to be me."

"He freely spent over $40K of my life savings and earnings."

"When I met this man, I only owed money for graduate school loans. Now, I owe a massive amount in credit card debts, for a car payment, and more. He 'robbed Peter to pay Paul' and kept it hidden from me."

"He took all the money we had. When his credit was no good anymore he forced me to ruin mine. He allowed our house to foreclose. And while we were in the marriage he constantly chose fun over bills, putting us in a precarious financial situation that I am now going to have to file bankruptcy because of."

Physical & Sexual Harm

Physical harm is more than physical abuse. Physical harm can also come from STDs and the long term health effects of stress. Many of the women contracted herpes, other STD's or hepatitis. Women experienced sexual damage and negative effects on their sexuality. Having been exposed to deviant sexual practice, humiliated about their sexual performance or bodies, compared to other women, cheated on, and often sexually harmed—most women felt they needed intensive sexual healing in order to overcome the affects of the sexually intimate relationship with a psychopath.

"He encouraged me to have my tubes tied (he did not like to use condoms) claiming we were in a committed monogamous relationship, while he continued to have unprotected sex."

"This relationship has taken a grave physical toll on my body. I have several medical conditions now. I look about 20 years older than I actually am."

Long-term Damage

Also significantly impacted is a woman's sense of self-esteem and trust. Remember, these are women who have very high levels of self-sufficiency and had a solid sense of self prior to the psychopath.

> *"I have no ability to trust and I tend to expect the worst from people. I assume they will hurt me and that I am not worthy of not being hurt. Most importantly, it has removed my trust in my own abilities to choose a partner."*

> *"I feel like I drew the "go to jail" card and have to sit there for a long time before I can really begin to live again."*

> *"I have long term PTSD and have been in counseling for a long time now. My therapist says I am not done yet. Who knows how long?"*

Reprieve: When Healing Begins

Recovery is an even greater challenge for these women who bear so much physical and psychological damage. When the relationship ends, women believe that the 'reprieve' from the constant gaslighting, infidelity and other pathological behaviors will be enough to kick-start her healing. Sadly, PTSD and other stress reactions have already taken its toll and set its course. Of course, healing can't begin until the constant trauma stops, so the reprieve is the first step in healing. However, a specific recovery path or treatment will be necessary for her to find her way back to herself. Women have lost precious time in intervening with their own aftermath symptoms by not seeking help early enough. With her level of resourcefulness, she will want to do it on her own and not ask for help, all of which slows her progress. Of course, many did seek help but found very little within the mental health field. Let's look at how *The Institute* has addressed meeting her needs.

Institute Levels of Care—Our Model of Care Approach for Pathological Love Relationships

The Institute has emerged as the leading support services and treatment provider for those recovering from the aftermath of Pathological Love Relationships. While it is beyond the scope of this chapter to be able to discuss all aspects of a complete recovery, in the remainder of this chapter I will highlight some of the profound aftermath symptoms that affect women most and how *The Institute* approaches her care. *The Institute* has developed our own unique Model of Care approach created from the hundreds of survivors we have helped so far. Our model of approach takes into consideration her super traits, stress disorder, exposure to unrelenting pathology, early childhood events, and her proclivity for choosing Pathological Love Relationships again in the future.

The Institute provides several levels of care depending on her needs and symptoms. Each level of care is designed specifically by *The Institute* and all support staff use our Model of Care approach.

o **Level 1** is our phone coaching program that utilizes life and relationship coaches (also survivors of these relationships) who are extensively trained by *The Institute*. Coaches work with women who do not have diagnosable disorders such as depression, anxiety/panic, or PTSD. Level 1 also includes the availability of teleconferencing support groups in addition to individual coaching.

o **Level 2** is licensed mental health professionals LCSW's, LPC's, etc. (usually survivors of these relationships) who are extensively trained by *The Institute*. The mental health professionals work primarily with women who do have diagnosable disorders such as PTSD, other acute stress disorders, major depression or other anxiety disorders.

o **Level 3** is the face-to-face support programs which include the 5+ day retreat programs offered several times per year, individual counseling with licensed mental health professionals in their own private practices (only available in some cities), and 1:1 support with Sandra in our NC location.

o **Level 4** is our intensive interventions which includes Intensive Outpatient Programming (IOP) with Licensed Mental Health Professionals 3-5 hours of therapy per day over the course of 5-10 day cycles (billable to some insurance providers) *or* our Residential Treatment Program approximately 5-10 day long which includes inpatient-like care including medication evaluations and treatment (billable to some insurances).

What Women Need For Recovery

Pathology Education: Foremost is the pathology education information that she, and most other persons have never been privy to because our country does not disseminate this information. The ability to understand the permanence, the relationship dynamics and inevitabilities, how to spot it in the future, red flags, intensity building, and other information on mental illness and personality disorders is critical.

Examining Patterns of Selection: Early childhood conditioning may have set her on a path for subconscious patterns of selection. Pathological family dynamics, normalizing abnormal behavior, or numbing of red flags can establish patterns of selection that are repeated over a lifetime. Women often can't name the subconscious traits, patterns, and attraction reactions they experience.

Knowledgeable and Consistent Support: The lack of trained professionals, paraprofessionals, support groups, and understanding family and friends impedes recovery. Getting her hooked up with trained coaches, counselors, support groups and giving information so that family and friends understand why this relationship is different than others can really jump start her process. We have developed products for family and friends so they can better understand what she has been through and how to support her.

Symptom Management: PTSD, depression, anxiety, and panic are common aftermath symptoms. It's hard for her to work, heal, or move ahead when her symptoms remain unmanaged. Since the women are very competitive and resourceful due to their super traits, most don't willingly want to take medication for their mood symptoms. However, after enough stress or a long exposure to psychopathy, even the strongest of minds depletes brain chemistry.

EMDR/Hypnosis: Since state-dependent learning occurs in trance states while she is internalizing experiences of him. Those experiences need to be altered the same way they were created. Hypnosis is a great way to restore her previous condition. Additionally, EMDR (Eye Movement Desensitization) is trauma processing—a gentle way to work through flashbacks and nightmares reducing their emotional power yet not re-traumatizing her.

Self Awareness: The women have unprecedented risk factors for being in Pathological Love Relationships connected to her super traits. Her greatest potential for future safety rests in a complete, deep, and thorough understanding of her traits, why they are risk factors, how they compliment a psychopath's traits, and how to guard these super traits from targeting.

Self Care: The focus of him and the onset of PTSD has obliterated her self-care. In order to build back her life she must also reestablish a routine of daily and weekly recovery activities that lead her back to her previous functioning level. Women are often so distracted with intrusive thoughts that they don't remember to take care of themselves. It's probably been a long time since they cared for themselves.

Intrusive Thoughts/Cognitive Dissonance Symptom Management: By far, the main symptoms that are disrupting her ability to function well are these two items. These are the symptoms women need help most with and complain most about. They are likely to be disorienting because in the past she was able to focus well and manage her thinking patterns. There are reasons why these symptoms have become so engrained that we will look at separately in a section below.

Relapse Prevention: Women never plan on going back to him or picking another one just like him. She didn't realize she was signing up for a lifetime with Satan when she dated him the first time and she certainly wouldn't seek another go around with another batch of evil. But that's exactly what can happen. Her risk factors mandate some intervention and prevention for her future patterns of selection.

Helping Her Achieve By Conquering Her Mind

Women don't feel like they have hit recovery until they can manage their most distressing symptoms of intrusive thoughts (referred to as I.T.) and cognitive dissonance (referred to as C.D.). Both of these sets of symptoms are related to PTSD which is an anxiety disorder and represent some of the strongest anxiety reactions.

Intrusive Thoughts

Intrusive thoughts are unwelcome involuntary thoughts or images that feel obsessive when the person can't stop or manage them. This is why so many of the women are labeled relationship or sex addicts—because their I.T.'s sound obsessive. Others think it's an addiction when it's really an anxiety reaction. I.T.'s are related to past- and future-focusing. When she rewinds the video tape and is replaying what happened previously in their relationship, her I.T. is past-oriented and can increase depression. When she is worrying about what he's doing, what will happen in the future, she is future-focusing and increasing her anxiety.

Psychology associates I.T.'s mostly to traumatic thoughts like replaying a rape. However, with these women, most of their I.T.'s are positive thoughts and images of him or the relationship. This is one way the women's symptoms are different than other victim groups.

Intrusive thoughts can trip adrenaline release in PTSD which then seems to feed a cycle of I.T's-->adrenaline-->I.T.'s-->adrenaline. The I.T.'s begin to make her look mentally ill, impact her ability to focus which negatively impacts her career, parenting, education, etc. Although it seems contradictory to logic, I.T.'s seem to have their foundation in her emotional *resistance* to accepting 'something'—or what I call 'what is.' While it would *seem* like focusing on what her resistance is would actually raise her I.T.'s setting off the adrenaline cycle, however, it's the repression of facing what she's resisting that keeps the loop of I.T.'s and adrenaline coming. To stop the intrusive thoughts, she must actually face what is at the core of her resistance. There are some predictable core resistances:

"If I really accept he's pathological/psychopathic then it's over. There's no hope."

"If it's over, then I'm alone. I'm so damaged, will I ever have another relationship?"

"Am I unlovable?"

"What does his disorder say about me, I picked him!"

"Will he be happy with someone else?"

I.T.'s are created, in part, by trying to stay away from information or feelings she doesn't want to deal with. The longer she doesn't deal with it, the longer she has I.T.'s.

"Anything we truly accept, changes us."[83]

---

[83] Eckhardt Tolle

I.T's eventually affect mood, causing or increasing depression and anxiety, so if her mood symptoms are problematic she must manage her I.T's. The only solution for I.T.'s and the anxiety and depression is mindfulness. The only place that depression and anxiety don't exist is in this present moment. Since anxiety is largely distraction, it feeds her resistance staying away from what she doesn't want to face. Yet mindfulness, which is 'experiencing this present moment' has no depression or no anxiety. Her emotional suffering is created the moment she resists the truth of something—him, her, the relationship, what he really is, what he's really doing, his inability to sustain change, or the end of the fantasy relationship.

Cognitive Dissonance

The women also have an unusually strong version of Cognitive Dissonance (C.D.) often misunderstood by others and therapists. C.D. is the holding of two differing belief systems at the same time. This defines the Pathological Relationship perfectly because she has held two differing belief system about the good/bad dichotomous psychopath. In fact, it was the holding of two different belief systems about the psychopath (he's good, he's bad) that created the initial split in her causing C.D. The reason why C.D. is so strong in the low/no conscience relationships is because partners must split in order to stay. In reality, she has held two different RELATIONSHIPS with the good/bad dichotomous psychopath! Each one of these relationships has required a different belief system in order to remain in it. These belief systems begin to battle each other increasing the intrusive thoughts which increase the cognitive dissonance, each feeding the other.

In order to reduce the conflict she is experiencing with C.D., she must change her attitude, belief, or behaviors in order to stay. This is usually done by justifying and rationalizing his behavior and as well as justifying and rationalizing her decision to stay.

C.D. is also increased and strengthened by several factors:

1. Staying in the relationship against her belief system that says she should go. This is created when a person perceives a logical inconsistency in their own thinking or belief system which obviously happens when the mask slips and she sees the dark side of the psychopath. Dissonance happens when one idea (he's good) implies the opposite of another (he's bad). Since the relationship

dynamics are largely the playing out of his dichotomous behavior, there is no other way for her to perceive this relationship except through cognitive dissonance. Noticing her own contradictory behavior (she beliefs one thing—he's bad, but does another thing—she stays) leads to anxiety, guilt, shame, anger, embarrassment and stress—all related to her aftermath symptoms.

To give an example of what we consider the opposite of C.D., is when our ideas are consistent and our 'walk matches our talk'— we refer to this as harmony, inner peace, psychological congruency. Before the psychopath, many of the women were very psychologically congruent. This is another reason why the experience of C.D. is life-shattering.

2. Thought and behavioral inconsistency also increases cognitive dissonance. Her inability to stay on the same thought page about 'who' he is and have one consistent view of him increases the 'ping pong' effect in her mind. As soon as she tries to get herself on the 'he's bad for me' page, up pops a positive intrusive thought of a time she perceives him as 'good.' When she tries to realign herself to get on the 'he's good for me' page, up pops an emotional pressure to find out he was cheating. She never stays consistently on one page about how she views him so she never really finishes a thought and never really connects to a firm decision about how to handle the relationship. Instead, she's pulled back and forth with the 'ping ponging' without ever resolving even one conflicting thought. Nothing changes because she never completes a thought without being pulled to the dichotomous opposite belief she was just having.

Behavioral inconsistency also exists. She is likely at odds with herself about her own conflicting behaviors. This is increased every time she does something that is against her own moral or behavioral belief system— which with a psychopath is often! These behavioral inconsistencies could be:

o saying she won't see him and then sees him
o breaking up and making up
o saying she will never loan him money and doing it
o saying she won't participate in certain sexual situations but then does it

The result of behavioral inconsistency is her mind is constantly trying to process these opposite emotions of hers. She also tries to process his opposite and dichotomous behaviors trying to make sense of his behavior and her reactions to him. But nothing gets resolved.

Since she was in a relationship with Dr. Jekyll and Mr. Hyde, C.D. completely makes sense. It was further strengthened by the constant dynamics required to be in a relationship with someone who had such opposite behaviors. These opposite behaviors in him required her to be opposite in her behaviors as well. She must equally have skills for the good side of him and skills for the bad side of him.

Fantasy

But handling C.D. is not the only thing that will help her achieve mental stability. She must also address the positive memories and the fantasies she has of *"If he would only...."* Or *"If I could ...."* then the relationship would work. Since the women are prone to positive intrusive thoughts (more so than negative ones) reviewing those thoughts in her mind connect to the emotions that were created during memory making with him. (This is the process of state-dependent learning we discussed in the hypnosis chapter.)

Re-running the video tape of a positive memory simply brings up the good feelings and causes more intrusive thoughts which then makes the cognitive dissonance start—because he ISN'T all good! The longer she keeps those positive images inside, the stronger the sentimental memory grows. The stronger the emotion, the more at risk she is of picking up the phone and dialing.

But the positive memory (and corresponding emotions) she has is largely fantasy. That's not who a psychopath is—that tender memory of a simply kind man. He is far from simply kind. Her thinking internally does not tap into what is rational, because inside, emotions and memory turn into a murky chemical cocktail flooding her in oxytocin and cranking up the intensity.

She must learn an ironic process of reframing her fantasy images of him. Referred to as *Provocative Therapy*—it challenges her insane loyalty, fantasy thinking, and the unusual dichotomous behavior of the psychopath that she has normalized. It uses exaggeration, irony, and helps her to self deprecate her unrealistic trust and absurd assumptions about the true motivations, for God's sake, of a psychopath! Even humor is woven in to sensitize her to her own absurdities when it comes to trusting the untrustable, loving Satan, or believing a pathological liar.

"You miss being in a relationship with a psychopath?"

"When you were little, you always hoped you would grow up and marry a psychopath, right?"

"You hoped your children would be raised by a sex addict psychopath?"

"You miss having degrading sex with a psychopath?"

"You wish you could give the psychopath just $10,000 more of your money, don't you?"

OK the answer to all those questions is a resounding 'No!' from her. This provocative reframing is a cold shower on a crusty-irrational-oxytocin-driven fantasy. Women have said they can feel an immediate shift when those kinds of verbal challenges are given. In their center-plex where emotions are experienced, they can 'feel a difference' often referred to as a paradigm shift. Her ability to reframe her own thinking will help her nip the fantasy thinking, positive memory flooding, intrusive thoughts and challenge the cognitive dissonance—all which rob her of the ability to heal.

Conclusion

We have looked at the damage from inevitable harm women need recovery for. This chapter has helped look at some of the items that help her begin the healing process. I am often struck by two things regarding the women:

o   how damaged they really are at a deep core level because that's what pathology 'does';

o   and how amazingly resilient the women are considering the deep damage.

However, that doesn't mean there isn't a lengthy recovery. Being damaged by the most disordered person on the planet does bring its costly consequences—one of which is—treatment can take a while. The good news is that *what* is wrong with her symptomatically is highly treatable and *she* is highly treatable and resilient. This is, after all, the woman who brings all those super traits to the task of healing. She has the internal great wiring for some strong temperament that will go a long way towards her own healing.

Yet what she needs also is trained and available professionals and paraprofessionals who can help her achieve her recovery goals. With 100 million people negatively affected by someone else's pathology, we don't have nearly enough treatment options and care providers for the victims that psychopaths are cranking out, daily. We need more people trained:

o   life and relationship coaches who can offer support
o   peer-facilitated support groups in communities across the country
o   licensed mental health professionals who are trained and have learned about pathology in graduate school
o   intensive outpatient, inpatient, and residential treatment programs

The Institute offers training for therapists, coaches, peer facilitators, women's organizations and agencies, and treatment centers. We welcome the opportunity to add more recovery options for women around the world.

Yet who is more important than the children who are so impacted by the psychopath's parenting? Let's take a look at what happens to them.

15 What About Inevitable Harm to the Children?

"Whoever inquires about our childhood wants to know something about our soul." — Erika Burkhart

Children are exposed to the same, if not worse, inevitable harm which means they too need healing through treatment. Women can recognize the utter disintegration of herself in the relationship with the psychopath but sometimes think he *might* make good father material for the children. As hard as it is for her to come to terms with his pathology as permanent, it is even harder for her to believe his pathology is so bad that he would hurt his children—overtly or covertly. Psychopaths, with all their proclivity for brain problems, skewed communication, impulse control disorders, addictions, and other mental health issues make just as bad (if not worse) parents as they do partners. It's criminal that our courts don't think so too.

What in the world can a psychopath give a child? That's the insane logic that society shares with the women—"All children need their father." Let me be clear, no child needs, or deserves, a psychopath. Not convinced? Let's see what types of pathological characteristics they bring to parenting when we look at Antisocials, Narcissists and Psychopaths.

Mentally check off *if any* of these represent qualities that a mother would WANT in a father who has access to her children.

___ Impulsiveness	___ Preoccupied with fantasies of power
___ Lack of consistency	___ Self-referencing their own uniqueness
___ Low sentimentality	___ Requires excessive admiration
___ Surface attachment	___ Entitled
___ Disorderliness with a lack of routine	___ Interpersonally exploitative
___ No empathy	___ Arrogant

___ Little helpful behavior toward others	___ Pathological lying
___ No compassion	___ Lack of remorse or guilt
___ No tolerance	___ Sexual promiscuity
___ Low responsibility	___ Lack of realistic long-term goals
___ Failure to conform to social norms and laws	___ Failure to accept responsibility for own actions
___ Deceitful, irritability and aggression	___ Many short-term marital relationships
___ Reckless disregard for safety of others	___ Revocation of conditional release
___ Grandiosity sense of self importance	___ Criminal versatility

Since pathology is marked by the inability to sustain positive change, grow to any emotional depth or develop insight about how their behavior negatively affects others, the mandatory parenting classes, anger management, batterer intervention, supervised visitation, and all the other ineffective illusionary management tools we use only put children through more torturous exposure to the low/no conscienced. Are we surprised what kind of actions pathologicals take against their children?

Dr. Kirkman revealed that women reported psychopathic men psychologically abused their children by:[84]

1. Lying to them;
2. Ignoring them;
3. Failing to provide for them;
4. Bullying and terrifying them;
5. Breaking promises to them;
6. Destroying their toys.

This is only the tip of the iceberg. *Why do we think that a person who is pathological enough to harm adults won't have pathology that will*

---

[84] Kirkman, CA (2005). From soap opera to science: Towards gaining access to the psychopaths who live amongst us. *Psychology and Psychotherapy: Theory, Research and Practice*, 78, 379–396.

harm children even more? These pathological disorders are in fact the misuse of power over others. Who is more powerless than children?

"When highly antisocial fathers reside with the family, children experience a double whammy of risk for antisocial behavior. They are at genetic risk because antisocial behavior is highly heritable. In addition, the same parents who transmit genes also provide the child's rearing environment. We found that a father's antisocial behavior accounted for his children's behavior problems independent of any genetic risk he may have imparted, particularly when he resided with the family and spent time taking care of the children." —Sara R. Jaffee, Ph.D. King's College, London

Pathological parents tragically influence their children's behavior. Kids go on to do what they see done while with him (or her). Their supervision is scant at best and children are expected to be their own adult. Since most pathologicals aren't older than 10-14 years old emotionally, it is the young-leading-the-young. Pathological parents choose to be a peer instead of a parent and will often treat even young children as if they are their 'friends.' Father-rite-of-passage impulsivity is common in which young boys are given beer, porn, prostitutes, keys to the car or are treated like a 'frat buddy.'

Young female children are used as servants—being made to clean up, cook, and care for the adult-yet-child pathological parent. Sexualizing of young girls emerging bodies is common. Of course, so is sexual abuse of both boys and girls. Considering that many psychopaths hang around other psychopaths, it's not common that the children are abused by his friends while in his non-focused supervision. They are also exposed to police raids, fights, dad going to jail, hearing sex going on in the next room, being driven in speeding cars without car seats, being left with people they don't know, eating junk food for days on end, and not keeping to a schedule or bedtime. The children come home ravaged from too much pathology exposure to a 'Jerry Springer' weekend. Months or years peel off the calendar as children have regular exposure to abnormal behavior and criminality. The child's own symptoms of impulse control problems, raging, gaslighting, lying, aggression, stealing, and defiance starts and mothers wonder 'why' their child is changing?

Yet pathologicals are just as likely to over indulge as they are to under care for their children. When pathologicals have higher levels of narcissism they often expose their children to excesses. One narcissist bought a 4,000 sq ft house next to his for his toddler so she could have an adequate sized play house and he furnished it with everything imaginable including a staff. At two years old, she doesn't have to take a nap, walk with supervision in the mall, or stay in a stroller because 'she doesn't like it.' To the degree that the narcissists' children are smart, attractive, talented, do well in school or sports, they are likely to be highly indulged. For children who are academically challenged, aren't interested in sports, or are nerdy or unattractive, they are likely to be ignored, unprovided for, or abused by the narcissist. To the degree that the child positively 'reflects' the narcissist in a good way is to the degree which the narcissist invests in the child. Antisocial, borderlines, and psychopaths are more likely to 'parentify' the child and make them care emotionally for the pathological. One psychopath said to his 13 year old daughter,

"Get me my beer! Get your slut-ass in there and cook something for me. From Friday at 5pm until Sunday at 5pm, I am YOUR business."

The courts act as if we have no clinical reference for what happens to children who are raised by the low/no conscience disorders. We know extremely well what happens to them. Why do we have Adult Children of Narcissistic Parents groups, treatment, books, and check lists of adult symptoms? If we don't know what children grow into who are raised by narcissists, why do we have checklist of adult symptoms? The same thing is true with Borderlines, Antisocials, Sociopaths, and Psychopaths. In all of our 'custody-political-correctness,' we want to pretend that all parents are created equal and bring to the table the same traits and skills to parent. Yet pathology does not bring those skills. They bring the toxic skills listed above—behaviors that harm children and add to the children's own proclivity to go on and develop the same pathology as the parent. If this book has highlighted anything it's that we don't need more pathology in this world.

We know what exposure to pathological parents (of both sexes) does to children whether the court will recognize it or not. There are books that highlight the profound damage. Here are some titles:

o *Surviving a Borderline Parent: How to Heal Your Childhood Wounds and Build Trust, Boundaries and Self Esteem*

o *Toxic Parents: Overcoming Their Hurtful Legacy and Reclaiming Your Life* o   *Children of the Self Absorbed: A Grown Ups Guide to Getting Over Narcissistic Parents*

o   *The Batterer as Parent*

o   *The Wizard of Oz & Other Narcissists: Coping With the One-Way Relationship in Work, Love & Family*

o   *Working with Monsters: How to Identify and Protect Yourself from Workplace Psychopaths*

o   *The Narcissistic Family*

o   *Understanding the Borderline Mother: Helping Her Children Transcend the Intense, Unpredictable and Volatile Relationship*

o   *Adult Children of Narcissistic Personality Disorder*

o   *The Psychopathy of Everyday Life: How Antisocial Personality Disorder Affects All of Us*

What disorders do we *think* the people and families have on day time TV talk shows? It's a portrait of pathology. We have watched the TV shows with our mouths gapping open at the atrocities of behavior, mental illness, and psychological abuse of pathological parents and the poor children being raised by them. Pathology has sadly become daytime entertainment when we believe 'no one is *really* that screwed up!' Yes they are, and the courts will allow them to abuse their kids through the act of parenting.

"At first in the relationship (he) did well, seemed to bond with my sons and played with them a lot. As the relationship progressed, he started to reject them, began telling me how he hated the dogs and ignored my son. At the end, told me he wanted to shoot the dogs and had physically fought with my then 15 year old son. He still got along with my daughter until she rejected him after he hit me and threatened me with a gun."

"He acted like the 'father of the year' in public with the baby, but the minute he got home, he would toss the baby (in the car seat) on the table and play video games."

"The kids were like servants that had to behave and do things perfect or else. He would control every aspect of their lives. They were never good enough, he never would say good job. He controlled with fear."

Blinded by the Courts

Of course, many women have recognized that pathology should have no part of parenting—but the court sees it differently. As often as she brought evidence to the table of his neglectful, even abusive and traumatic behavior with the children, the courts rule as if the skills he brings to the children are actually parenting skills and not merely criminal skills. The courts apply cookie-cutter approaches as if all parents have the same proclivities or problems. Psychopaths are shuffled through the system like a normal soccer dad—treated as if he brings the same love and sanity to the child as a normal dad does.

For his chronic criminality, he is guided through an illusionary treatment program consisting of providers who don't recognize psychopathy. So he is put in anger management, counseling, group therapy, batterer intervention, drug treatment, or mediation for high-conflict cases. Dozens of attempts and years go by as the psychopath continues to be given opportunities to destroy his children. Unqualified and untrained people write reports about his 'achievements' in treatment—an example of his profound gaslighting abilities to even the seemingly professional who are suppose to know better.

The protective mom is labeled as a parental alienator for trying to spare her child from exposure to sheer evil. She's labeled neurotic, selfish, and uncooperative. She's sent through psychological testing, while the psychopath isn't (or if he is, the psychologists use the wrong testing instrument and he looks normal). When he screws up again, he is merely put in 'time out'—supervised visitation until the paid supervisor is charmed too. With all the treatment and social service support he has had poured into him, he comes off sounding more insightful than a grad student. With her PTSD, intrusive thoughts and high harm avoidance—she looks like a neurotic mess while he is calm, cool and utterly pathological.

Organizations like the Protective Mothers Alliance and Parents Without Custody highlight our societal and judicial failure recognizing and believing what pathology does to children. When the non-pathological parent is stripped of their parenting rights or abilities because the psychopath is so convincing in court and the courts remain untrained, we have another generation of inevitable harm with mounting numbers of new cases of pathology emerging in our already burgeoning pathological society.

"He used his kids as pawns and encouraged them to hate their stepfather and view their mother as being in the wrong. He portrayed himself as a big victim of her unfair attitudes and rules and encouraged his kids to also view her in that light. But he would always end his criticism of her by saying, 'But I'm not saying she's a bad mother.' Yeah right..."

"He screams parental alienation but he alienates. He screams neglect, but he neglects. Whatever he accuses me of, he is doing. I am hopeless because I never see the court seeing this for what it is."

Are We Surprised?

Children develop their own set of pathological behaviors, modeling the psychopath's own pathological world view. These disorders in children, which are often a precursor to adult psychopathy or other low conscience disorders include Oppositional Defiant Disorder, Child Conduct Disorder, and Reactive Attachment Disorder. Here are some of the symptoms in children who replicate the symptoms of their pathological parent:[85]

Oppositional Defiant Disorder

The child often loses temper, argues with adults, actively defies or refuses to comply with adult rules, deliberately annoys people, blames others for misbehavior, touchy and easily annoyed, angry and resentful, spiteful or vindictive.

In more extreme cases (or as the child ages):

Child Conduct Disorder

The child often bullies, threatens, intimidates others, initiates physical fights, has used a weapon to harm others (brick, broken bottle, etc.) been physically cruel to people or animals, has stolen while confronting a victim, forced someone into sexual activity, deliberately set a fire, deliberately destroyed other's property, broken into someone else's property, lies to obtains good or favors, stolen items of nontrivial value,

---

[85] American Psychiatric Association: *Diagnostic and Statistical Manual of Mental Disorders,* Fourth Edition. Washington, D.C., American Psychiatric Association, 1994.

stays out at night despite parental prohibition, runs away from him, truant from school.

Reactive Attachment Disorder

The child is excessively inhibited, hyper-vigilant, or ambivalent and has contradictory responses to caregivers, does not have appropriate attachments (such as shows excessive familiarity with strangers or lack of selectivity in choice of attachment figures). *Pathogenic* (here is a clue in this word alone!) *care* is evidenced by one of the following: persistent disregard of the child's basic emotional needs for comfort, stimulation and affection; persistent disregard of the child's basic physical needs, repeated changes of primary caregiver that prevents formation of stable attachments.

Who does this sound like? These symptoms sound a lot like the low/no conscienced. Why do we believe that children aren't influenced by exposure to pathology? We have seen the profound syndrome-like behaviors including PTSD that the women emerge with from a relationship with the child's father. Yet courts will believe that children, with tender and susceptible developing personalities, will not be negatively affected even though their mother was? Not surprisingly, children also emerge with significant PTSD which manifests itself in either a victim persona or with pre-pathology antisocial-like behaviors in Child Conduct and Oppositional Defiant Disorders.

Wake up courts! Sociopathy is created from toxic early childhood environments. This toxicity is largely a child's exposure to how the low/no conscienced think, feel, relate and behave during parenting. That means, sociopathy can be formed in children from exposure to other socio/psychopaths. Since the psychopath's behavior is chocked full of antisocial actions and belief systems, we shouldn't be shocked to find children sponging up these ideas such as racism, sexism, exposure to his sexual addiction/deviancy, his open use of drugs/alcohol, uncontrolled rage, or other impulse problems such as speeding, spending, and seducing.

As children are parented by the low/no conscienced, our society just keeps cranking out more and more pathology through exposure.

o   Women continue to have children with psychopaths who have genetic risk factors for passing on pathology to their children.

o   Children are raised by psychopaths and the low/no conscienced which produces social risk factors for acquiring pathology from exposure to his pathological world view and psychopathic parenting styles.

Somewhere, this insanity must stop!

Conclusion

The Future of Psychopathy Focused Education

But it will only stop when there is a full frontal assault of public education in this country. Women can't avoid what they don't understand. Therapists can't diagnose what they don't know. Courts can't rule differently until they understand (and believe!) the permanence of pathology. Young teens can't make better partner selections if they don't know how to spot. Victims can't heal if they can't find knowledgeable help.

The Institute believes this country needs to invest in:

o   Victim Research and best approaches training for other professionals
o   A National Ad Campaign for Public Psychopath Education so people can learn to spot, avoid, or break up with those who will inflict inevitable harm
o   Legal and Judicial Training so that courts cooperate with what is realistic behavior for psychopaths and actively protective his victims and children
o   Identification Training of Pathology for anger management, batterer intervention and other services that psychopaths are likely to filter through
o   Better Pathology approaches when considering child custody and willful exposure to a parent's pathology

The Institute holds high hope that this country will get it together and provide the education that everyone needs in order to avoid or heal from inevitable harm. The women and children deserve that much. If we want to see pathology diminish, we must address the problems that pathology creates.

"Every beginning is a consequence. Every beginning ends something." — Paul Valery

The Women's Stories

"There are years that ask questions and years that answer."

— *Zora Neale Hurston*

Rebecca's Story

My husband of 24 years passed away unexpectedly when both of us were merely 49 years old. My children were grown and out of the house. I relocated to an area and didn't know anyone and had very little support from others. I was very lonely and hurting and a friend suggested that I use an online dating service. As naïve as I was, I gave out way too much information about being a widow, a professional and lonely. I received a note and no picture from a man who said he lived in my area but was out of town much of the time on business. He gave me his phone number and I called him. We talked for hours that first night and I thought that I had found my soul-mate.

I was leaving for a cruise and we talked before I left and spent much of the time onboard ship emailing him. After the cruise, he picks me up and suggests that I go look at real estate with him (I suppose to impress me). So we looked at million dollar homes and said he had just sold his house and hadn't purchased anytime yet. Within a week, without discussing it with me, he had moved in and asked me for a 'sign of trust' in our relationship. I wasn't sure what that meant but I wrote him a check for $70,000 that he said he would keep in his wallet and not cash.

I owned two cars that were paid for and he felt they were 'unsafe' for me to drive and I should get something better. He said to maximize the return on my two cars I should trade them in on a high end vehicle so he negotiated a trade where I turned in my SUV and a Corvette and added another $40,000 to the price and got a new BMW 645. In order for him to sell it for me to get my money back I had to put it in his name. He's still driving the car two and a half years later. He never intended to sell it. I now have a leased vehicle that I pay for monthly and he drives around in the car I paid for.

I am a very intelligent woman with a master's degree in taxation and my Certified Public Accountant license (CPA). I should have known better but I felt powerless to say "no" to this man. These two episodes were the start of a lot of money going from me to him. In the course of two and a half years I have given him over $500,000. At the time, the real estate market was doing well in Florida and I owned three properties that were appreciating in value and I was able to get home equity loans when my cash ran out. He was always borrowing money and would say he would repay it. He convinced me to add his name as owner to the most expensive property that I owned.

Dealing with him was chaotic and exhausting. He could be the sweetest guy and make me laugh and I would feel happy and content. He would leave the house and say "I'll be right back" and I wouldn't see him for day, even 2-3 weeks.

He would show up on Saturday evening, we would go out to dinner (I paid) and then he'd get all dressed up and leave until 2 a.m. in the morning. He would never tell me about how he spent the money or where he had been. He led me to believe he had been with the CIA or other highly secretive government operations. He also preached a lot of Christianity to me and told me repeatedly that I was a very negative person (usually for confronting him about the money, his lies, or where he's been) and I should think more "positive thoughts."

The chaos with him affected my work. He would call me at work and ask for money or want to talk. I lost my job with a national CPA firm that had great benefits and I ended up joining a smaller local firm because I lost my ability to focus and make decisions. My confidence and self-esteem were shot! He had me questioning everything that I did and usually whatever decision I made, was the wrong one. So then I couldn't make any decisions at all. I was paralyzed.

My stress kept increasing. He didn't help around the house and then would be gone for weeks. I would just get used to being alone again and he'd show back up and the whole cycle would begin again. I think he did this to keep me off-balance.

While in this situation, I was diagnosed with breast cancer and I believe the stress of dealing with him and the money issues contributed to the cancer. During my treatments he would say he was 'standing with me' but would take my ATM card and get money out of my account without me knowing it. He would drive me to the hospital and drop me off at the front door for a procedure and then would go home and go back to bed.

During my cancer treatments while I couldn't work, I had to withdraw $80,000 to pay all the mortgage payments and resulted in a large balance with the IRS for withdrawing the money from my 401k. I wanted to sell the real estate to get some cash flow but every time he would get upset and tell me I shouldn't sell at that time.

I have now filed bankruptcy. I walked away from about $1 million dollars in real estate because I couldn't afford to pay the mortgages and monthly bills. My credit is shot. I had to borrow money from one sister to move away to another state. This is a big change from having $400,000 in a savings account like I use to and owning my cars and house outright.

Even despite all this, moving away from the area was the most difficult decision I ever made. I knew it was the best thing for my emotional health but it hurt dreadfully to know I would not see him again. I loved the man, or the man I thought he was. But my life is most definitely changed for having known him and loved him.

I couldn't have been able to break away from him without moving across the country. There is just something about him and I feel as I am addicted to him. There was financial abuse but also this emotional addiction to him. Every time he asked for money even though I knew I didn't want to do it, I would do it anyway and it created internal strife for me.

Today, I am a much less a trusting person. I don't want to get into a relationship with anyone. I'm in therapy trying to understand why I allowed this to go on. I can see he came into my life at a time when I was very lonely and he satisfied that need some of the time. I do believe I'm healing and I have hope for the future.

Christine's Story

We met online on a Christian web site. He's been married once before and had two daughters with his first wife. They were high school sweethearts and he claimed he never loved her and married her because he felt pressured to. After two weeks of dating he wanted us to be exclusive and I didn't really feel comfortable with that. He said the relationship would have to be over if we weren't going to be exclusive. He said he cared about me way too much to have me seeing other people. We dated for two weeks and it was intense right from the start. He lived in a nearby state and drove an hour to me every weekend. Sometimes he would just show up and "surprise" me during the week. I felt special and looked forward to those days with him. He was very romantic during that time.

He told me about his childhood and I felt so sorry for him. I thought I would be the one to help the rest of his life be better. He told me his ex-wife made him feel left out and she paid too much attention to the children. We got engaged after dating only six months. He began saying very cruel things to me but it seemed that when we weren't together I got separation anxiety, like I just 'had' to see him. It was painful at time and I would cry a lot. It never dawned on me that this wasn't normal.

I saw his cruelty to his sister and found out that he use to beat his former girlfriend. He said that was a long time ago and he had "found God" and was different. He also said that she had been violent to him and it was an act of self-protection. My girlfriend set up a luncheon with his ex-wife so I could hear first hand from her what it was like to be married to him. I didn't believe her and thought she was biased. I felt like we should slow it down but he said no he couldn't wait that long to be with me. He missed me so much when we were apart. I remember how unhappy I was during the engagement, not at all how I thought it should be. After being engaged for only one month we got married.

Our honeymoon was in Vegas where I told him I didn't want to go. I waited in the car an hour for him to gamble to get money for our hotel room.

As the relationship unraveled, we went to counseling and we started a daily Bible study. It only lasted for a short time. Then I became pregnant. After the baby was born, he'd have rages about nothing and disappear for days. We separated.

Then I found he was watching teen porn and would come and ask to take our one year old daughter "out for a ride." I asked the courts for supervised visitation which I did get for about five months. Then the state ran out of funds for the program and now he has asked and gotten one over-night visit with her and a four hour visit on another day. It is horrendous and a nightmare. I feel a lot of guilt when it comes to my daughter and not being able to protect her. I left so that I could protect her but I feel like I've failed her because I can't protect her through the courts anymore.

He even managed to have me arrested. He showed up late one time to drop her off. He had shut off his cell phone so I couldn't reach him probably to just make me frantic with worry. When he finally showed up, I was so worried and he was very nonchalant about what he had done. I touched his arm as he was leaving pleading with him to leave his cell phone on the next time he had the baby. He filed charges for me touching his arm and had me arrested.

It's been tough and I pray for strength that I will need to endure this custody issue with him. The last thing he said to me was, "If you think it's rough now, it's going to get much worse for you…"

Lisa's Story

I met him through work. He said he was in an unhappy long term relationship and had one other relationship years prior. He's highly intelligent, charismatic, has an excellent education, very sexually charged, and an excellent lover—but also lots of narcissistic traits.

When we were alone he would circle around me as if I were prey. I thought it odd at the time but I just chalked it up to "intensity." He pretended to be very insecure and said it was my warmth and love that kept him sane. "You are the only one I have ever been completely honest with," he said while I found out he was still with his long term girlfriend the entire time we were together.

We were on again off again because he would not commit to the relationship. There was definitely a sense of intense attachment with him—like I couldn't live without him. I had never felt level of uncontrolled intense attachment that way before which should have been a red flag to me.

His long term relationship girlfriend was offered a job in Singapore and he decided to go with her but she went on ahead of him. She left on Saturday and he was in my bed on Sunday talking to her on his cell phone very intimately right after he had sex with me!

He moved to Singapore and I was devastated! As soon as he got there he began emailing me saying he regretted his decision but was 'helpless' to change anything. He was coming back in a few months to attend someone's wedding and was living for the day he could see me again. He emailed me daily with love letters and said he told her he wanted to break up. She found out about us and he then decided he wanted a committed relationship with me.

He came to see me for 11 days and it was blissful. We talked about marriage. He wanted to meet my daughter and talk to her about us being a family. He wanted me to buy an airline ticket to Singapore so I could come there at Christmas. His long term girlfriend arrived here for the same wedding he was attending and he insisted on picking her up at the airport. I was nervous about that but he kept texting me all day long saying that he loved me.

He called me the next day and said his girlfriend was sitting there with him and he ended the relationship with me on the phone. I was reeling! I felt as if I had been emotionally raped! He went back to Singapore with her. He started sending spyware to my personal email address. He broke into my email account and deleted it. I filed a complaint with my email company, they checked into it, and it had, in fact, been broken into. He is an I.T. engineer so it wasn't hard for him to do.

He would leave me messages in my emails. I would delete an email and it would be replaced in my inbox with a message from him. I thought I was losing my mind! I had my computer rebuilt six times and each time they found it loaded with his spyware.

He sent me an email at Valentine's Day which was bloodcurdling in its claim of 'true love' for me. He bombards my computer with spyware and sends cards pronouncing his love to me! I responded with a text saying I would go to the police if he continued to contact me.

Then his rage began. He began sending me pornography for eight months. He was investigated and it was proven to be him (or her together) sending these emails and breaking into my computer. I became so destabilized I ended up in the psychiatric hospital. I was diagnosed with Post Traumatic Stress Disorder. It's been two and a half years of recovery so far and I still wonder if I will ever be the same woman as I was before I met him.

Susan's Story

I'm a high management level marketing executive. I was separated from my husband with whom I had four children ranging in age from 3-14. I traveled a lot for my job and met a man on one of the flights. He was in uniform, heavily decorated with metals. We were on the same layover for the next flight so we had a drink in the bar.

He was a Colonel in one of the military branches. He was physically fit, strong and aggressive, and single minded in his focus. I was sure that was what got him to the rank of Colonel. He asked for my phone number and I said no but took his. It was several weeks later when I thought getting to know him better might be okay with me. He didn't live in my town, in fact, he lived several states a way but jumped on a plane and came to see me.

He was intensely sexually aggressive—assuming that I would have sex with him. I was in no way ready but I was becoming frightened by his aggression. He was ravenous and animalistic in the sex. To be honest, I had never experienced anything like that.

We spent several days together. When not in bed, he listened to my stories about my separa-tion and began militantly organizing my life, children, and job. He was intrusive in my life that way—after all, I was an executive I knew how to organize people! He was also obviously jealous of my soon-to-be ex-husband. He talked a lot about himself then too— mostly a glowing history with the military and how he climbed the ranks in record time 'squashing those below' him to get to where he is today.

After that time together, he would call me constantly. I am in an executive position in my job and must stay focused. I work hard—over 50 hours a week. He was a constant distraction. I wondered why the military "let him" never work! Didn't he have a job or something to do, I wondered?

I knew something was up when he sent me in the mail a headphone set for my phone. In the box was also a video. It was porn; he said he had the same video and we were going to have phone sex together. I had never even watched porn nor was I interested. I declined and he pursued. Almost every weekend he was flying to see me. Or would meet me at layovers I had in airports, rent a room and we would have this "animalistic sex." He began bringing porn to me when he came to see me.

Within a few short months phone sex and porn were my everyday experience. In the evenings, he would call and we'd put in the new video he sent and stay on the phone for hours and hours having phone sex. He then bought vibrators and other items when I complained that my vagina hurt and I didn't want to continue. He thought these items would be 'gentler' on me. But the phone sex was escalating and he was getting verbally very graphic about what he wanted to do to me, other women, then animals…

One weekend he wanted to try marathon sex and I stayed on the headphone set for 36 straight hours. He asked for group sex, stronger porn, and I began to worry about what else he was doing when I wasn't around. I instinctively knew not to allow him around my children.

My job performance plummeted. For the first time in my entire career I got a negative review, missed my promotion, and bonus. I was exhausted. And when I looked in the mirror I looked like a drug addict—strung out on stupid sex and no sleep. I was spending less and less time with my children.

I would even take my lunch hour and my head phone set to the car, to the bathroom, or home. I started researching sexual addiction wondering if I was one now. I knew he was.

I would break up with him but couldn't change my phone number because it was a corporate phone. But I did block his calls. He continued to send letters, calls to my home phone, packages of videos, etc. When I didn't respond I noticed one day on my way home I was being followed. It was him. He had flown from the military base and rented a car and was now pursuing me. I called the cops and of course, being dressed in military garb, they just asked politely "that the colonel remove himself from the property."

Off and on for two years I tried to get rid of him only to be stalked, phone tapped (I believe), and harassed. I also think he sent others to follow me. He would send porn to my corporate phone and threatened to continue to do that until I responded to his phone calls. I already knew his level of aggression and feared him physically now.

I started "faking" the phone sex. I was repulsed by him. And when I actually stopped and got some distance and just listened to him, I knew he was psychopathic. Hearing him panting on the phone saying very deviant stuff like "I'd do anything for you…I'd kill an animal to show my devotion to you."

They say there is an epiphany moment in our lives—that point where everything becomes crystal clear and you turn a corner. My therapist called it a "paradigm shift." When I turned that corner and heard him in a new way, I didn't know how I would get out with my life but I knew I had to get out. I found The Dangerous Relationship Institute online and began working with them to get out.

I was treated for sexual addiction that I had in fact, developed. It was sad to see where a normal woman ended up on this journey with a high powered psychopath. During the sexual addiction treatment, they helped me develop an exit strategy. It was humiliating to ask for help from my ex-husband to get rid of this guy, to have to tell my company that I needed sex addiction treatment, that I needed vagina surgery for repair of injuries. Working the 12 Steps and having to really look at my neglect of my children was heart wrenching.

Today, I am now facing treatment for Post Traumatic Stress Disorder. I still fear him—I have flashbacks of this horrid sex life and deviancy. I am always afraid he is following me or having me followed. I have problems concentrating and haven't been able to fully return to normal in my job performance. My understanding of PTSD is that I may always have some residual effects of this. This highly decorated soldier was definitely a life changing ambush.

Appendix A: Comparison of Sociopathy vs. Psychopathy[86]

Below is a table showing a comparison between the personality traits used to diagnose sociopathy (in the DSM IV-TR) and those used to diagnose psychopathy (the PCL-R criteria which is the Psychopathy Check List designed by Dr. Robert Hare).

DSM IV APD/Sociopathy Criteria	PCL-R Psychopathy Criteria
"a pervasive pattern of disregard for and violation of the rights of others"	Grandiose sense of self worth
Lack of remorse or guilt	Callous/lack of empathy Parasitic lifestyle
Symptoms present prior to age 15.	Early Behavior Problems Juvenile delinquency
Failure to conform to social norms with respect to lawful behaviors as indicated by repeatedly performing acts that are grounds for arrest.	Revocation of conditional release Criminal versatility
Deceitfulness, as indicated by repeatedly lying, use of aliases or conning others for personal profit or pleasure.	Pathological lying Conning/manipulative (Glibness, superficial charm)
Impulsivity or failure to plan ahead.	Poor behavioral controls Impulsivity Promiscuous sexual behavior Lack of realistic, long-term goals
Irritability and aggressiveness, as indicated by repeated physical fights or assaults.	Poor behavioral controls

---

[86] Contributed by Liane J. Leedom, M.D.

DSM IV APD/Sociopathy Criteria	PCL-R Psychopathy Criteria
Reckless disregard for safety of self or others.	Poor behavioral controls Irresponsibility
Consistent irresponsibility, as indicated by repeated failure to sustain consistent work behavior or honor financial obligations.	Lack of realistic, long-term goals Irresponsibility Failure to accept responsibility for actions Many short term marital relationships
Lack of remorse, as indicated by being indifferent to or rationalizing having hurt, mistreated, or stolen from another.	Lack of remorse or guilt Callous/lack of empathy
NONE	Shallow affect

This chart helps us see how similar antisocial personality disorder/sociopathy, and psychopathy are and that similar traits make up definitions of both.

Information and Resources

The Institute for Relational Harm Reduction

A provider of professional training and survivor support services for those emerging from relationships with Axis II/Cluster B and Psychopathic partners.

Survivor Services

o   Community Workshops and Lectures
o   Books, Workbooks, e-books, CDs, DVDs
o   Phone Coaching and Counseling
o   Therapist and Counselor Referrals
o   Support Groups
o   Retreats
o   1:1 Intensive Support Sessions
o   Intensive Outpatient, Inpatient, and Residential Treatment Programs

Professional Training Services

o   Books, Workbooks, e-books, CDs, DVDs
o   Therapist Training and Certification Program
o   Life and Relationship Coaching Training
o   Peer Support Group Facilitation Training
o   Agency Staff Development Training
o   Keynote Addresses
o   Workshop Facilitation
o   Treatment Center Development

www.saferelationshipsmagazine.com